Hoofprints in Ed

~ Nobbut Thirty Year ~

Dedicated to the Fell Pony

Sue Millard

HAYLOFT

First published 2005

Hayloft Publishing Ltd, Kirkby Stephen,
Cumbria, CA17 4DJ

tel: (017683) 42300
fax. (017683) 41568
e-mail: books@hayloft.org.uk
web: www.hayloft.org.uk

ISBN 1 904524 34 6

A catalogue record for this book is available
from the British Library

Printed and bound in the EU

Papers used by Hayloft are natural, recyclable products
made from wood grown in sustainable forests.
The manufacturing processes conform to the
environmental regulations of the country of origin.

All photographs by the author unless credited otherwise.

CONTENTS

The Greenholme herd of Fell ponies in early spring.

Introduction

The story I tell in this book is simple. It's about the Fell ponies and their breeders, the land, and the cycle of the seasons. Perhaps I should explain how this book came to be written. Over the years, as for various reasons I have become acquainted with more and more far-flung horse owners, enthusiasts and buyers, I have realised that the local practices and history of Fell pony breeding are as foreign to many people within Britain as they are to people overseas. Chris Thompson says: 'some people are not as lucky as us, to have the fell.' So as the ponies gain recognition elsewhere, there is a growing need for us to share background information about how they are kept in their homeland of Cumbria and Northumbria.

How am I qualified to do that? Well, living in Greenholme, I am surrounded by fell commons: the Howgills, Roundthwaite, Birkbeck, and Crosby (which, however, no longer carries horses). Greenholme is also within ten minutes' drive of the group of fell commons running south from Bampton that includes Martindale, Heltondale, Askham, Shap, Ralfland and Kentmere. These high bare moorlands circle the Eden Valley, the 'Eden' of my title.

I have been a user, admirer and owner of Fell ponies for over 30 years. However, only part of this book is about my own opinions and memories of them. I felt it was important to draw on the knowledge of breeders, who could remember and judge ponies and activities from much further back than I could, if I hoped to capture a snapshot of current and past practices in keeping 'the old breed of pony that has roamed the northern hills for years.' There is nothing better for passing on such knowledge than the eyewitness statement which puts an activity into its context and gives practical explanations for something always having been done a certain way.

So, one by one, month by month, people let me fit my appointments into their busy lives. I called at farmhouses; I entertained visitors. My interviewees were charming, helpful, funny, wise, shy, cautious, self-deprecating, intelligent, kind and informative. With my tape recorder on the table they talked widely of ponies and people, reminisced about events and places, straightened each other's memories and explained puzzles where facts were missing, told me terrible

> Fell ponies are believed to have originated on the border between England and Scotland during Roman times from the crossing of imported war stallions with the local Celtic ponies. They were originally brown in colour, though over the last few decades black has become predominant, followed by brown, bay and grey. They are primarily a working breed with activity, stamina, hardiness and brains that enable them to live and thrive in tough conditions out on the fells. Their average height is 13.1-13.2 hands, with a limit of 14 hands and no lower limit.
>
> (Fell Pony Society promotional leaflet, 2003)

tales with huge relish and then squawked with anxiety when they remembered that I might quote them. Most of the breeders I interviewed had a rather similar range of knowledge to impart so I could not use the technique used by Melvyn Bragg in *Speak for England* of allocating one chapter to each protagonist. I had to break the narratives down and string relevant sections, like beads, on the thread of a topic.

An interview with one breeder would fill gaps in the story told by another. A brisk exchange within a family or between two friends would need scripting like a play when it came to be written up. I have tried to retain that liveliness, the vigorous expressive language, the local dialect and place names. The result is not and should not be 'BBC English'. It is a drystone wall, not a plasterboard partition; it is the real thing. Read it, hear it in your head, and savour it as I did.

Every person I interviewed suggested other people I should meet and listen to! The word *pony* lets you into a network that extends world-wide. If I had not set a simple filter on my information, that is, 'at least thirty years breeding Fells,' I could have gone on tracking down Fell pony people forever. I am quite certain that I shall have missed listening to someone important; I make my apologies now.

The interviews were punctuated by the tiny whirr of the recorder, the clink of tea plates and, usually, the noise of appalling weather outside. I was, after all, talking with breeders of Fell ponies, mostly hill farmers whose work lies outdoors at the mercy of rain and wind; they could only spare time to talk to me when storms or the early dark of a winter's afternoon kept them from their work. The tales became detective work, history flavoured with personal opinion, and fact spiced with anecdote. I'm only sorry that, because of their general niceness, my interviewees did not wish to offend anyone and when they edited their words they insisted on cutting out some of the bits I found most wickedly fascinating.

Henry Harrison, President of the Fell Pony Society and third generation breeder, writes in the 2005 FPS calendar, 'What is it about the Fell pony that is special? Besides its hardiness, thrift, strength and being sure footed, it is the personality of the Fell pony that means so much, a kind natured pony, ever eager to please and provide good company.'

When interviewing Henry I was struck by a phrase that Ivan Alexander used to measure the time he had spent helping with the Sleddale ponies, 'which is nobbut thirty year.' It made my neck hair prickle. It fitted exactly with my time filter. Yet in his interview Henry said, 'We're still learning!'

'The Knowledge' about Fell ponies lives in the heads of those who own and breed them, and I am glad they were willing to share it. My humble thanks go to all of them for their generosity. Piecing this book together from their gifts has been hard work and a total delight. The book is theirs, rather than mine.

We need to blow our own trumpets more about our working native horses and ponies. We have the best in the world! (Charlie Parker, Roandale Dales Stud, Gilsland, Cumbria).

ACKNOWLEDGEMENTS

In addition to all the contributors of interview material who are named in the book, I am very grateful to the Council of the Fell Pony Society who gave permission for me to use material from their archive of Fell pony photographs; to Laura Hart (Chair of the Educational Committee of the Fell Pony Society and Conservancy of the Americas), who spent a week's holiday in proof reading for me; and to Mary Thomas, who managed to find gaps between her full-time job and her Dartmoor stud to do the same.

My thanks must also go to the many friends who made friendly enquiries about the book's progress and suggestions for its development. You know who you are! Despite your urgings I have not added the contents of the Fell Pony Museum (www.fellpony.f9.co.uk) to this book; that can be a later project, when I have recovered from this one!

Sue Millard, Greenholme,
February 2005

GLOSSARY OF TERMS

The farming community in the old counties of Cumberland and Westmorland (now known collectively as Cumbria) and Northumberland, use traditional terms and local dialect pronunciation. My neighbours use these expressions daily, but the 'non-Cumbrians' who helped by proof reading chapters for me have asked so frequently 'what does THAT word mean?!' that I thought it necessary to provide some translations. All these words and phrases are used in the interviews.

Allotment
An 'allotment' is a large area, mostly unimproved, but walled and distinct both from the fell and the farm. Allotments are useful in that stock can be allowed to run freely on a large acreage. A stallion can, if necessary, run with the mares, which is hardly allowed anywhere on a true fell which is shared with other farms. Often an allotment is owned by a farmer or a smallholder who actually lives some distance away. Cumbrian hill farms often own extra patches of land here and there, bought in times of prosperity and hope when the bank balance looked safe enough to stretch a little; when that is the case, their land is seldom all inside one ring fence. This patchy ownership has been blamed as a complicating factor in the spread of foot and mouth disease in 2001, since it involved a great deal of travelling about the countryside each day past other people's stock.

Back-end

Autumn (also, the hindquarters of an animal).

Back (verb)

To start the training of a young horse under saddle; also, to ask a horse to move backwards.

Bagging up

The increase of size in the udder just prior to foaling (or lambing or calving for that matter).

Bait

Food taken during the working day, either for man or horse; 'bait-bag', the bag in which a man carries his midday meal to his work place.

Beast [bee-ast]

A cow or bullock.

Beck

A stream.

Bent

Fine, hardy grass (several species) suited to poor soil and high rainfall; 'benty' describes the older, tufted growth which turns dry and fades to almost white in autumn.

Bone

The traditional way of measuring the weight carrying ability of a horse or pony is to measure the circumference of the foreleg below the knee. This measurement of the narrowest and least changeable part of the leg is known as 'bone'. It actually measures the cannon bone plus the tendons behind it, and used to be more accurately expressed as 'bone and sinew'. It does not strictly measure the bone itself, but it gives a reasonably effective estimate of the weight bearing capacity of the foreleg, which takes more than half the pony's own weight and a good deal of that of the rider. It therefore gives a fair idea of the strength of the pony's physical makeup.

Tendons should stand well back from the bone; the cannon bone area appears broad and strong from the side, yet proportionally narrow from the front. The front aspects of the hock and knee are flat, rather than rounded or dimpled.

Bray

To beat something – whether animal, child or inanimate object such as a fence post!

Byre

A building designed to keep cows in stalls over winter. The old traditional pattern is designed to hold two to a stall, tied to opposite sides. The cows have a rope or chain around the neck with a toggle fastening; the rope or chain is looped through an iron swivel and the swivel joins in turn to another iron which circles a vertical wooden or steel stanchion. This enables the cow to stand or to lie down without too much constriction. There is usually a feed channel in front of the cows to be filled twice a day, and a muck channel behind to be emptied. Cows were let out from old byres once a day for water, but more modern ones have automatic water bowls operated by the cow pressing a lever with her nose. Solid stone-built byres with low roofs are usually warm in winter, but they are devilish to muck out because their narrow doorways are built for wheelbarrows only, not tractors.

Cake

Any proprietary compound animal feed, made into pellets or 'nuts'. Derived from 'cow cake' or 'oil cake' – the term for a by-product, from which linseed oil had been extracted, which was used as a 20th century cattle feed.

Clashy

Bad weather – heavy rain and strong winds.

Cleanse, cleansing

After foaling, the mare expels the placenta or afterbirth; she 'cleanses'. The afterbirth itself is also known as the cleansing.

Common

Most of the fell areas supply grazing rights held 'in common' by more than one farm, and some big fells are divided into four or five areas, which are themselves known as 'commons'.

Commoner's Association

Group of farmers who, usually because of their tenure of certain farm land around a named fell, also hold commoners' rights on the fell; and who agree policies for the management of stock turned out there.

Cover, covering

Mate, mating – of horses: a stallion 'covers' a mare.

Corn

Oats, or occasionally barley or other grain feeds. (Hardly ever does it mean maize or Indian corn. That is usually referred to as flaked maize or by its old trade name 'Uveca'.)

Cow clap

Cow dung (which lies flat as though 'clapped' with the hands).

Crammling

Scrambling, climbing awkwardly but determinedly.

Cumbria

Largest county in England, formed from the old counties of Cumberland and Westmorland, and parts of Lancashire and Yorkshire.

DEFRA

Government Department for the Environment, Food and Rural Affairs; formerly MAFF or Ministry of Agriculture, Fisheries and Food.

Dowry

Money or goods brought by a wife to her husband on marriage.

Dyke

A land boundary, usually a stone wall or a hedge, rather than a ditch.

Entire

An ungelded male horse.

Fell

The 'fell' is the top of the hills; the lower stretches of the fell are known as the 'fell bottom' and the higher as the 'fell tops'. The fell is extensive. There is no point in labouring to subdivide it into small parcels, because its feeding value is small and animals must be able to range widely to pick up what they need. For instance, the Howgill fells, which are divided for ease of reference into the four commons of Ravenstonedale, Langdale, Brant Fell and Tebay Fell, cover thousands of hectares. Theoretically, ponies on that fell could be anywhere in the ten miles from Tebay to Kirkby Stephen. Even a small fell such as Birkbeck measures 750 hectares (1,600 acres).

Fell-Galloway

The term Galloway had probably come into popular use in Shakespeare's time; he certainly used it in 1598 (*Henry IV part 2*). Galloway is a former horse producing region of Southern Scotland, just over the Border from Cumberland. Dent suggested that in the 17th century there may have been a common confusion in England between the names 'Galloway' and 'Galway' (Southern Ireland). Evidence of its actual spelling and usage in the 18th century comes from apparent trivia such as advertisements in the *Cumberland Chronicle* or *Whitehaven Intelligencer* in 1777 seeking the return of stolen 'horses' which the owners term either 'Scotch' or 'Galloways' – not Irish or Galways. The advertisements give identifying details which show that, surprisingly, these dark brown or bay 'horses' are often only 11.2 to 13 hands high. Scottish Galloways were said to be fast, tireless, very sound, and able to move quickly over rough country. Cumbrian racing Galloways are in the foundation stock of the Thoroughbred but as some were sired by Barb horses, the term must also be a generic one of size and use, rather than a strictly reproducible breed. What is clear is that these little saddle horses were valued, because when they went missing, owners offered rewards for their return. The word in more recent times was applied to any general purpose horse. 'Fell-Galloway' is an old term for the local ponies bred on the fell.

Fell right

All the farms surrounding the open land have a 'fell right' which allows them to turn their stock out to graze 'in common with their neighbours'; for instance there are ten farms with rights on Birkbeck. Originally the capacity of the fell right corresponded with the acreage available in-bye to support stock in winter. Along with the right of pasture went rights to cut peat, to take wood for house repairs, to fish and to feed pigs on acorns and beech-mast. These were all regulated through Manorial Courts, the humblest level of local government. The system was in existence for over 400 years, but since 1965, each commoner holds rights registered with the county council. The Register defines the quantity and type of stock that each commoner is entitled to graze. Commoners may be members of an association which makes the policies for that fell. They may agree, for instance, on which environmental schemes the fell should enter. The commoners do not own the fell, which may be privately owned or belong to a body such as the National Trust. Ownership usually retains the mineral and sporting game rights. Public access is traditionally permitted and is now formally included by British law.

Fell wall

The 'fell wall' divides all the enclosed pasture - allotments, the in-bye, the meadows and any arable fields - from the harsh mountain land above. A good example of the fell wall can be seen to the west of the M6 motorway between Tebay and Shap, or in the Lune Gorge where the motorway skirts the west end of the Howgills. In winter it always seems that the frost and the snow lie more heavily on the fell above the wall than on the in-bye land, and in spring, particularly, the difference in the growth of grass can be very marked with the close-cropped in-bye greening up long before the fell loses last autumn's shades of faded taupe and fawn.

Field house

Stone building in the higher fields of the farm, usually designed to hold cattle in an under storey, and hay above. Often, access to the upper storey is by a ramp at the back, up which the horses could pull haycarts in summer to save the grass for winter use, making use of the inclined plane to spare muscle power lifting the crop.

Flait, Flairt

Frightened.

Foal pride

The mare's first oestrus following foaling, roughly nine days after the foal was born.

Followers

Offspring, progeny. Some fells, eg Birkbeck, do not divide into stints (*q.v.*); instead they permit adjacent farms to run so many female animals plus their offspring or 'followers' under a certain age. '20 ewes and followers' equates flexibly to 20 ewes plus between 20 and 40 lambs.

Fother

Pronounced with a voiced 'th' to rhyme with 'bother', this is the softer Cumbrian version of 'fodder' - any long fibred animal feeding-stuff, traditionally hay but also straw with treacle (molasses) on it, or more recently silage or haylage.

Furnish

Of a young animal, to develop a good covering of muscle over the basic bone structure, and to look mature.

Gapping

Mending the gaps in drystone walls that occur after frost has lifted the ground and then thawed, or after stock have leaned on or climbed over the wall.

Gathering

'Gathering' mares from a big fell prior to weaning foals can involve a drive by quad bike of twenty miles or more to bring the herd down from the fell onto in-bye land.

Geld

Of a mare, barren or not put in foal.

Gelding

A castrated male horse.

Garth

A small enclosed field; a paddock near the farm house.

Ghyll, gill

A deep, steep, narrow valley cut by a small fast stream. Some are small, others are several miles in length. They are a notable feature of the Howgill Fells.

Guineas

A custom of horse auctions is still to take bids in this very old currency. One guinea - £1 and 10 pence, formerly 21 shillings.

Happed up

Heaped or wrapped up – eg, trapped in drifted snow.

Haver [havver]

Oats. Mashed haver is rolled or crushed oats.

Heaf (sometimes 'heath')

Stock, especially sheep but also ponies, are traditionally 'heafed' or 'hefted' to a particular area of fell - that is, they live 'at' the fell most of the year and have been carefully shepherded to accept a certain area as their regular beat. The dams pass on the tradition to their offspring and the herd or flock is thus tied by heredity to its own territory.

Hemmel

A farm building to house cattle (or ponies) loose indoors

especially during the winter. A Scottish Borders rather than Cumbrian word.

Hoggs

Young female sheep; yearlings before their first clipping-time.

Hogghouse

Shelter or other building for sheep. (Nothing to do with pigs!)

Horse sales:

Appleby Fair, Fair Hill

This is a world famous gathering of travelling people. Some of them are true Romanies, but many supposed 'travellers' are merely using the fair as an excuse for a week's holiday and a spot of sharp dealing. Thousands of visitors come to see the caravans, the stalls and and the countless horses, trotters, coloured cobs and ponies. Fair Hill now held on the weekend of the Epsom Derby, ie in early June. It is known locally for high horse prices, low quality harness, and rough behaviour. Occasionally, a fine animal from the many horses 'flashed' here will appear in shows of the highest class. Several auction marts run horse sales throughout the year, but the ones selling Fells are:

Cowper Day

Cowper Day is a horse sale in Kirkby Stephen. The date, as with most of the autumn horse sales, is in October, and the method of sale is an auction, the animals being sold through the ring, individually, to the highest bidder above the owner's reserve price. The sale died away in the 1960s but was revived in the 1990s. It was a useful outlet for Fell, Dale, and cob type foals, as well as unbroken and older stock such as stallions who had reached the time to 'change hands' after four years with one owner. Like all horse sales it could be a wild day's entertainment and not universally approved by the townspeople.

Hawes horse sale
Autumn sale at Hawes, North Yorkshire.

Penrith horse sale
Recently instituted autumn sale at Skirsgill Mart, Penrith, which is now the venue for the Fell Pony Society's own sale.

Wigton horse sale
Autumn sale at Hopes Auction, Wigton, which was for many years the venue for the Fell Pony Society's own sale, organised largely by Jimmy Bell.

Howk
Variant of 'hook' - dig up.

Hull
Any small building that can hold an animal. Usually rather short of space, built of stone with a slated or stone flagged roof, and unlit except for a small window and a wooden half-door. May be for birds, as in 'duck hull', or for young beasts, as in 'calf hull'.

Hundred-weight (cwt)
Measurement of weight; 8 stone or 112 pounds.

In-bye
'In-bye' (often called 'inside' or 'inside land') is any more-or-less improved land that is enclosed. 'Within the boundaries of the farm' might be a good translation.

Intakes, outgans [IN-ticks]
These are stretches of fell edge; the points at which fell stock are driven down to the lower land. Often, catching pens are built to make stock handling easier. In some places, they are called 'outgans', describing the opposite movement, the way the stock 'gans' or 'goes' out to the fell. Cumbrian dialect betrays its Norse roots in such ancient words. 'Fell' is itself of Scandinavian origin.

Kin-bred
Inbred - for example, father-daughter, sibling-sibling, or mother-son matings.

La-al
Little, small.

Laid in
Animals kept indoors. Cattle for winter, or ponies for work, are said to be 'laid in'. (Keeping animals 'inside', usually means in a field, ie 'not out on the fell', rather than in a building.)

Laik, laik on
Another direct descendant from Viking days: to 'laik' or 'laik on' is to 'play'. Often used about the training of horses in a relaxed way: 'you'd get 'em used to things, just laik on with 'em a bit.'

Lish

Fit, supple, active.

Long backed

A pony which appears long from shoulder to rump appears to have 'a rib mair' (an extra rib). If excessive, length is criticised as a weakness for weight carrying, but a degree of length is liked for comfort in riding.

Lowsed

Let out, loosed; used of stallions, bulls or rams, being let out to mate with their females.

Luck

Something, usually money, given back by the seller to the buyer on completing the sale of an animal, 'for luck'. Traditionally it was a penny piece. Sometimes it can be used to bargain with - a buyer would say, 'I'll give you £200 for the colt if you give me £5 back for luck.' Luck can be goods, harness, or even another animal. It depends on the generosity of the seller; it may be worth 1% off a pony's cost, or the idea of 'luck' may never be mentioned at all!

Lugs

Ears - Scandinavian again. Ear marks (notches, slits and holes) were a traditional way of indicating legal ownership of animals - so lug, 'law' was used to describe the earmark, and hence the ear itself. This gives a strong clue that the use of earmarking to denote ownership is at least a thousand years old. Fell pony ears are supposed to be small: if they poke out when a man closes his fist about them, then 'lugs is ower lang' (too long).

Mart

An auction sale; 'market'.

Meadow

A field where long summer grass is mown, and preserved for winter feed as hay or silage. Ideally it is flat, but more often in Cumbria it is steep or rolling ground!

Meat

Often used in the sense of 'food'. 'Sheep meat' is short sweet grass, pasture, herbage; 'green meat' for horses is grass or other green, growing foodstuffs.

Midden, middin

Heap of manure waiting to be spread on fields; can get big in winter when the ground is too wet to take the weight of a muck cart.

Nobbut

'Nothing but' shortened to 'nowt but' shortened to 'nobbut' - barely worth talking about; 'only'. The 'o' is short, as in not, and the emphasis is on the first syllable.

Nowt

Nothing.

Once over [Once ower]

'In the old days', 'once upon a time'.

Owt

Anything.

Paddle

To trample about on wet grassland and turn the sward into bare muddy soil, (also 'poach').

Paster, pasture

Grass to be eaten directly by cattle or sheep, (also 'eatage').

Pennines

Long mountain range running north-south down the centre of the North of England; forms the dividing line between Cumbria and Yorkshire.

Pony

The word 'pony' does not appear to have been used in Britain until relatively recently. Dr Johnson's dictionary of 1755 lists it but he admits he does not know where it came from. 'Poney' appears in advertisements in the *Westmorland Gazette* in 1838. The local pronunciation is sometimes 'poWney', with an oW sound as in 'flower power'. Since 'colt' can also sound locally like 'coWt' with the same oW sound replacing an L, it could be, as some dictionaries suggest, that *pony* comes to us via Scotland (from 1659), from the French *poulenet*, a foal, or a young, small horse. But the breeders use 'pony' and 'hoss' (the Scandinavian 'hross') interchangeably as though they are the same thing, and until quite recently Fell ponies were not so often called Fell ponies but Fell-galloways, *q.v.*, ie a Jack of all trades 'bred on the fell'.

Potter

Traveller; an itinerant trader, especially in tableware; the local word for a gipsy.

Puddle

Mud, wet clay (also 'clart' or 'clarty').

Pulled-off

Also called 'swinging'. Often a foal is taught to lead obediently by being 'pulled-off' - it is tied up on a head collar or halter until it stops fighting the restraint. After that it is led about by the rope and if it follows, it is considered halter-broken. Some places always do this by hand - walking with the foal while it bounces about, or taking a dally in the rope around something solid; some tie the foal to a stout post or tree, to a ring in a wall or even to a farm tractor.

Quad

Four wheeler farm motorbike, used to travel fast to feed or round up stock over fields, allotments and fell land; often tows a trailer that can carry hay to sheep, or bring sick ewes and lambs to be treated at home.

Quid

English colloquial term for 'pound' (£ sterling). Like 'sheep' it is a noun with no 's' for the plural: 'a quid', 'two quid'.

Ratch, ratching

Seek, search, look for; sometimes, seeking for mischief, looking for something to do.

Scour, scoured; also skittered, skittery

Diarrhoea, or the state of suffering from it.

Scran

Find for yourself; scrounge or steal food (verb). Can be any kind of food; but often means tasty bits and pieces, titbits (noun).

Seaves

Rushes - soft rush (light green stems) and, more usually in the North of England, compact rush (dark green) are plants with cylindrical stem-like leaves, one to four feet tall, and clusters of brown flowers halfway up the leaf in summer. The centre is made up of continuous pith, which used to be peeled and used for a wick in a tallow-dipped 'rush-light', where it was supported along its length by a last strip of leaf. Ponies will eat seaves.

Serve, service, serving

Mate, mating - of horses: a stallion 'serves' a mare. A mare who does not conceive 'does not hold to service' or 'breaks'.

Sheep trod

Narrow path made by sheep walking through vegetation as a regular route; usually it only grows very short grass due to wear and nibbling. A sheep trod is most easily seen on 'white ground' or among heather. Here the majority of the grass or heather will be 6-12 inches long, while on the sheep trod the grass will be only one inch long. Among bracken, which grows much taller, sheep trods are difficult to see unless you are following one through the vegetation.

Shiller-bed

Gravel or scree. Shap granite, crushed and used on paths, is often called 'pink shillers'.

Silage, haylage

Relatively recent methods of preserving summer grass. Formerly it was cut and sun-dried to become hay, and stacked, either outdoors and thatched, or in a large barn. The next development was for it to be trussed or 'bottled'; then made into small bales. Round or square big baling followed when mechanisation progressed. Silage follows the same processes as haymaking, but the cut grass is only wilted, not dried, and the product is stored damp. It is preserved either in a silage 'pit' under a large sheet of polythene, or baled and wrapped in plastic sheeting, either of which keeps out air and thus preserves the grass in a comparatively fresh state. It is a faster process than haymaking and so very useful on fell farms where the weather can be unsettled for much of the summer. Haylage is very similar but is dried for longer.

Snigging

Pulling out timber from a woodland using horses. (Could be related to 'snaking', from the motion of the tree trunk across the ground).

Spain, spean [spee-an]

To wean a foal, lamb, calf or other young animal off its dam.

Square up

Start a fight or sort things out; squabble to establish dominance in a herd of ponies.

Stagg

Young horse or pony of about three years old.

Ridden Fell ponies at Sizergh Show 2004.

Lune Gorge, showing the division between in-bye and fell land.

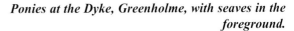

Ponies at the Dyke, Greenholme, with seaves in the foreground.

Heather in bloom on Sunbiggin Tarn Pasture, showing the difference between heather and 'white ground'.

The western edge of the Howgill fells.

Bert Morland with Lunesdale Rebecca, photograph courtesy of Fane Murray.

Mrs Dargue, Alice Robson and Peepings Heather at Dufton Show, August 2003, photograph courtesy of Gwendy Byas.

Above, senior breeders: Jimmy Bell (Waverhead), Frank and Marjorie Wales (Lownthwaite), Her Majesty Queen Elizabeth II (Balmoral) and Bob Charlton (Linnel), photograph courtesy of Christine Morton.

Below, waiting for the ponies: Barry Mallinson, Thomas Capstick and Charlie Parker at an open day at Murthwaite, photograph courtesy of Laura Hart.

Stint

A measure of the grazing on a fell; a stint may for instance support one cow, one pony, or three sheep. Different fells define stints in different ways. A fell farm usually has a right to so many stints, linked to its original land area within the farm boundaries. A small farm will have fewer stints than a large one because it can carry fewer stock in-bye.

Stinted to

A mare that is in foal will be described as 'stinted to foal', or alternatively 'stinted to' the stallion who served her.

Stone

Measurement of weight = fourteen pounds, or about six kilograms.

Stirk

A young cow or bullock. A flexible term from about two months old to a year or so. Often used generally, as in describing a bunch of young cattle as 'la-al stirky things'.

Swung

See 'pulled-off'.

Take over

When a new tenant or owner takes a fell farm, the hefted sheep flock that belongs to the farm is 'taken over' with it, valued as part of the land because their heredity ties them to their area of fell. Other animals such as cattle are not hefted and may be either sold away from the farm or bought individually by the incoming farmer.

Trap

Two wheeled vehicle drawn by horse or pony. From the characteristics of some vehicles (governess car, and some floats) of constraining passengers or driver to enter through a back door or by lifting a seat; if something went wrong you had trouble getting out of the vehicle, ie you were trapped.

Tups

Male sheep; rams.

Twine

To complain, moan, grouse or grumble.

War Ag

During the Second World War the British Government set up the 'War Agricultural Committee' to ensure maximum domestic food production in Britain when imports were all but cut off. This involved bringing all possible land into arable production.

Whin

Gorse, a sharp-prickled green shrub that grows on poor acid soils.

White ground

Dry ground on the fell which grows grass rather than heather. In winter the old growth dries out and fades to off-white, which stands out very distinctly against the near-black of the heather, the red-brown of bracken and the dark green of 'seaves' or rushes. The ponies prefer white ground and avoid heather.

Yam
Home

Yan, ya
One; for instance, in a shop, 'gie us yan o' them' or at the start of a story, 'I remember, ya day…..'

Yows
Female sheep; ewes.

Yoked up
Harnessed to a cart or trap or farm implement.

Mr. A. Smith's Townend Rally FP51093C, winner of the three year old class at the Stallion Show 2004.

THE BREED STANDARD

Height - not exceeding 14 hands (142.2 cms).
Colour - black, brown, bay and grey. Chestnuts, piebalds and skewbalds are debarred. A star and/or a little white on or below the hind fetlock is acceptable. An excess of white markings is discouraged, but such ponies are eligible for registration.
Head - small, well chiselled in outline, well set on, forehead broad, tapering to nose.
Nostrils - large and expanding.
Eyes - prominent, bright, mild and intelligent.
Ears - neatly set, well formed and small.
Throat and Jaw - fine, showing no signs of throatiness or coarseness.
Neck - of proportionate length, giving good length of rein, strong and not too heavy, moderate crest in case of stallion.
Shoulders - most important, well laid back and sloping, not too fine at withers, nor loaded at the points - a good long shoulder blade, muscles well developed.
Carcass - good strong back of good outline, muscular loins, deep carcase, thick through heart, round ribbed from shoulders to flank, short and well coupled, hind quarters square and strong with tail well set on.
Feet, Legs and Joints - feet of good size, round and well formed, open at heels with the characteristic blue horn, fair sloping pasterns not too long, forelegs should be straight,

Mrs. C. Morland's Lunesdale Evening Star FP2720, Fell Champion at Tebay Show 2003.

shoulder and flexing the hocks, not going too wide nor near behind. Should show great pace and endurance, bringing the hind legs well under the body when going.

General Character - the Fell pony should be constitutionally as hard as iron and show good pony characteristics with the unmistakable appearance of hardiness peculiar to mountain ponies, and at the same time, have a lively and alert appearance and great bone.

well placed not tied at elbows, big well formed knees, short cannon bone, plenty of good flat bone below knee (eight inches at least), great muscularity of arm.

Hind Legs - Good thighs and second thighs, very muscular, hocks well let down and clean cut, plenty of bone below joint, hocks should not be sickle nor cow-hocked.

Mane, Tail and Feather - plenty of fine hair at heels (coarse hair objectionable), all the fine hair except that at point of heel may be cast in summer. Mane and tail are left to grow long.

Action - walk, smart and true. Trot well balanced all round, with good knee and hock action, going well from the

Scale of Points	
Height and colour	5
Head, nostrils, eyes, ears, throat/jaw and neck	10
Shoulders	15
Carcase	20
Feet, legs and joints and hind legs	25
Action	25
General characteristics	25
(October 2002 - used by permission of the Fell Pony Society, www.fellponysociety.org.uk).	

23

FAMILY TRADITION

The characters whom I will introduce here are all from farming families. Through faith, resilience, habit, bloody mindedness or whatever one wants to call it - they carry on the habits of a lifetime.

This book 'reaches back in order to go forward' (Bragg, 1976). When we look back, we measure time in many different ways. Some people recall years. Some recall decades, or generations. It is common to mark periods of time with rhymes and mnemonics, and even more so by outstanding characters and events. In the interviews which have contributed so much to this book, the landmark phrases 'in my grandfather's day', 'before the War' and even 'before the First World War' crop up again and again.

The most recent phrase is 'before foot and mouth'. The outbreak of this disease of cattle and sheep paralysed British stock farming between February and September of 2001, especially in Cumbria, Northumberland and Devon, and in some areas its effects are still being dealt with three years on. But disasters such as this, of weather or disease, long hours, low returns and the hard physical work of farming have not daunted the farmers who breed Fells.

Breeding, rearing and handling stock is in their blood, so old farmers seldom really retire; they usually turn into 'dog-and-stick men' who hang over the shoulders of the younger generation, or keep and breed smaller numbers of animals 'for a bit of interest'. They carry on, stubbornly resistant to diseases and ministries and governments, and even in the face of family who tell them with the best of intentions that they should give the ponies up. In response, one breeder said defiantly, 'But I like having Fell ponies about. I would be lost without them.'

How We Got Started

YOU'VE got to be interested in them to carry the Fell ponies on, and it's got to be in the blood. There's a lot of fun in it as well; you get a lot of pleasure out of them. (Chris Thompson).

The Dargue family (Peepings ponies)

MRS Elsie Dargue is the widow of Jos Dargue; her daughter is Pauline Robson, and grand-daughter Alice Robson. The herd runs on the East Fellside of the Pennines in Cumbria, ranging higher than 2,000 feet, and has been in the family's ownership since before 1880.

The Dargue family cannot say when the ponies came into the family, but they can identify exactly when additional ones were brought in by marriage. The Dargue family Bible records that Thomas Dargue of Bow Hall married Anne Shepherd of Murton Hall on 6th June 1820. The family say she brought a dowry of twenty grey Galloways. Anne was born on 4th June 1800, but there is no date of birth for Thomas. In 1856 Thomas and Anne had a son called John who was Jos's father. Jos was born in September 1919.

Mrs Dargue: 'The ponies came to Jos's grandfather, Thomas Dargue, when he got married to Miss Shepherd from Murton Hall. They already had them at Bow Hall [pronounced as in Flower Power]. It's a long time ago. Jos's father was born in 1856. He was sixty-three when Jos was born so you're going back a long way. And then his uncle had them you see: Shepherd Dargue. He was always known as Uncle Shepherd. He was the main pony man; he lived at Bow Hall. I don't know just how he came into them. Jos was nine when Uncle Shepherd gave him his first Fell.'

Pauline: 'Dad never called them Fells.'

Mrs Dargue: 'No, he called them Gallowas [Gallowers]. He always called them Gallowas.'

The late Jos Dargue, photograph courtesy of Fell Pony Society Archive.

Mrs Elsie Dargue explained this during a get-together at Derrick Byas's home in Knock, in which the three generations of the family took part. Derrick became friendly with Jos Dargue in 1980 when he came to Cumbria as a forestry contractor. 'Jos wasn't so fit and I gladly helped out, especially with ponies.' He started helping with such jobs as gathering the Peepings ponies from the fell, then bought himself an unregistered yearling colt which he later trained for forestry work.

The Wales Family (Lownthwaite Ponies)

FRANK Wales and his daughter Christine Morton run the Lownthwaite ponies on the East Fellside of the Pennines in Cumbria. Their ponies can range higher than most of the others with Cross Fell (2,700 feet) as part of their territory. They are close behind the Dargue family time-wise, and probably better known, through showing Fells extensively over the years.

The flanks of the bare Pennines were streaked with snow from a recent fall as I drove to Milburn to interview Frank Wales. On that brisk early spring afternoon heavy rain drove in sweeping veils across a slate-grey horizon. When the showers cleared and the sun glowed in shifting patches on the pale upland winter grass, the Lownthwaite herd could be seen as fourteen black dots high up on the fellside.

Our family have had ponies since 1889. We called them Gallowas. There were Galloway cattle, Galloway sheep, and Galloway horses - ponies. When I was a boy they called them Gallowas, Fell-Gallowas. But they're Fell ponies now.

I don't know where our family's stock originally came from. I think when the family came to the farm, it was common for all the farms to have these ponies. They had them for traps, for going to marts.

The farm belonged to Appleby Castle and we were tenants. In 1924 - maybe - Lord Hothfield went to Monte Carlo and lost £14,000. So when he came back, he'd to sell four farms that were outlying, on the outskirts, to pay it off. So

Christine Morton with Lownthwaite Star Trek, photograph from the FPS archives courtesy of the Wales family.

that's how they got Lownthwaite bought. They would take the sheep over with the farm, but they didn't have many sheep. The cattle they would buy. We don't really know if the ponies went with the farm like the sheep, or if they were to buy, we don't know. (Frank Wales)

The Lownthwaite name is first recorded in the Stud Book as a suffix on 6367 Jenny of Lownthwaite, foaled in 1929, whose grand-dam was a 'Fell pony, by Crossfell Hero'.

Henry Harrison (Sleddale ponies) and Ivan Alexander (Lune Valley ponies)

HENRY Harrison's ponies run on the fells between Shap and Ullswater, Cumbria. In this interview he was supported by Ivan Alexander. Henry's family have bred the Sleddale ponies for generations. The date of the Sleddale herd is not known but certainly before 1920; Ivan Alexander's Lune Valley prefix is first seen in 1970 but he, like Henry, has a lifetime's experience of his local breed.

The Sleddale prefix is the first Fell stud name that I ever became aware of. I rode a grand brown gelding, bred by Henry Harrison, in the pony-trekking string with which I worked every summer during my university years.

Henry is a quiet-spoken, reserved man, and it was helpful to have someone else there to fill in the background and spur him

Henry Harrison.

to expand on some of his remarks. He is at least a third-generation Fell pony breeder, but just like the Dargues and the Waleses, Henry cannot pinpoint the origin of his ponies.

Well, my grandfather had them like. I can't tell you before that, but I know my grandfather had them. Now and then, years ago, we had quite a lot; most we'd ever was about forty I think, once over like. But not then, earlier days, they hadn't that many. Oldest certificate I have is dated 1932; there would have been others before that. (Henry Harrison)

The Heltondale ponies

IT is a matter of great regret that one of the most frequently heard names in Fell pony breeding, the late Sarge Noble, is no longer with us to give his account of the breed with which he will be forever associated. Sarge died in 1996, so when I asked to interview Mrs Greta Noble, a former President of the Fell Pony Society, she said with a wry smile: 'You're ten years too late.' I explained that I would be asking questions such as how the family got started breeding Fell ponies and she laughed and said, 'Sarge didn't need to get started - it was all there for him!' But she preferred not to talk about Fells, in case what she said was taken amiss as being Sarge's words. 'I had very little to do with the ponies. I was just 'the lad', in the background.'

You cannot discuss Fells however without the Noble family's name and the Heltondale prefix cropping up again and again. When Sarge was born, in 1923, his parents

Thomas and Annie Noble lived at Moora Hill, below Keld Head in Heltondale. Thomas died in 1949 and in 1961 Mrs Noble, Sarge and his brother Thomas moved to High House, Butterwick, retaining land at both places to make a 100 acre farm.

In between the two World Wars when farming went flat, they couldn't give the Fell pony foals away... But Sarge's father more or less kept the breed true, and he bred them pure on them Heltondale fells. And then after the 2nd World War when it got popular again, and folk started wanting a

Pictured below, the Fell Pony Council in 1991 showing some of the people who contributed to the book: Top, L to R, Mr Peter Boustead, Mrs Molly Laing, Mr Sam Wood, Mr Frank Wales, Mr J Wykes, Mr Eddie Wilson, Miss Betty Walker.
Middle, L to R, Mr Thomas Capstick, Miss Rachel Bell (secretary), Mrs Gwen Williamson, Mr R Bellas, Mrs Elizabeth Ball, Miss Mary Longsdon.
Bottom, L to R, Mrs Ailie Newall, Mr Jim Bell, Mr Jos Dargue and Mrs Sylvia Hasell-McCosh.

pedigree Fell pony, Sarge's father had the nucleus. That's why you can't hardly buy a pony now without somewhere on its pedigree, a Heltondale pony. (David Trotter)

This is an over simplification, because it completely overlooks the Peepings, Sleddale, Linnel, Lownthwaite, Waverhead, and Townend studs, where the breed survived tucked away in similarly remote places, but it is true that Heltondale, as an area, has been producing Fell ponies 'time out of mind'.

The Noble family first registered their ponies with the suffix 'Keld Head' in the 1930s. Around 1946 in the Stud Book Volume XXV, several ponies were registered with Heltondale used as a suffix. The pedigrees given, which go back three generations, include other ponies with Heltondale suffixes, who are all first registered in that volume.

Like many early entries they descend from mares whose names are known but not individually registered in the Stud Book. You can see whole families of ponies who appear in the Stud Book in a batch around then; dams, daughters, granddaughters; and the date of a prefix appearing in the Stud Book often has little to do with when the family began to breed Fells. Rather it indicates a period when there was enough interest and money to spare on registering ponies at home. Often, ponies were not registered until they were sold.

...all our money went on sheep... Well there wasn't any spare money to do anything. (Mrs Elsie Dargue)

You know, in them days they couldn't afford to register them, could they? It was five shilling I think to register them. (Mrs Frances Bell)

Hence, although the earliest recorded use of the Heltondale prefix or suffix for the Noble family is only seen in the Stud Book in the 1940s, the Stud Book cannot show fairly the length of the Noble family's involvement. It is the same for many breeders: until quite recent times, the registration of a prefix and a pony name were costs that could rarely be afforded.

Sarge showed extensively and had champion ponies at many of the shows. His Heltondale ponies have been used very extensively as foundation stock by other breeders.

Sarge Noble with Tebay Campbellton Victor, photograph courtesy of FPS Archives and Mrs Greta Noble.

The Wilson family
(Townend ponies and Carrock ponies)

THE Townend ponies run on the Caldbeck Commons between Haltcliffe Bridge and Caldbeck, Cumbria. Living at home during the summer, in winter the mares roam over 10,000 acres including land rising to over 2,000 feet. Eddie Wilson's daughter Glenis Cockbain now runs her own Carrock ponies near Keswick, Cumbria. Margaret Wilson and Glenis shared this interview, and some information comes from an article Margaret wrote for *Native Pony* magazine, published in April/May 2004.

Registrations of the family's ponies began early, with 2505 Fanny of Southerfell, 2399 Nelly V (foaled 1905) and 2394 Plly VII (f. 1906) being registered in 1912 in the fell section of the National Pony Society Stud Book Volume XIII. These mares were bred by Eddie's grandfather J G Wilson of Stone Ends House, Hesket-New-Market, and owned by his father E J Wilson of Town Head, Mosedale.

The family moved to Haltcliffe View, where Eddie was born in 1923. The Wilson family then used Haltcliffe View as their prefix, as recorded in 1928 for 5883 Haltcliffe View Polly. However, Eddie Wilson was best known for the Townend prefix, which became famous with the show-ring success of such ponies as 8248 Townend Polly III and Townend Flash II 5278.

Eddie Wilson died in 2003. I was privileged to study as a trainee judge with him more than once; he was kindly and

Margaret Wilson and Glenis Cockbain.

generous with his knowledge and I wish I could have seen him in his prime showing his ponies. Apparently a lady judge once asked him to show his pony's trot again, just for the pleasure of seeing him run!

The Bell Family (Waverhead ponies)

MRS Frances Bell is the widow of Jimmy Bell; she and their daughter Barbara breed the Waverhead ponies on land near Caldbeck. The family owned Fell ponies from the mid 1890s onward. The first registrations of Waverhead ponies were in 1947, but they were bred from others bearing family prefixes including Colemire and Bank House and the suffix 'o' the Hill.'

This is another interview for which I wish I could have used a time machine. The late Jimmy Bell, who died in

2002, was a stalwart of the Fell Pony Society, and one of its best known members. In his showing heyday he and his daughters Nancy and Barbara could turn out up to ten ponies from the farm, perched on its bare sweep of hillside between Caldbeck and Wigton. They would drive long distances to shows and march round several in-hand classes before the daughters performed a lightning change into riding clothes to present their mares under saddle.

Mrs Bell enjoyed fame for her hospitality at the Fell Pony Society's Breed Show and Annual General meetings. I was reminded of this when she and Barbara entertained me one evening by their wood-fired range while the wind and rain battered the house, and she pressed me to eat heartily of a late supper of ham sandwiches, tea, shortbread and fruit cake.

Frances: Granda Bell, Jimmy's father, he was a character. He used to tell about his father coming up Kingston Hill one day in a flat wagon with a Fell pony, and they'd to draw in the side because there was too much on - his two sisters and him; when he was just two year old. He was born in 1893; he died in 1979, at 86 year old. He always had a pony. He rather changed his prefix later on; he had Colemire, which was land he had round Wigton; then him

Waverhead Gypsy and Barbara Bell at Breed Show 1970, photograph courtesy of FPS Archives.

31

and Grandma went in to look after Bank House, Midland Bank, in Wigton; there was a solicitor's, upstairs, and they lived in the house adjoining, and they cleaned the bank. He was postman and he used to deliver a lot of grocery stuff on his bike, and scrubbed all the bank steps, and if any kids walked over them well he brayed them! His prefix was Bank House, then. And then he had what he called 't'ranch' that was land and a cow or two and a sheep or two.

Barbara: Just down from Brookfield, Cuddy Lonning they called it. There was sheds and all sorts but they knocked them all down when they built on it.

Frances: Granda Bell had o' the Hill as well, and then in '46 we married and he handed over three to Jimmy - Jenny o'the Hill, Bank House Polly, and Bess. Jenny o'the Hill was Jimmy's first Fell pony, as his own, when Jimmy was six year old. Granda could rhyme them off, the breeding of them. That's the bloodline that we still have, Pearl and all them.

Bob and Sarah Charlton (Linnel ponies)

FOUNDED by Robert Blackett Charlton who bought The Linnels near Hexham in 1890, the Charlton family's Linnel stud produced Dale and Hackney type ponies as well as Fells. The herd runs on the farm and on rough allotment.

The first Linnel registrations, in Vol XV (~ 1918) were of Linnel Heather 888, a transfer from the Dales stud book, and Linnel Fellsman 889, bred by Swinburns of Gowbarrow Hall. In contrast to the other breeders in this book, these were registrations of stallions rather than mares. Mare registrations

followed not long after, in 1923.

Linnel Fell stallions were exported to Spain in 1926 or '27 alongside stallions from other studs, most of which no longer exist. From the 1940s to the 1960s the Linnel prefix outnumbered most of the other registrations in the Stud Book. This was not just because Linnels bred a lot of ponies. Mr Charlton dealt in them too; he bought many unregistered stock from other breeders. In some ways he acted as a clearing house, buying and paying the fees to register ponies that might otherwise go unrecorded, then selling them on with their papers.

Back in t' fifties like, Bob Charlton's grand-da used to come round and buy all the foals up and then register them back at Linnels. (Bill Potter)

However, by 1989 the numbers at home had dwindled, and it was Dalemain and Heltondale stock which, with bought-back Linnel ponies, formed the nucleus to regenerate the stud.

Sarah: When Bob and I inherited the stud when father in law died, we had the old stallion [Romany Boy], one breeding mare, one barren mare and a gelding.

Bob: So really our stud is new. We bought back four or five Linnel ponies - that we could find - not what we would have chosen. That's why I went and bought from Sarge [Noble] and Sylvia [McCosh] and so on.

Bob plans on writing a history of the family stud to follow up his grandfather's well known book *A Lifetime with Ponies.*

Chris Thompson (Drybarrows ponies)

CHRIS Thompson and his brother Joe originate from Askham, south west of Penrith, where their family have owned Fells since before the First World War. Their ponies run on the fell adjoining Heltondale and can roam as high as the summit of High Street at 2,700 feet.

The Drybarrows herd runs on Askham Fell, between Shap and Ullswater. Joe is well known as a sweet-voiced tenor at hunt sing-song nights, while Chris is more retiring, but both talk knowledgeably and with evident pleasure about Fell ponies. The family's older prefix was Askhamgate.

I always liked working with horses. It was just because they were Fell ponies, the fell rights were there, that I took the job on, you know, of breeding them and looking after

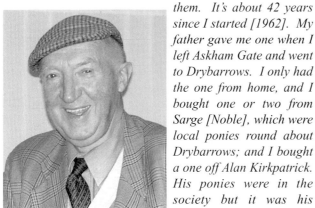

them. It's about 42 years since I started [1962]. My father gave me one when I left Askham Gate and went to Drybarrows. I only had the one from home, and I bought one or two from Sarge [Noble], which were local ponies round about Drybarrows; and I bought a one off Alan Kirkpatrick. His ponies were in the society but it was his

Chris Thompson

daughter who had them. He had them at Hullock Howe. And I also bought a one - the breed would originate from Sarge - off Anthony Barker at Patterdale, who was huntsman, once over.

My father had them all his life; and his father before him. I think they started, there was a farm sale at Town End at Helton, Mr Hunter, and that would be very early on before the First World War, before the society was founded. He bought three ponies there and he just left them on their own ground where they'd been taken from and that's where they originated from. (Chris Thompson)

Mrs Ailie Newall (Dene ponies)

MRS Ailie Newall has kept her late husband Gerald's stud of ponies for nearly 60 years on farm land and rough allotment at 750 feet above sea level. The farm, Todridge, is close to the Roman road, Dere Street, as it runs north from Corbridge, Northumberland.

I married in '50 and the ponies were already here. I think Gerald had 36 to 40 ponies; he had a Linnel stallion, Linnel Radiant, changed to 'Dene Radiant'; and he'd had Fell ponies from a boy, before the War; all sort of through Bobby's [Charlton's] grandfather. (Mrs Ailie Newall)

In those days it was permissible, and quite common, to change the name of a pony that was already registered; that is no longer allowed.

He also started off Sylvia [Hasell-McCosh] with her Dalemain ponies. He was very enthusiastic about getting young people into the society.

I have my husband's stud book here. In those days, people quite freely crossed their ponies with Dales. Roundthwaite Lucky Jim's half brother went to the Dales Society to get them smaller.

After we got married, we decided we would cut the ponies down. So we gave up the Dales, and we gave up the brown ponies, and just kept the blacks. That would be about 1950. (Mrs Ailie Newall)

Ted Benson (Adamthwaite ponies)

TED Benson's Adamthwaite ponies ran on the south east side of the 2,000 foot Howgill fells between Sedbergh and Tebay, Cumbria. Adamthwaite itself lies at over 1,000 feet. The herd was started in 1948 and the mares and young stock used to run on the fell above the farm.

Ted Benson, probably best known for breeding Adamthwaite Lucky Star who stood in the Fell Pony Society's Enclosure in the 1960s, has been retired from farming for many years and now lives in a modest bungalow in Shap, looking out over the wind-swept open moorland of Ralfland Forest. Once again, it was Sarge and Thomas Noble's Heltondale breed that was the foundation for Adamthwaite.

I always liked ponies or horses of any sort; I used to knock about amongst farmers who kept them (Fells) at Caldbeck, sort of amongst them that way, but I never had any of my own till we got to Adamthwaite in 1948. I started

off with Nobles' breed from Helton. First one I had was Heltondale Princess. I bought it off Mrs Laing. She couldn't keep it off roads, that's why she sold it. It would stray down roads. I think Princess was just about best mare I ever had. She was brown. I never had more than about five or six mares in all the time; I didn't go in for keeping a big lot. My first priority was sheep farming. (Ted Benson)

Bill Potter (Greenholme ponies)

BILL Potter's Greenholme ponies run on Birkbeck Fell, east of Shap Fell, Cumbria, on rough, wet land rising to over 1,000 feet. His family was breeding ponies in 1940; Bill's herd dates from 1957.

Bill is a fairly close neighbour of mine, hence the Greenholme prefix. He was my first interviewee and an enthusiastic participant in this project. I was surprised to learn how many places he had lived in as a boy: he went to several different schools - all now closed through lack of numbers - as his family moved from Greenholme to Sedbergh and various points in between.

Father's father was kicked - he'd been to Orton and was kicked by a hoss and was killed at Whitebrow, up at Ullock Bank, Greenholme. That was father's father, my grandad.

We've always had ponies as long as I can remember, but in the early 50s we hadn't any registered ponies. They were by Hardendale Model - that was Bill Brunskill's. Him and Uncle Kit used to sit together at school. Bill Brunskill had Hardendale Model, and Kit used to take his mares to that

Bill Potter spectating at Appleby Show, photograph courtesy of Laura Hart.

stallion. *Far back as I can remember of our own, there was a pony called Shelt, and a pony called Nancy, and they were two dark brown ones. (Bill Potter)*

1683 Hardendale Model was foaled in 1927. He was dark brown with a star and a little white on his off hind fetlock.

Kit would have them when he started farming; they farmed up Studfold, Fell End, had ponies there like. We've always had them plus the fact when we were gaan to school at Midwathstead George Potter had them at Bretherdale Hall; they were called Stead ponies. (Bill Potter)

'Studfold' is a highly appropriate name for a pony breeder's farm - it is a very old name meaning 'the mare enclosure.' George Potter's father and Bill's father were cousins and Bill still has relations living in Bretherdale. Most of Bill's foundation mares for his own herd were Heltondale bred, bought from Sarge Noble.

I started breeding my own when we came to Ewelock Bank [Ullock Bank] - 1954 it would be - bought my first one from Kirkby Stephen for 11 quid. *Then I bought another one after that for 16 quid, and after that I bought them off Mr Noble - I think it was 36 quid for first 'n off Sarge, and I must have had dozens off him since. (Bill Potter)*

Bert Morland (Lunesdale ponies)

BERT Morland's Lunesdale ponies run on Roundthwaite fell between Shap and Tebay, Cumbria, where the land rises to nearly 1,500 feet. His herd was started in 1956.

Bert always acknowledges his debt to Ted Benson as his mentor in the early days of his interest in breeding Fell ponies. Like most of the breeders interviewed, Bert is a FPS judge; he is also on the National Pony Society's panel, and travels widely as judge, showman and clinician. He is keen to maintain the traditional type of all the British native ponies. Some of the material used here is from his book *A Lifetime in the Fells* which is gratefully acknowledged.

> Kaber... a large village green, up and down which I remember running with a Fell pony called Hartley Castle Dolly, belonging to the late Mr W J Dent, of Kaber Fold... In 1958 I purchased my first Fell pony, an unnamed black filly foal from Mr Mark Ireland of Newbiggin-on-Lune for the sum of £14. (Bert Morland, *A Lifetime in the Fells*).

There's a lot of confusion about the Galloway, isn't there? The Galloways - there's some call Fells Galloways, and there's some call Highlands; there's the Garron and the

Galloway Highland. Going back a lot of years they used to talk about them that way, but I've never seen what they called a Galloway... (Bert Morland)

Like most of the other studs, the Lunesdale ponies have been frequent show champions, their progeny are well known all over Britain and they are now also establishing themselves overseas.

David Trotter (Tebay ponies)

DAVID Trotter's Tebay ponies ran mainly on the north and west of the 2,000 foot Howgill fells between Sedbergh and

Tebay, Cumbria. The herd was started in the late 1960s, but largely sold out in 1997-98.

David is a larger-than-life character whose ability to absorb large volumes of bitter beer and retain his cheerful temper constantly amazes me. He is one of the few contributors to this book who is not a judge in an official sense, but his ability to describe the make and shape of

David Trotter in his favourite horsey waistcoat.

ponies, and their behaviour and character, have proved to be extremely valuable. His long-suffering wife Gilly would, I am sure, often have 'given him away with a pound of tea' especially when he spent money that was earmarked for household improvements, on well bred and expensive Fell pony mares. She reminds David of her ironic greetings to these mares on the fell: 'Hello, Three-piece Suite... Hello, Carpet...'

Like so many others, when he started off, David bought Heltondale stock from Sarge and Thomas Noble:

Blow me, when did we start? Somewhere about 1968. Heltondale Star Bright was first, then I went and bought two mares and a stallion off Sarge: Heltondale Laddie, Heltondale Mary II and Heltondale Snip. (David Trotter)

Thomas Capstick (Murthwaite ponies)

THOMAS Capstick's Murthwaite ponies run mainly on the south east side of the 2,000 foot Howgill fells between Sedbergh and Tebay, Cumbria. The herd was started in 1963.

Thomas Capstick called in one afternoon to talk about ponies and share his knowledge of the Howgill fells. He is a gifted photographer. His images of Fells are regularly seen in equestrian magazines, because he goes out long distances onto the steep hillsides and captures the ponies in their natural environment. Looking at other people's earlier photographs it comes as a shock to see him with long hair and dressed in period costume, taking part in historical re-enactments. But he always had a Fell pony in hand. Thomas' family were not Fell breeders as such:

We were at Murthwaite. I got my first Fell pony in 1963. I wanted a bike... I'd never had a bike - I wanted a bike! Mind, I wanted a pony... I'd never had a pony either! And Dad said I could have a choice - a bike or a pony. We had a work horse; it was called Vic because it was born on Victory Day - 60 years ago; a Clydesdale cross, got by a dual purpose horse called Renown. Ted Harper, my great uncle, had it at Garsdale Foot. When I decided I would have a pony instead of a bike, Dad got Ted Benson to buy one from Cowper Day at Kirkby Stephen. It would be the last Cowper Day - they've revived it since. He gave 40 guineas for it, it was a yearling filly, but it wasn't registered. It was off Tom Atkinson.

That first pony, I called it Flicka - that was because there was a programme on television when we were kids, My Friend Flicka. It's funny, I'd such a fascination for horses and ponies. I'd a scrapbook; I mean there wasn't many magazines [Horse and Hound; Light Horse] and I'd this scrapbook and I'd only two or three photographs in it that I'd got out of Farmers' Weekly; we used to get Farmers' Weekly secondhand off Ted Benson, that's how poor we were! We used to get a bit of a magazine from school, Animal Ways. It cost a penny; it was about, well the pets you could have I suppose. I don't know whether it was a monthly, a weekly or what it was, but occasionally I used to get that. It was just a two or three page thing. Of course sometimes that would have a photograph of a horse or pony and I would cut that out for my scrapbook. I would say it has been burnt by now; it hadn't so many. As I say - you were never allowed comics, Beano or Dandy or whatever, we never. You know they [Thomas' parents] started with very very little; I know they didn't have furniture for quite a while. I know furniture was just bought secondhand. (Thomas Capstick)

Barry Mallinson (Hardendale ponies)

BARRY Mallinson's Hardendale ponies run on enclosed fell at Shap, at the 1,000 foot contour, and on some limestone land near Raisbeck, Orton, Cumbria. The herd was started in 1971, but some ponies can be traced in family ownership back to 1918.

I used to see Barry Mallinson helping Stan Mawson and his sons and grandsons to bring Dales type ponies down off Loupsfell allotment. Just before Hawes horse sale, they would walk them past our house along the old drove road. I encountered Barry again when I bought a Fell-cross colt foal from Stan in 1987; Barry helped to deliver it by leading the mare into our cattle building and then nipping out smartly with her while we shut the door in the colt's face. I got to know him a little better during a judging trip to Kentucky, USA, in 2003. He is another who acknowledges Sarge Noble's position among Fell ponies:

1971 it was when I started. I was sixteen year old - it was with Billy [Bill Potter - Barry's uncle]. I was helping

him, and then I ended up I just went to Sarge's, bought a mare in foal, untouched, and he threw yearling colt in for luck; which they did in them days; they were worth nothing.
(Barry Mallinson)

Some further interviews

I am also including, later in the book, some first-hand observations on pony activities of the past, in particular from the late Horace Wilson, of Orton, and from Les Thackeray, who farms at High Scales, Scout Green.

Finally, I had an interview with a local veterinary surgeon, Paul May of the Paragon Veterinary Centre. His public link with the Fell pony is his identification in 1993 of an immuno-compromising disease that is now commonly known as 'Fell Pony Syndrome.' He has shared work with others in this area of research. Liverpool University was the first to begin research into the problem. Academic papers have so far been published in the *Veterinary Record, the Equine Veterinary Journal* and the *Veterinary Clinical Pathology Journal*.

These then are the characters whose words will make up the bulk of this book. They will take you from the tops of wind-swept hill ranges down into the quiet valleys, and from the shores of the lakes to the fertile ploughlands of the Solway plain. They move effortlessly back into the furthest history of their Fell knowledge which still informs the practicalities of day to day husbandry; and throughout, they will tell you of the farming year with the ponies that they have bred for generations.

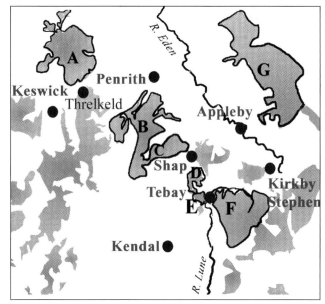

Figure 1: map of the fell commons
A Caldbeck *(Townend)*
B Askham, Barton, Fusedale, Heltondale, Kentmere, Martindale *(Heltondale, Drybarrows)*
C Mardale, Ralfland Forest, Rosgill, Shap, Swindale *(Sleddale)*
D Birkbeck *(Greenholme)*
E Roundthwaite & Bretherdale Commons *(Lunesdale)*
F The Howgills *(Adamthwaite, Murthwaite, Tebay):* **Brant Fell, Tebay Fell, Ravenstonedale & Langdale Fell**
G The Pennines *(Lownthwaite, Peepings):* **Dufton, Knock, and Murton on the west (Front Fell) divided from Back Fell on the east by Cross Fell, Great and Little Dun Fells.**
The unmarked fell areas do not carry pony herds.

WHERE THE FELLS ARE BRED

Very few Fell pony breeders - and none in this book - live in the Lake District, the central fells of Cumbria whose dramatic, volcanic scenery inspired Wordsworth's and Coleridge's poetry. The Fell pony's home stretches from the rolling wildernesses of High Street and Askham Fell, across Shap and Orton to the grassy Howgills; over the Eden Valley to the North Pennines; the Northern Lakeland fells; and beyond them the Border country of Hadrian's Wall stretching into Northumberland and the Borders of Scotland.

The Eden Valley and Border country are fertile areas, where agriculture has been a mixed activity for many

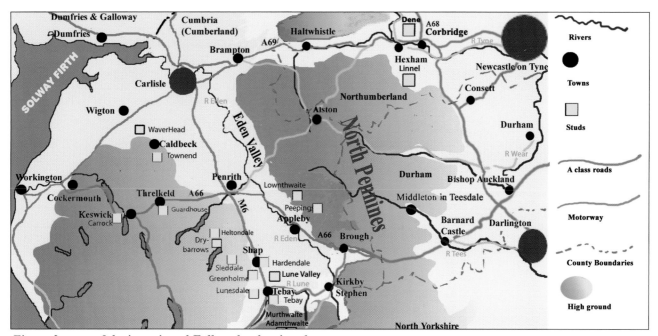

Figure 2: map of the interviewed Fell studs, showing the north end of the Pennines and the Eden and Lune Valleys.

39

Figure 3: map of Northern England showing high ground and locations of interviewed breeders.

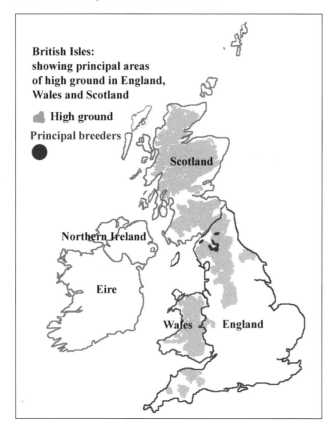

British Isles:
showing principal areas
of high ground in England,
Wales and Scotland

High ground

Principal breeders

Scotland

Northern Ireland

Eire

Wales

England

*The Williamson family's
Townend Ruffle and Greenholme Kitty.*

The Greenholme ponies on Birkbeck Fell in early spring before the grass gets going.

Heltondale Dainty and foal,
photograph courtesy of Thomas Capstick

Lune Valley Lauren FP3551

centuries. Most of the Fell breeders in this book run pure-ly grass fell farms, with cattle and sheep as the mainstay, and one or two have milked dairy cows as well.

Some of the home farms have had land under the plough, especially under Government compulsion through 'the War Ag' (War Agricultural Committee) during the years of the Second World War, but they have never been solely arable. Most breeders of Fell ponies live on the less generous farms, where an important factor is the use of a fell right to take animals onto shared grazing on the hill, away from the farm's lower, relatively confined land.   The fell right enables them to turn out sheep and lambs, sometimes cattle and of course Fell ponies, so freeing-up in-bye grassland to take a summer hay crop. Not all the pony breeders have a fell right, but most do. There will be much more about the fell and its uses in later chapters. It is worth looking first at the breeders' locations.

Most interviewed breeders are in the north and east of Cumbria, with the exception of two in Northumberland. There is one group along the edge of the northern fells of the Lake District, roughly from Keswick to Caldbeck. Another little cluster is in Northumberland, at Hexham and Corbridge; a third along the East Fellside of the Pennines, to the east of the Eden valley; a large number on its west side, from Askham south to Shap, Greenholme and Orton; and another group around the edges of the Howgills from Tebay to Ravenstonedale, east of Sedbergh.

Peepings

TO get from Dufton Fell over to Milburn Fell, for a pony, is quite difficult, 'cause you've got such as Rundale cutting through, on the low side where it's decent footing; and by the time you get to the top of Rundale you're into mosses, soft ground. So for ponies to actually get round, they need to be sort of intending heading in that direction. But hav-ing said that, ponies are now spending more time this side of Rundale than what they used to. They never used to come to this side of Rundale. They used to come from High Cup across as far as Pussgill and back again; and then usually from High Cup down the stream and back towards Bir'dale [Birkdale, south of what is now Cow Green reservoir], that's where they always traditionally ran. But they're now getting to run further towards Milburn side than what they used to do. I think it's mostly to do with quad bikes on fell; they've got a new grouse keeper up there does a lot on bikes, and ponies don't like them - it's disturbing them off their natural heaf. They won't have owt to do with them and they just get out of t'way. And keeper's up on that side reg-ular. It tends to push them to this side. (Derrick Byas)

If you found a horse in the middle of pure heather there was something wrong because they didn't normally go onto t'peat. So basically they would follow Front Fell, which was all white [fine hardy grasses]; they'd go down side of High Cup and into High Cup and they'd go down what they call High Cup Plain at back, and what they call the Street - Maize

Beck. Basically they followed Maize Beck down towards Bir'dale - that was their traditional range. It's starting to alter now, but again they're following white ground and avoiding the heather. (Dargue Family)

Lownthwaite

Frank Wales: They can go twenty miles. It's seven miles to t'Back Fell [east of Cross Fell].

Christine: The last ones that we lost, I picked up at Helbeck - Brough - once you get to Helbeck there's the Army fence that pushes them over to Barnard Castle. And the A686 that cuts right across.

Frank Wales: Our ponies are heafed; they don't go over the top. They'd only go maybe six mile out. But if people put strange ponies onto the fell they 'tice our ponies over the top. It's like heather and peat. They die, if they get on a peat break - it's like a mat that grows heather, there's peat all round it. We once had seven died of thirst on a break because they daren't come off. (Wales family)

It IS soft underneath. Waleses lost some of their horses because they got over t'Back Fell in a drought, and then, by back end came and it come wet again, they couldn't get back off there - they actually died on t'Back Fell. I don't know whereabouts because I wasn't there. (Derrick Byas)

Linnel

An old chap called Johnny Nichol, he's come here all his life;

and he remembers as a boy turning ponies for father and grandfather. He used to have some land at Natherton which is half way between Hexham and Newcastle and he used to run a lot of ponies there. Just ran them loose back along the A69... imagine doing that now! And the men used to come out of the pub at Corbridge, the Angel, to turn them down across the bridge. (Bob & Sarah Charlton)

Dene

The A68 is Dere Street, the Roman Road. That high part, 'The Fell', was open moor, but they've dug it up now, ploughed it. It used to be heather - lovely. When I was first married, first came here, there were no trees, nothing - the prevailing wind is west and it's really pretty awful! (Mrs Ailie Newall)

Sleddale

Ivan: They could get on top of Rossgill Moor and that was as far as they could get, wasn't it?

Henry: Yes, on there, that's right. But they could get right over top here and then down to Haweswater.

Ivan: Did you once have one at Kentmere an' all? They're inclined to go to Swindale more - you set off to breed them in Swindale, didn't you? (Henry Harrison and Ivan Alexander)

Drybarrows

They sometimes get around Rough Hill [Ruffle] but they also go the other way onto High Street as well. We're straight onto the fell at Drybarrows. A steep pull up from the road... You rise from 600 feet to 1200 you see.

They can come down to Barton and they can go to Patterdale. They have their own little patch. Well they normally go on our own fell and up onto Low Cop and then High Cop. They have been sent round into Cawdale and round that way onto Sceugh. Not so much on Helton Fell because there's that piece comes up from Widewath and Scales, that rather divides it. They tend to hang to the Sceugh fell and onto Loadpot.

There's about fifteen breeding mares. The young ones I have in-bye at present; well since foot and mouth, I took allotment ground for them and kept them off the fell and just let the mares with the foals at the fell. (Chris Thompson)

The Heltondale ponies ran on similar areas to the Drybarrows ponies. Like the Sleddale ponies, some went as far as Kentmere, while other little bands separated into Martindale and Fusedale on the edges of Ullswater.

Waverhead

We have no fell right, never have had. The fell wall divides us. They used to come over onto Ellerbeck there, but they [the farmers] don't really like them on this side. They go on the other side, and really they're supposed to be on that fell, but occasionally they come onto Uldale. Johnny Little had quite a lot on t' fell; he'd a fell right, but his used to come right down into t'village, because storm would drive them this way. There was a man in Caldbeck - Tom Wilkinson - used to always just have one pony, a nice, old fashioned type. It used to be tethered in the village. (Mrs Frances Bell)

Townend

Our mares can go over to the other side of Carrock Fell as far as Caldbeck, which is about six miles. The fell itself is 3,700 hectares. (Margaret Wilson)

Murthwaite

The fell is actually known as the Howgill Fells. You see it's split into four different fells: Ravenstonedale Common, Langdale Fell, Tebay Fell, and what they call Brant Fell, which is from Carlingill right down Howgill and back to Cautley, to just up to Cross Keys. It's collectively known as the Howgills. Really, we only have rights on Ravenstonedale Common, but because there's no fences, there's nothing to stop them from going right down to Sedbergh, and they do. Two or three ponies seem to go down to Sedbergh, on a regular basis, and there's some come onto the Fair Mile which is still part of Brant Fell. I'm in the east on Harter Fell, that's where my sheep run, and the ponies just spread. Ravenstonedale Common is 3,800 hectares. Langdale common'll not be quite as big; Tebay common'll not be quite as big; but Brant Fell, which is from Howgill and back up Cautley, 'll probably be the biggest.

The Howgills is quite unique in the type of fell that it is; it's not peaty, so you get a nice green grass, you know, there's no heather, or very little heather; it makes it a very good fell for ponies. There's a rocky bit in Black Force and a bit at Cautley Spout but really they're the only rocks; there's a few shiller-beds; a few stone outcrops; no, a tremendous area for ponies; it is. The only trees that survive are those that are in these rather inaccessible gills; they're only mountain ash, and they're there because the sheep can't get at them! There's very very few. It's practically a treeless fell.

There's some bracken on Howgill and on Cautley front and a little bit on our side on the front; you tend not to find them there, and you certainly tend not to find them on very very steep areas; it's as if they know their limitations, or they sense the danger. (Thomas Capstick)

Adamthwaite
The only bit we hadn't any right on was on Bluecaster. All the rest, they could run right round Tebay and Howgill, 17,000 acre. Where would you find ponies? Oh anywhere - we never had much bother finding them, specially t'older mares. We could find them very often within sight of Adamthwaite, but the younger ones, when they got turned away at spring, they could get away to Howgill or Fair Mile. (Ted Benson)

Tebay
Our ponies could run right through to Sedbergh, and Cautley. [Heltondale] Heather Lad used to run Longdale Bottoms, and on this side, and onto Fair Mile, was [Tebay Campbellton] Victor. They seemed to just keep to the herd; Heather Lad would come sort of out along the bottom, perhaps up Yewdale, this way, and then go back again. Victor,

he'd have his, just sort of on this end, up to where we call 'Dick Mawdesley's ground' that drops into Yewdale; then go over that top into Fair Mile and into t' Howgills. (David Trotter)

Lunesdale
It's six mile to the top - goes nearly to Huck's Brow, except there's an allotment in between. With the hills and hollows, a map measurement doesn't give you the correct acreage. It gives you a lot more acreage on the ground. (Bert Morland)

Greenholme
It all slopes away north - it isn't very well sheltered either when you get up there. It bloody isn't. There's no trees when you get yonder, and best bit is up a back of Shap Wells there, the wood that they planted, and it's that damn wet - they can't get up to within two or three hundred yards because of t' bog, it's soft, wet. Down from Wasdale Bridge - right to the wood - corporation ground - between that trod and t' wood, you can hardly walk, it's just bog. They like to try to get into there to shelter like, but it's ower wet for them. River drains it a bit, it's driest on t' beck edge. (Bill Potter)

Hardendale
I'd some land up to Keld, so I'd rights on Ralfland. But against motorway, that's classed as fell. There's three of us has rights on it, three stints; it's enclosed fell, it was common land before the motorway was built. Up at Raisbeck

there's no shelter, that's the trouble, it's all wide open; it's just growing is my wood, but if bad weather comes in t'other way, if they do stay out, they just paddle it up. So they might just as well stand inside for six weeks and go onto good grass. Surprising how it grows in March. I've never known anything grow like it [limestone pasture]. Grow grass! Lot better than Shap. (Barry Mallinson)

Other beasts on the fell

SHEEP and cattle numbers have gone up as well as down. Farms will only keep what there is a market for. There have been strong influences, such as the temptation to increase numbers to qualify for Government subsidies, or the drastic compulsory culls of foot and mouth in 2001, but even on one fell, farm practices vary. On some heafs the ponies have the fell to themselves over winter, and little competition for food, because the in-lamb sheep are brought down in-bye, and cattle housed. Some farms leave their sheep out all through the winter and only gather them to the lower ground for lambing. On some fells cattle are put out in the summer months, and on other fells, there are none at all.

Pennines

Mrs Dargue: There was no cattle at all at any time. But sheep were all brought in beginning of November and they weren't out any more till lambing time. Well the hoggs used to go earlier, about April.

Derrick Byas: Yowes and lambs went up end of May, June.

Mrs Dargue: But there was no cattle at all.

Derrick: If you got snow and a bad east wind on that fell, you got them 'happed up' as Jos put it. So there was only ponies - they stopped out all year round. (Dargue family)

There were sheep, and cattle; not geese in my day. There was a lot of sheep at fell, far more than there is now. But how did eighty horses survive? Our sheep used to stop at fell till just before lambing. On my pony I used to take a bag of cake in front of the saddle, you know, in front of Silverband mine, and chuck it out for them on't fell. It would be four miles. I spoiled my saddle, cause it stretched the front bridge. (Frank Wales)

Shap

Henry: You never saw cattle on t'fell then. Years and years ago, there was as many sheep as there was just before foot and mouth. There was three farms up Swindale; they would have well over a thousand breeding sheep that I know of. We had one or two ponies used to go and bother other people's sheep, kind of thing; they maybe were a bit of a nuisance. So you're better bringing the ponies in.

Ivan: Cattle, when they've been out on the fell lately, I think they've been substituted rather than living off - like they were often fed at fell, weren't they, rather than living at fell. But I suppose in a roundabout way horses have as much right on fell as sheep, and if you wanted to feed your sheep, you took that chance.

Henry: We weren't forced to bring the ponies in, just brought them in for neighbourly's sake really. Ponies knew where sheep was being fed; they weren't daft! (Henry Harrison and Ivan Alexander)

Crosby Ravensworth Fell

There was sheep, cattle and horse. All breeds. Every breed, there was. Now there's no cattle, and very few sheep; and horses have been off for a while. What ruined Crosby fell was the cattle. There used to be beautiful heather; it was best heather there was. If they'd kept the quantities to what everything was registered for, there'd have never been any problem with it. (Barry Mallinson)

Tebay Fell and the Howgills

I know of quite a few heafs that have gone that would have a few hundred sheep out. There's definitely less. We're getting more twins nowadays in our flocks, so they stay in, and suckle the lambs in-bye. I've no suckler cows now, but I used to put them out in the spring, just before lambing time. Less work, and mostly because I calved my cows in February and March, and I used to put 20-something cows out and just feed them a big bale of silage. Then when I spained my calves of a back-end, the cattle went out on the fell bottom, again with supplementary feed. But the ponies used to clear off, about the middle of March. So by the time you put the cattle out, there wasn't many ponies coming to your silage. These last two years they've been taking rather

longer to go, just into April; but as soon as there's any fresh grass, they go, rather than stay. (Thomas Capstick)

Mostly ours stopped on fell, but fell came right down to yard gate; there used to be a bit of a planting, a few old larch trees, just out of fell gate, and they used to come into there in winter at nights, and I used to feed them in there. They didn't bother my own feeding sheep there; I used to feed them in there and then take sheep hay further up fell. So they didn't bother them, but if they were going to bother anyone else, such as at Murthwaite, I let them into the allotment to feed them there. (Ted Benson)

Sometimes we'd do a deal and we'd get a few cattle and we would have cattle on, but not permanently. And then I got a few Herdwicks. As for cattle on the fell - there were two farms used to put them out. There were more sheep out then; well, every farm. From here to Brockholes, that was where Bybeck used to run their sheep, out on that breast; well there isn't a sheep out there now. As these farms get sold, to off-comers sort of thing, that aren't farmers, they're not running sheep. There'll be no sheep on this front nearly to t' Fair Mile. (David Trotter)

Askham Fell and Helton Fell

There were just sheep on the fell; there wasn't a lot of cattle put out. There were three farms would put out, on our own fell where I could see. Sarge and Thomas [Noble] would put cattle out on the fell when they were at Heltondale. Well some of them were Galloway cattle, just as hard as the Fell ponies. They just had hay; it wasn't that there was any concentrates or anything fed. Yes, there could be more sheep out then. Since foot and mouth they haven't gone back, not to the quantity that there were. (Chris Thompson)

Birkbeck Fell

In 1972 I had 72 ponies. The stock numbers on the fell weren't as high. Plus the fact that here, my ponies are the only hosses on t'fell and my sheep are t' only sheep on t' fell in winter, so I can feed them, but them that's on Howgill side they get nowt, not a bite. (Bill Potter)

Bill's reasons for not feeding the ponies out on the Howgills are several - quite apart from the fact that Birkbeck is right outside the farm gate, while the Howgill ponies are seven miles away. The Howgills, unlike Birkbeck, are a shared fell, so feeding ponies out there can cause trouble; the ponies are on a bigger range, and can travel widely to find food; they can also get into shelter in deep ghylls and thus need less food to keep warm in bad weather, instead of being lured out into the wind to feed at the fell wall. This shelter is something they don't have the advantage of on Birkbeck. Yet Birkbeck at one time supported two dairy herds.

When Uncle Kit came here [Stoney Gill] in '54, he used to milk 18 cows, and fell was his cow pasture. You could actually hear him, when it come to three o'clock, you could hear him shouting of his cows, from here, to Ullock Bank.

Anywhere near Ullock, we used to set 'em off. He used to boast about how high his butterfats was in them days. (Bill Potter)

When I went to school, John Robertson at Bracken Hill, his milk cows used to ga to t'fell through t'day. There again, there wouldn't be as many sheep out I don't think, then, as now. I can remember John Robertson shouting o't cows at nine o'clock at night, and once you could hear him shouting, if they were over our side, we could see them setting off; he never come for them, just shout on 'em; and away they went. They would go in paster for t'night, milk 'em and put 'em to t'fell. Kit [Potter] used to supply Shap Wells [Hotel] in those days; I can remember them ringing up at three o'clock or half past one night, wanting milk. And Kit said, 'Wey, you silly buggers, t'isn't milking time yet!' but he went to t'fell and got two or three cows in and milked and got plenty, and then they were put back to fell and then he set off again later to finish t'lot like. But not so often! (Ivan Alexander talking with Henry Harrison)

The milking cattle pastured on Birkbeck were Shorthorns, a hardy dual-purpose breed. Ivan added: 'You're talking of mid sixties when folk got to caking them, for t'hill farms. Your sheep never got cake, they just got hay.' Nobody in Greenholme milks today.

To sum up, on the Pennine commons, no stallion, ram or bull could run with the herd, and this is a rule of very long standing. Crosby Fell used to carry a lot of horses but it has now been cleared. The Howgills have a fairly recent rule that forbids stallions running on the fell, and the same is true of Birkbeck. Roundthwaite does not permit stallions either. Only on the Helton and Askham fells, there seems to be a limited right to put out a stallion during the breeding season, but he is brought back in-bye for the rest of the year.

Ponies share the grazing with sheep on all the fells, with larger numbers grazing during the summer than in winter, as the ewes and lambs are turned out to free the in-bye land for hay and silage-making. However, there are fewer sheep out on the fell now (2005) than there used to be. One of the main reasons cited is that, four years ago, there were massive 'contiguous' culls, intended to prevent further spread of disease from infected farms during the foot and mouth outbreak. Sheep numbers have not gone back to the levels that they were in 2001. One of the other reasons for falling sheep numbers on the fell is that, with better management at tupping time, more are carrying twins, which cannot easily be reared by a ewe living on the fell; so after pregnancy-scanning the flock, farms turn out only the ewes carrying single lambs, while those with twins are kept down in-bye. In a few areas, cattle as well as sheep used to be turned out to graze on the fell during the summer, but in almost all areas this is no longer the case.

As with all things, a balance needs to be struck. The high grazing pressure of a few years ago has begun to decline. The breeders interviewed can recall a period before that, when there were relatively few stock put out, with a mix of mainly sheep and a few cattle and ponies, and with almost no supplementary feeding the fell commons sustained everything. They point to subsidies on stock numbers as the motivation behind increased grazing in recent times, until the foot and mouth outbreak. But the political arguments underlying general hill-farming practices are, fortunately, not within the scope of this book. Ponies have never attracted any subsidies, so the numbers kept are driven by the limits of the fell right, by market pressures and by breeders' wishes and opinions and their ability to manage the herd.

What does a Fell pony look like?

Over coffee one day, I was talking with a work colleague about what I had been doing recently with Fell ponies, and of course, he asked the inevitable question: 'So tell me - what makes a Fell pony a Fell pony?'

I trotted out the usual remarks about the pony type and the strong bone and silky feather; the well laid shoulder, the 'backside like a cook', the length of rein, the long, straight mane and tail. He listened attentively and objected, 'But you have been besotted with these animals for over thirty years! What is it that makes them unique?'

I found a brief answer for him, about liking their hardiness, toughness, and compact power, and the fact that the ponies, like alpine plants, are so well tuned to the area in which they have always lived. However, his question set me thinking: how much information do we manage to impart to people who are interested in learning about Fells? Do we really describe their qualities adequately?

Type

MOST of the outward characteristics of the breed of course are detailed in the FPS breed standard; a breed being a group of animals which are physically alike and genetically similar, distinct from others of the same species and which, when you breed them together, predictably reproduce the type. Breed status may or may not have anything to do with the 'pedigree' status of registered stock. The Polo and Riding Pony Society (1893) which became the National Pony Society in 1914, took responsibility for registering mountain and moorland ponies, as pure hardy types from which to breed polo ponies by crossing with Arab or Thoroughbred sires. The ponies then were only classified by their origin in various areas of Britain.

One difficulty with the FPS breed standard is that it assumes the reader already knows what the word 'good' means in several different contexts - good length of rein, good bone, and so on. So I asked the breeders to elaborate on what they personally liked. It was easiest to begin with the outward characteristics, so those form the main topic of this chapter, but as Bob Charlton said, 'I can't just say they're fat, black and hairy, can I!'

Over and over again came the phrases 'it was a real pony', 'a proper pony'. But pinning down how the Fell pony differs from other breeds, or even how a pony differs from a horse, is very hard to do in words. There is something about a Fell pony head that is quintessentially 'pony' - pricked ears, bright prominent eyes, breadth across the forehead, a kind yet alert expression; depth of jaw without a coarse throat; a straight profile that is neither Roman nosed like a cold blooded horse nor dished like an Arab, and quite a sharply defined, open nostril above a neat muzzle. Fleshiness around the head, or drooping lips, are not liked and completely loppy ears are unknown, probably because such characteristics would cause more rapid heat loss in bad weather than a neater, 'dryer' outline. There's also very often a quickness of movement, expressed as 'full of fire', that distinguishes a Fell as a pony rather than a horse!

I reckon really that the Sleddale ponies are the only true ponies that have always, constantly, been a true pony. (Mrs Newall)

For Jos, they wanted to be blocky and thickset; not these light 'uns; they wanted to a be a good thick pony that could do some work. He wanted them square and he wanted them blocky and he preferred them below 13-2 as over. Well set up, workmanlike. (Derrick Byas)

Bob: There were very few breeders just breeding the riding type; I suppose you could say we were sort of leaning that way. But I do think a lot of the old fashioned breeders have realised that their market has got to be something that would get you home for dinner and not be late. Whereas a lot of them probably - I'm not saying they wouldn't but they didn't look as though they would. Because you can go back, fifty or a hundred years, and I wonder about those trotting ponies that pulled the record times and all that, they were probably great big hefty things but they still did the speed. But really you should start at the feet and work upwards; make sure they're sound. I like a leg on each corner! (Bob & Sarah Charlton)

Frank: Charlton's ponies then were more riding type, like Mrs Newall's. They're more the older fashioned type now.

Christine: You can still see two types though, can't you? (Wales family)

The mountain ponies of Cumberland and Westmorland differ considerably in type, the result of promiscuous breeding by farmers and others possessing mares.

Judging from the nature of the locality, which in most parts is rugged, hilly and exposed to nearly every keen blast that blows, one would expect such ponies to be similiar in build to those of Wales, endowed with surety of foot and endurance, combined with a constitution of iron.

As a matter of fact, these features are strongly developed in the mountain ponies of the counties to which they belong. The indiscriminate selection of stallions has been one of the principal causes of the diverse specimens of fell ponies that one sees in visiting the district.

These ponies do any sort of work, such as harrowing, going to market, ploughing, muck-carting etc, etc., frequently existing on the mountain-side without any forage beyond that of their own gathering.

In colour they are mostly black, brown, bay, more rarely grey, and quite exceptionally chestnut, without white markings, though a star on forehead is frequently met with. The withers as a rule are fine, the chest deep and the shoulders of good slope, making good riding ponies of the weight carrying class.   (*All About Horses*, 1911)

I do like to see a nice round open eye, and a nice broad forehead. We used to get a lot of Roman noses, but you don't get those so much now. But the jaws sometimes aren't shaped; you know, I like to see a nice outline of the jaw-

bone. I like a good deep girth, and that's another thing, some you could drive a double decker bus under them. They've got so much hair now, it looks as if they've more bone. They've got better flat bone, because some of them used to have what I called the 'cannonball knee', a great round hock, which stopped them from really moving for-ward; the back legs were trailing, they just go up and down instead of covering the ground, you know, picking it up and going, with the back legs getting under and pushing them off. No, they have changed, very much so. Change of people, change of breeders, a lot of the old fashioned studs going out. (Mrs Ailie Newall)

Winners of the Northern Group at the National Pony Society Show at Islington, around 1930. Roy B Charlton (centre) with Ted Turnbull, stud groom at The Linnels.

Fell pony type has changed a lot; over thirty years. They used to be short legged, thick bodied; rather narrow feet; a coarse, heavy coat on them; they seem to have lost that now. I think better end of them could be as good, better than they used to be; better feet, better ankles, better hind legs. ...No, I think taking them on the whole, they'll be rather better than they've ever been, specially feet and legs.

Well what I always looked for was same type as a good Clydesdale; good broad feet and a good pastern; not too long, not too stumpy; good hind leg; and if you'd all them, you weren't so far wrong. (Ted Benson)

There have always been good ones and bad ones both then and now! But less attention seems to be paid now to bone, joints and action. (Glenis Cockbain)

Shoulders

BERT Morland, who has given his share of educational clinics, always makes a point about the shortest line on the outline of a pony's body being the line under the neck, from throat to brisket, while the longest outward curve should be the topline of the neck, from the poll to the point where the wither drops into the back. That gives a pony a long, well sloped shoulder which in turn provides scope for elastic movement. 'Good length of rein', therefore, comes from a well laid shoulder, not a long neck.

Shoulder is very very important. If shoulder's wrong everything's wrong. It's a case of if you get a good riding shoulder you can get some action. They want to be sloped rather, they're better workers and everything. (Bill Potter)

Heads and necks

To be typical the head ought to be small, but big or coarse heads are more frequently met with in mountain ponies than any other breed of pony...

Large ears are more general than small ones. The legs and feet are generally of the best, there being plenty of muscle, bone and wing sinews.

For protection the coat is necessarily long and dense, the hair on the limbs being rather long, but it ought not to be coarse in texture.

As previously stated, there is a good deal of difference in the quality and type of these Border mountain ponies, some being excellent, others bad, and a third class indifferent.   (*All About Horses*, 1911)

I don't think the head wants to be too big. Neck nicely joined onto the shoulders. (Chris Thompson)

I don't like ponies with short stuffy necks; I like something in front of me. We've got a few plain headed ponies and I don't particularly like the plain heads; I think the pretty head is the first thing you look at. (Bob Charlton)

You want a nice head - not too long; there are quite a lot with long heads; good bone, plenty of bone, nothing less

than eight inches. (Barbara Bell)

It had to have pony characteristics. I didn't like them with big heeds and big lugs. Dalesy, aye. If you breed that into them like, you're gaan naewhere. I always liked heeds - I know I get criticised a bit by folk when I'm judging, if I say, lugs is ower lang. I like a big bold eye and a big wide nose and they criticise me because I say I like its heed. It's what comes into t' ring first is its heed, it's got to look nice and sweet. I get criticised quite a bit because I like a nice pony head. (Bill Potter)

Length of back
There's a difference of opinion about the length - some people like them short coupled. But you've always got to be able to put a saddle onto them, haven't you, if you want to ride them? Whereas the short coupled ones, they liked them for the collieries, they reckoned they were stronger you see. (Chris Thompson)

I like a thick 'un, I'm not a reet riding type man; you know, I like them short coupled. They reckon riding type has a rib mair, like a good rider wants to be long backed doesn't it. And a good short coupled 'un they maybe don't make the best riding ponies. (Bill Potter)

I like them short, nicely coupled up - not too long. But if you get too short-coupled up, you don't get a good ride because it's all just 'going' together. (Barbara Bell)

I'm not mad keen in any horseflesh on things that are too short. The old fashioned thing of - you know - short coupled and so on - certainly for riding, I think they're uncomfortable. They don't want to be great long lanky things, but if you think about the ones that are slightly longer, I don't notice any difference in any form of disability or lameness or back problems. I don't think it's got anything to do with the length of the back; it is how they are stuck together. (Bob Charlton)

Hind quarters
CURIOUSLY, nobody gave me any comments about the hindquarters on a Fell pony! Twenty years ago I heard Jim Bell say he liked a pony to have round, smooth quarters,

round like an apple. Looking from the side, Fells don't have a flat croup like the hot- or warm-blooded breeds; it

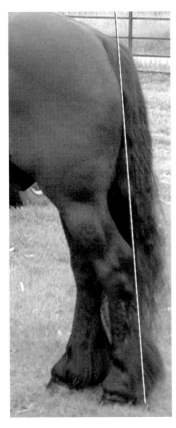

slopes down to the tail with a muscular outward curve. In youngsters, particularly on the fell in the depths of winter when they are a bit thin, the quarters can look as though they fall away, but all this changes dramatically when they 'furnish' with muscle later in life and start doing serious work. The point of the hock needs to be cleanly defined, and the front of the joint should be flat rather than round. If you imagine a vertical line up the back of the cannon bone to the hock, then extend it upward, it should not lie further back than the point of the buttock.

Bert Morland told me when I was a trainee judge that, looking at the pony from the back, he wanted to see hocks that lay a little closer together than the 'book description' of good conformation, where the tip of the hock is supposed to lie vertically below the point of the buttock. The cannon bones stand vertical as far as the hock and then the pony widens out dramatically with muscular gaskins and quarters. Many horse books show the hoof placement ground plan as 'four square', but Fells often stand slightly wider at the front than at the back, though it can be hard to see this because of their impressive tails. It is a fault to go 'wide behind' or to swing the feet out from a true line, but we are very spoiled in the fact that few Fells move crookedly; they nearly all go straight! When Mrs Newall looked for 'a bit of nice action, free action,' she was also looking for 'a bit of lift in the hock as well as the front end.' A good Fell 'goes back and front' with lots of power from the back end.

Feet

If you hadn't got good feet you hadn't got a horse. Jos wanted good blue hard hooves - most important thing was good big feet. Jos used to reckon if you'd too much feather you'd nae hoof. He used to look at a pony and say, 'look at all that woolly stuff round - there's no hoof underneath it.' (Derrick Byas)

Good hard black feet - nice - not round boned...(Chris Thompson)

Feet must be in proportion, neither narrow donkey feet nor walloping great 'dinner plates'.

Lots of 'back ends' at a breed show.

I like to see a genuine spread of foot. I know that mare that we lost, she had a good foot and she always bred a good foot. (Barbara Bell)

It's surprising, like I follow a lot of ponies on me quad - if ground's wet and you follow them away, it's surprising how fifty per cent of them has white soles. Back and front! I didn't realise this, cos when you're standing in the ring and judging, if you don't pick it up it's a blue foot, but Arthur Heighton, t' old blacksmith from Barrow, he said, 'Pick that'n up Bill.' Picked it up and sure as eggs it was a white foot underneath, its sole was as white as white. And I said

to him, 'is it any softer for putting shoes on?' 'No,' he said, 'it isn't, not a bit different,' he said, 'if t' outside's blue, they're just all t' same.' But there's a lot of ponies with white soles. You wouldn't realise. If you're just standing looking standing on ground, you wouldn't notice. (Bill Potter)

I enjoy watching my own farrier when he trims and shoes my two ponies. The gelding's grey-green-slate colour feet he can clip and rasp level in no time; the soles are white. The mare has much the better shaped foot, more open and round with excellent quarters. Both the walls and the soles are dark slaty blue and the farrier has a much harder job to clip off the excess foot and level it. The difference between the gelding's hooves and her blue-slate ones seems to be in the resilience of the horn. The extra power the farrier needs to put into the clipping tool and the rasp is quite clear to see. Which does he prefer? Don't all horses' feet wear the same no matter what colour they are? He grins to himself and cocks his head in approval over the foot that is causing him the extra effort. 'I could shoe them all day, with this 'blue' horn, and never complain. You dream of shoeing feet like these. It's quality.'

Bone

AGAIN opinions vary about whether there have been changes in the amount and quality of bone the ponies have: Mrs Newall considered that ponies used to have 'average bone; they weren't like little carthorses, they were an active pony, strong but very active.'

I don't know how much bone ponies used to have but I certainly think they've got quite a lot of bone. Eight and a half, nine inches, something like that. I think often good bone looks less than round poor bone - but weren't there always round boned ponies? I do think there is some eccentricity about flat bone - maybe scientifically, performance wise, flat bone is stronger - but there'll be some damn good-moving round boned ponies. (Bob Charlton)

Bill Potter thinks ponies have slightly more bone than they had. 'They are rather thicker and heavier. But it isn't as good a bone. It's thicker, and then it's rounder. It isn't nice flat bone.' Chris Thompson thinks they used to have 'probably rather more bone than some of these have today.'

What can be drawn from such widely varying observations? Just that the variation in bone has always been there and that it still is there! Some have more and some less, some more quality and some less, just as they always had. Different studs just have different preferences and different opinions about what constitutes 'good bone' with reference to Fells. However, the breed overall has notably good bone which often measures more than that of riding-horses that may be several hands taller.

Action and movement

ALL the breeders mentioned qualities such as hair, colour, bone or feather, but action and movement were less often cited as Fell attributes. However, those who did discuss them were decided in their likes and dislikes. Fells do need some action; it is mentioned with pride on the old stallion cards; it made them nimble on hilly ground and enabled fast times in trotting races. The Fell does not lift knees and hocks as high as the Hackney or even the Dales, but there must be lift to give the ability to move forward and it must come equally from all round, back as well as front. Mrs Dargue observed that for Jos, 'They hadn't to be daisy-cutters.' Glenis Cockbain agreed that, 'They always had a bit of action.' Thomas Capstick singled out ponies by Heltondale Prince 3751 as having exceptional movement and Barry Mallinson specifically praised the action of some Sleddale ponies.

I'm a stickler for movement; if they don't move I don't want to know. While some people, they don't mind if they trail the back end, well I can't be doing with 'em. They don't get a second look from me. If conformation's correct, the movement's there. It's when your conformation's wrong, that your movement's gone. If you've a straight shoulder, you've no movement. And if they're stiff, too far through the hock, you've no hock action; that's why they lift their legs from the stifle. They're horrible. And then the leg comes way out behind and then they have to retrieve it with the stifle to get it forward again. Well, anything like that's going to go rheumaticky one day. You get stifle wear and that. A lot of it's bad conformation to start with, because they're using muscles and joints that they shouldn't. (Bert Morland)

Height

THE breed standard limits Fell height to under 14 hands (142.2cm). It is the only large British pony breed using this measurement as its top limit; Welsh ponies change at 13.2 (137.2cm) from Sections B and C up to Section D Cobs, while Highlands limit height at 14.2 (147.3cm) and Dales and Welsh Ds no longer have a top limit. For the Fells, the height limit has been variable over the years. For example, in the first groups of ponies registered as Fells between 1898 and 1905, all the stallions were 13.2, while the mares ranged from 12 hands to 14.1$^{1/2}$ with most around the 13.1 mark. Around 1924 the FPS ruled that mares must measure under 13.2 hands, but later the height limit for both mares and stallions was set at 14 hands and this is still the rule today. Frank Wales says, 'Ours were a stronger made type. But fourteen hands would be the biggest and some would be less.'

Mrs Dargue: There was a man - he came from Buckden in Yorkshire - he was a member of Parliament; he wanted them to be 14 hands - he would have liked 14.2! He and Jos, they were quite friendly and that, but he was used to riding roughshod. He didn't get away, Jos managed to keep it 13.2 for quite a while! But eventually - some of the other breeders wanted them bigger for riding - well if you're out voted, you've to give way, haven't you? But Jos never approved of it. (Dargue family)

Only a few breeders made these comments on height, yet it has been a point of argument about ponies, on and off, ever since it became a dividing criterion between show classes; for instance, the *Cumberland and Westmorland Herald* describes the in-hand pony class at Ousby Show in 1880:

> The first prize for the pony sweepstakes also came from Penrith, it being won by Mr Davidson, of Shepherd's Hill, with his nice fine-actioned black animal. Mr Hall, of Melmerby, was second with a rough-legged pony, a well known prize-taker. This beast is six years old, and has been in the possession of the exhibitor since it was a three year old. In commencing its career in the ring it was awarded two seconds, but since that time it has on ten occasions earned winning brackets. Mr Hall lodged a protest against Mr Davidson's pony, on the ground that it was above the height specified in the conditions (14hh and under), but we understand that the pony had been measured previous to being shown, and the height was found to be correct according to the rules.
>
> (*Cumberland and Westmorland Herald*, 1880)

Wigton horse sale was always a very big event, a three day job in the back-end. Two-and-a-half year old colts, they used to go onto the farms down round Wigton, arable farms, and they used to grow out into quite strong general purpose horses, 14 hands like. Farmers down there used to buy one, break it in, keep it another year or two, then bring it back, and it would go into Carlisle, for bread vans and so on. They were beautiful types, I used to like to see them, real good stuffy, strong sorts, far more stuffing in them than what they have now. They would get down among seed grass hay, near to t'plough. They would get a bit extra feed when they were broken in. If you take a pony down, from up here, maybe down Penrith, and put it in a pasture down there, in 12 month it had doubled its weight. Bone and everything, not just flesh; swell out, doing well. They say a Fell pony shouldn't increase in size wherever it goes, but they do! (Ted Benson)

Wendy, she used to come up from Cheshire to Appleby Fair Hill, and she would buy one or two of ours and take them down to Cheshire onto good going; oh, she said they just outgrew theirselves. Well this is one reason why they had to lift it from 13.2 to 14 hands. While they're on the fell you see, they just keep to that size; Nature does it! But folk were taking them off the fell and putting them onto land where dairy cattle were running; if they bought a mare and a foal, by the time foal was a yearling, it was as big as its mother! And it just kept on going. (David Trotter)

I think it probably has tended, itself, to go rather more for the riding pony. It's the market that does it though isn't it; if you've a little stumpy pony, well it's somebody's preference, but I think - well little people can ride little ponies, but big people can't ride them can they? And you've got to have something to sit on when you get onto them. (Chris Thompson)

From a marketing point of view, Chris Thompson's concept of the bigger pony having more uses is perfectly valid but as Bob Charlton said at a recent FPS General meeting, the smaller pony is just as robust and will do as well in most disciplines as the bigger one; 'it isn't height that carries weight. A well made pony of 13.1 is up to just as much weight as one of 14 hands.'

Colour

FROM 1898 onward the Polo and Riding Pony Society registered ponies from the Fell area, where brown and bay were the commonest colours, followed by black and grey; a few 'broken-coloured' piebalds or skewbalds; creams, roans, duns or chestnuts. Chestnut and broken-coloured ponies were debarred in 1940. The last examples of other alternative colours, red roan or blue 'grey' roan, were registered in 1952 and 1966 respectively and the permitted coat colours settled to brown, bay, black and grey.

Browns

'In the early days they were nearly all brown, with black points; there were mair brown 'uns than black 'uns,' says Bill Potter. Ted Benson remarks, 'The brown un's, they always had a thick coarse coat.' 'Brown' is a slightly misleading term as it may sometimes be used to describe a near-black with a brown muzzle, and sometimes quite a bright bay with black points (legs, mane, tail, tips of ears, nostrils). Some colours are very characteristic of certain studs, and brown is very typical of the Sleddales: 'Henry Harrison, he had browns; his father always had them,' says

Chris Thompson. Peter Robinson used to worry in the 1970s that blacks would swamp out other colours, and so attempted to breed only browns for that reason, but Chris says, 'I don't think the browns will die out.'

Henry: Black un's are smart - and very dark browns. A good dark 'un! Our ponies were mostly bay, dark bay. It was just way they were bred.

Ivan: When they first started, they must have been brown, brown; all the time I've been helping out here [Thorney Bank] - which is nobbut thirty year - you've used very little brown as a stallion apart from Adamthwaite Lucky Star, and yet they're still coming brown. So they must be brown bred away back for it still to be coming out. I think it's bad to beat myself. There's some nice grey horses. They're all right, but not my cup of tea really. I think dark brown, personally myself, is top of the list. (Henry Harrison and Ivan Alexander)

Blacks

Black has always been a sought-after colour and Mr W W Wingate-Saul's breed description of 1898 stated that not only were 'the best animals' often 'jet-black' but black was the commonest colour, though actual registrations do not support that. However, some studs were notably black-based: Margaret Wilson says that the Townend ponies were 'brown and bay in the early days, but hardly any after that. Almost all of ours were black.' The Stud Book shows that four of their early ponies were brown. In Volumes 44, 45 and 46, Townend registered nineteen fillies and only four were brown; and only one out of their eighteen colts was brown. All the rest were black, as were the Waverhead ponies: Mrs Frances Bell remarked that Red House Dusty was the first brown mare they got. She was by Waverhead Rambler 4101 out of Mrs Hoodless's black Section B mare 14589 Red House Mandy, and bought in by Jimmy Bell as a youngster. Lownthwaite ponies too were black: Frank Wales says, 'Ours have always been black. I always remember people bringing horses in off the hill, off the fell, and there was eighty-something of them, and people all knew their own, by the colour.'

The local colour effect is less pronounced in other studs: Chris Thompson has 'always had that colour range, blacks and bays. I've even had bay stallions.' 'They weren't all black; no, we'd browns and greys. Gilly always liked a grey,' says David Trotter. Like other breeds which are predominantly black, Fells occasionally throw-back to chestnut: 'Occasionally I have had a chestnut one. My father had a breed that used to throw chestnuts too,' says Chris, and Bob Charlton says, 'Scientists say it is quite possible, still, to breed a chestnut pony... my father bred a chestnut, about 40 years ago. We took it to Kelso [horse sale], quickly...'

While there is still a common misconception that all Fells are black, the old adage that 'a good horse is never a bad colour' can be applied to Fells as it can to any other breed. Bert Morland says: 'Ted Benson didn't mind what colour if the pony was correct. And I'm the same; it doesn't matter if it's a light bay; to me, if the conformation's right the pony's right.'

The brown ponies, the very dark ones, would stand winter better than the blacks. They would come in better in the spring. And the greys didn't do as well, no they didn't. (David Trotter)

Greys and roans

Jos always wanted grey ones. I think we had a brown; he bought one off Mr Charlton but he didn't like it and he let it go. There's one's picture hanging up on the wall - Strawberry Girl - she won races carrying twelve stone over three miles - and she was grey. They've been black for a long time; but Jos always wanted a grey one. (Mrs Elsie Dargue)

Strawberry Girl won several trotting races in the early 1880s and her top prize was £60 in the Borough Stakes at Blackpool, a huge sum in those days: in modern money it would be over £25,000. Prints show her as a light grey. She also looks to be a rather of the light-boned 'Wilson pony' type. While looking through the registration certificates we found Peepings Swell's great-great-great-grand-dam Murton Lass who was a 'grey by Telegraph.' Telegraph is noted in several early entries as being 13.2, while one entry in the Stud Book Vol X adds that he was a 'half-bred Arab owned by Mr Bomfield-Soulby.' However, Jos Dargue, who wanted to breed a grey, never got one despite the colour having been a family tradition and a badge of speed.

Mrs Bell makes much the same remark about the rarity

THE CELEBRATED TROTTING PONY, "STRAWBERRY GIRL,"
13 HANDS 2 INCHES,
The Property of MR. JOHN WILSON, Liverpool.
KIDDED BY CHARLES BARNETT

Winner of many Handicaps, including the Borough Stakes of £60 at Blackpool, on Tuesday, July 17th, 1882, beating Eighteen others; also the North Lancashire Handicap of £140 at Blackpool, Tuesday, July 17th, 1882, beating Sixteen others in the First Final Heat, none of them being within the distance, were all disqualified. Won the First Prize at Farnworth Show in both Saddle and Harness, in September 1881; also the First Prize at Altrincham Show in both Saddle and Harness; on September 25th, 1881. Won the Silver Cup, value 10 guineas at Bootle Show, for the Best Pony in Harness under 13 hands 2 inches; also the First Prize at Farnworth, in September, 1882, for the Best Pony in Harness, under 13 hands 2 inches.

of grey Fells at one time:

We didn't have them [in the breed] for a lot of years. Billy Winder ['Mountain' ponies at Caldbeck] always used to have the roan breed - the very very old roan. I can't remember any other person with that dark, dark roan. There was this iron grey from his last roan mare - very, very dark. And Joe Wilkinson, he was very very in with the Nobles, he said old Mr Noble, Sarge's grandfather or father, used to drive a very dark iron grey. (Mrs Frances Bell)

A major distinguishing characteristic of a roan is that its

head is often darker than its body colour, whereas greys tend to have lighter coloured heads. Alison O'Neill, née Winn, who was brought up at Dent which is south of Sedbergh, used to ride a Fell pony in the 1970s that was roan; it was dark coated all winter and did not fade with age like a grey. All the local ponies then, she said, were brown or roan. Not far away on the south-eastern Howgills, Thomas Capstick says:

I sometimes used to go over to Tunstall's to Frizington White Heather [4209] with mares. I didn't get many greys - I suppose I didn't take many mares, just one or two; funny thing is, you often got bays, still can get bays out of greys. But then, he was got by a bay stallion: Merry John [3709]. (Thomas Capstick)

Minute single-hair white 'ticking' in the coat on flanks and quarters can sometimes be seen on brown, bay or black ponies, yet they never actually grey-out. Such tiny white markings are not as intense as 'roan' colouring, and they are not regarded as a fault.

White Markings

Just as with bone, opinion varied a lot about how much white was wanted on a pony. Jos Dargue would not have kept a stallion with a white foot; but although Frank Wales would never breed off an animal with a white front foot or a blaze, he says, 'most of them had a bit of white on the back feet. We didn't mind it on their back feet. Or a star; because t'was used, you could identify them.' Mrs Newall observes: 'They would just be very very small stars or a little bit of white on the back foot. They often have a bit of white, but we've got it almost out of the breed over the years because nobody liked it. It is in the genes; but when you were judging you took that into consideration as a fault.' Mrs Bell agrees: 'He had one with white on, had Jimmy, from a mare that he sent to Mr Baxter's stallion. She was a bonny pony but she'd two white socks and a white star. If there was three in a class she was third, if there was ten in a class she was tenth. And that's why he was so much against white.' Bob Charlton asks, 'Do you put a pony 'down the line' because it's something you definitely dislike, when the rest of the pony's brilliant?'

The Stud book did not always note white markings so during some periods we can't check exactly how many there were with white feet or a star. Thomas Capstick says, 'My first pony had a star, but it had no white anywhere else. But there were plenty of other ponies that would have white on them.' Bill Potter estimates, 'in the early fifties, 75% had white on them! I don't mind it with two white socks and a gert [great] white star as long as it hasn't three white feet. If it's there and pony's good enough well there's nowt you can do about it.' He points out that white markings will disappear for generations then pop back when least expected: "My foal's got a white foot, where's it come from?' I say, 'It's no good looking back three generations; look four if you can,' and it's usually in there.'

White markings are part of the breed standard. When

people talk about breeding them out, there's no point; it's there and it'll always be there. White markings have always been in the breed and little bits of white should not be marked down in the show ring if the pony is good. (Glenis Cockbain)

Feather and beards

ALTHOUGH opinions varied a lot over the relative amounts of bone over the years, comments on feather were remarkably similar: successful show Fells now have more feather than their predecessors. The original demand for silky quality was explained by Frank Wales: the silkiness made the pony easier to keep clean and less liable to infections of the heels, so it was more saleable to farmers and the Army, which was a big buyer in the early years of the 20th century: 'The Fells had silkier feather then. It was most important for the Army, was to have silky feather. Some of our ponies would go to India as packhorses.' And Christine agrees, adding: 'Your old farmer wouldn't buy a horse that had a lot of feather. Or a long mane and tail.'

Derrick Byas: If you look at photographs of the 20s, 30s and 40s, none of them had a lot of feather. Peepings Raven, he's an old hoss now, so he's got quite a bit of feather, but as a young hoss, he wasn't particularly over the top for feather. Which is how Jos liked them. They have to have the right sort of feather.

Mrs Dargue: Jos didn't like these hairy ones. It had to be nice and silky. He didn't like these frizzy and thick ones.

Derrick: Jos wanted a bit of silky feather at back. Virtually nowt in summer and a fair bit in winter. These that you see with hair right down the hooves, is way over much - they should shed right back.

Mrs Dargue: I know my Dad didn't like Clydesdales with too much feather because they got cracked heels. (Dargue Family)

Bob: I am anti curly feather, full stop. Straight feather drains better, and consequently you don't get trapped muck and gunge. They stay cleaner, but I think there is a bit of eccentricity about too much feather. I don't like feather that goes right up the back of the leg.

Sarah: Grandfather-in-law bred it out - he didn't like it. Just a little bit at the heel to drain; it was neither good to man nor beast! It's a pain.

Bob: Feather is only one point among many. I don't particularly like this feather that goes right over the coronet and halfway down the wall of the hoof. But I don't think that should be the major judgement about whether it's a good pony or not. (Bob & Sarah Charlton)

Again, opinions vary! Everyone wanted silky feather, but the quantity differed. David Trotter: 'It didn't matter if there was a lot or just a bit, but it had to be nice straight silky feather.' The main requirements were the silkiness and straightness.

They didn't like really thick, rough, hairy legged uns, they were too coarse; if it was in ringlets, it was out.

Ponies in the yard at Lownthwaite, around 1950, with Mr. Harry Wales. Photograph courtesy of Christine Morton.

Doesn't matter how much there was, so long as it was nice and straight. Once it started to curl, it was out. They thowt they were Dales. (Bill Potter)

I have had a pony faulted because it had a wavy tail. Most of my ponies don't have that. Another thing is, my ponies don't grow a great beard, or even a moustache. And I've noticed a certain stallion that I did use once, that pony, the dam, *her daughters have grown beards and have still got beards even in the summer. I've known quite a few in the shows I've gone to in Cumberland, there's quite a few have beards in the summer; well that never used to be. (Mrs Newall)*

Bert Morland says, 'Feather, and your beard and moustaches, and your spat [hair over the coronet]; they're all

T B Capstick with Look at Me, 2003, aged four. He was Champion at the Stallion show in 2002, 2003, and 2004.

characteristic points.' Thomas Capstick adds, 'They varied a lot, but they can vary a lot today too. It's become very fashionable to have them with a lot of nice feather on.'

However there are places where the soil conspires against the breeder whatever his preferences. Ted Benson continues: 'There's something on Adamthwaite, but mares used to always lose all the hair round the coronet, as if something had eaten it away; I never knew what it was.' The Bell family said that their ponies 'had nice fine soft hair,' but the heavy wet land at Waverhead removed it: 'They used to come up from Colemire, with their hooves covered; and from day one when they came up it got less

and less every day! It really disappointed us.' Chris Thompson agrees: 'Out on the rough fell ground they never find that poached ground you see. And it doesn't matter what you put on it, you can't always preserve that hair.'

Although the amount of feather is a major point of argument, the breeders all pointed out that the main requirements of a Fell are that it should be a strong, well balanced, versatile, active pony. The ideal animal has flat, strong bone, and round, hard, blue-black feet. All the breeders

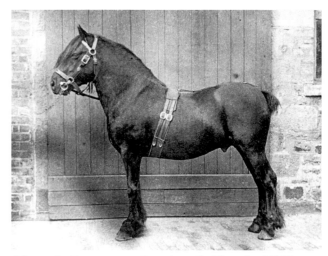

Mountain Ranger was Premium Stallion for Middleton-in-Teesdale in 1912 and again in 1916, 1917 and 1918; for Keswick in 1922; Shap 1923, and Best Fell at Penrith Agricultural Show 1923 and 1924. Photograph courtesy of the FPS Archives.

wanted straight, silky hair in the mane, tail and feather but there were differences in how much they thought was typical, particularly on the legs. It was generally the older-established and mostly northerly families who preferred the least amount of hair, while some of the more recent ones further south have selectively bred for more. Certainly in old photographs the amount of hair is much less than on some successful modern examples of the breed.

Some breeders have hardly ever bred anything other than blacks, while others like and breed all colours (black, bay, brown or grey) and some are known particularly for brown ponies. Some breeders and judges have ponies of a lighter type, some smaller, some taller; some breeders prefer ponies to be heavier, and some more hairy; some will countenance quite a lot of white markings, others prefer few. That range of colour, size and type has to be acknowledged. All these makes and shapes fall within the breed standard and the variations have always been there, including 'fell ponies and field ponies' and 'good 'uns and bad 'uns!'

Changes over the years

OVER the centuries the type of Fell that is sought has changed a little. Big ears and big heads used to be frequent; the FPS newsletter of 1968 said that, 'Breeders are paying more attention to producing real 'pony' heads with small

1923-1927	Black	Brown	Bay	Grey	Pied	Total #s	White feet	Percent white feet
Stallions	21	20	1	0	1	43	13	23%
Mares	37	35	9	0	3	84	11	12%
All	58	55	10	0	4	127	24	16%

2002	Black	Brown	Bay	Grey	Pied	Total #s	White feet	Percent white feet
Colts	118	9	5	11	0	143	27	18.9%
Fillies	122	14	5	10	0	151	26	17.2%
All	240	23	10	21	0	294	53	18.0%

Pony colour distribution, 1923-1927 compared to 2002.
(FPS Stud Books)

prick ears and large prominent eyes, while retaining the depth, action and freedom of movement so beloved by Fell pony men.' This has not been carried to the extremes seen in some breeds, but a common-headed pony will seldom win in the show ring today.

Colour is the most obvious change. The range of colours is smaller and differently distributed. In NPS Volume XIX the National Pony Society recorded that, between 1923 and 1927, the proportion of black pony registrations was only slightly larger than that of brown (46% to 43%). Bay (8%) was a more frequent colour for mares than for stallions; four black-and-white ponies were registered (3%); and there were no greys, though in other NPS volumes grey and dun were registered, red and blue roan too. Today, brown, bay and grey together account for only 20% of registrations; approximately 80% of ponies registered are black and the other colours have become ineligible for registration, if not vanished entirely.

In Volume XIX, 16% of all the ponies registered had a white foot or feet. Eighty years later, when the recording of markings at registration time has become so much more stringent, the percentage overall has only risen to 18% and though fillies show a slightly rising trend over the past decade, colts show fewer markings than the stallions of 1927. This suggests that white markings are something we really need not fret over too much!

Forty years on there is still some variation in bone and feather, with heavier feather becoming fashionable in the show ring and perhaps even a 'breed badge' for the less knowledgeable spectator. Depth, action and free straight movement are certainly still evident in the majority of ponies and it is to be hoped they always will be.

WHAT MAKES A FELL UNIQUE?

There are outward characteristics of a Fell, as we've seen in the previous chapter, and there are inward ones. The simplest answer to the question 'what makes a Fell pony a Fell pony?' is that they are ponies who can survive happily on the fell; live safely in a high, open environment, thrive on sparse grassland and know how to escape bad weather by using the lie of the ground.

However, as such things always do, this obvious answer hides many qualities which breeders and owners know but which they seldom articulate and which were much more difficult to draw out. There are several reasons for this. Only half of the breeders interviewed find the time to train their ponies in any discipline, other than in-hand showing. Some, like Henry Harrison, Barbara Bell and Thomas Capstick, have seldom handled anything other than Fells, or the occasional Dales, Clydesdale or Clyde-cross cob, and it is hard for anyone to identify characteristics that are 'special' when they have had little chance to compare the Fell with other breeds of pony or horse.

The temperament is good with them, for riding. If you've got love for horses, you tend to like every type of horse, but I prefer Fells to Dales, they're a sweeter, truer type of pony. I think a Fell is a comfortabler ride, a smoother ride than a Dales is. (Barbara Bell)

I like them to be sharp, and go when they're asked to go, but

WHAT MAKES A FELL UNIQUE?

I always think they look rather placid. (Thomas Capstick)

I think you'll go a long way before you'll find anything that's as hard and as tough as a Fell pony. And versatile, they'll do anything. (Chris Thompson)

...getting them to look right, and the right conformation and all the rest of it, is not the only thing about Fell ponies. Some of the little diddly ones with the wrong hair, and maybe a slightly long back or whatever, they're just as hard and tough and do the same job. (Bob Charlton)

...they live a natural sort of life; and they've no sort of 'blood' in them, same as your Welsh pony, it has a bit of Arab; and they've such a good temperament and hardiness. And they make a good all round pony you see; for a riding

Peepings Wild Rose, aged 26 years, photograph courtesy of Gwendy Byas.

school they're quiet enough and a decent size for a kiddie to ride, and yet they're strong enough to carry an adult, and they don't cost as much to feed. (David Trotter)

Lots of girls that I've had, who've looked after hunters or been in racing stables and they think they're lowering themselves, when they've come to the Fells - in the end, they say they're so interesting, because they've all got character; each one has a different character and its own little quirks. (Mrs Ailie Newall)

You get the same phrases coming out over and over again - 'hard,' 'tough' and 'fit.' There is quiet astonishment that anyone would spend good money on rugs for horses, when Fells grow their own; buy expensive worming medicines, when the free-roaming Fell can avoid overburdened grazing by wandering to find what she needs on the hill; or install closed-circuit television monitors to oversee foaling, which the Fell mare can manage perfectly well on her own.

Ponies continue to enjoy their work well into their twenties, and mares foal and 'do well' on the fell until an age when most other animals would be retired: in late October 2004 when I interviewed Mrs Newall, among her mares was 'Beauty Blithe, now ancient' who had a four-week-old foal trotting by her side.

There's old [Lunesdale] White Rose up there, is she 24 this time, summat like that? And she's as flexible as could be. She's fit as fire. (Bert Morland)

[Peepings] Wild Rose was foaled '78 and we've still got

her; she's 26 year old and up on the fell. She's as fit as fit can be - you wouldn't take her for 26 anyway. (Derrick Byas)

My oldest mare'll be about 22 I think and still breeding. I kept Packway Princess until it was - 29 I think. (Thomas Capstick)

We have a mare now that's 24 with a foal. (Frank Wales)

Breeders are proud of their mares' longevity and fitness for their tough environment, yet find it awkward to define what they 'know' about the mental qualities of the ponies, as opposed to their physical makeup. Pony behaviour is known, understood and taken as read in any situation. That knowledge is learnt by hands-on experience and lifelong observation of pony behaviours and family practices; stockmanship is taught from childhood, not just by handling ponies, but also cattle and sheep.

Survival is a quality upon which breeders insist. It should be possible in a Fell pony owner's daily routine, especially in the better half of the year, to walk to the fell wall or drive up on a quad bike, and just 'look' the herd. To owners of stabled or paddock-kept horses and ponies it may come as rather a surprise that if the ponies are all there, upright and eating normally, all you do is go away again!

There's quite a range of Fell ponies and I always think there are two types: there's a Fell pony and a field pony! Fell pony will do on the fell, whereas - well I've a one now that I bought, that has never been on the fell, and it hasn't done anything like the others. He was bred over on the east side [of the Pennines, in County Durham] and he's not going to 'do' as the other ponies are; he's inside actually on hard feed at present to see that he does come around. (Chris Thompson)

The breeders don't neglect poorer doers, but neither do they keep and breed from them. Chris Thompson's most recent 'field' pony is now doing well in a kinder climate in South West England. David Trotter also tells how this major characteristic, survival, was defined by the judge to justify his placings at one show:

Our Lynn was showing [Tebay Campbellton] Victor as a two year old and he was up against a mare in the championship. Mare won her class and he won his class... who was judging em? Dargue, one of them old lads... 'I'll tell you what it is,' he said, 'you've got a very good mare there;' but she was way up [tall]; 'but if you threw those two to the fell, and forgot about 'em,' he said, 'which would come in best next spring?' Well, Victor would. He said, 'well that, for me, that's best.' Even though they were nephew and aunt like. (David Trotter)

The story (opposite) of 15144 Lownthwaite Star Trek, illustrates that survival and hardiness can go hand in hand with show quality. She was foaled in 1972. (see photo in chapter 2 of Lownthwaite Star Trek).

Hardiness is essential, so the lack of it more or less disqualifies a pony to be called a Fell. The influence of the fell environment, and the way ponies are allowed to look after themselves on the fell, is very strong. This is usually

'...Star Trek was awarded the Supreme Championships at the Cumberland County Show and the Fell Pony Society's Summer Breed Show. However Star Trek's illustrious career on the show circuit was to be cruelly cut short by a freak accident. Frances [Wales] awoke one morning to say that she had to go and see Star Trek, perhaps it was a dream or a premonition. Star Trek was found sheltering behind a wall. It was instantly obvious that all was not well, Star Trek was unable to move. Frances's dream was rapidly turning into a nightmare. The vet was summoned and he pronounced that she had a broken shoulder, it was thought that she might have caught her shoulder on a stone protruding from a wall or fallen on a stone or that she had been kicked; but no one will ever know. Antibiotics kept infection at bay, but nothing could repair the shoulder; it would set solid. Star Trek survived but she would henceforth walk only on three legs.'
(www.lownthwaitefellponies.co.uk courtesy of Christine Morton)

explained by breeders by a comment on how a pony that *wasn't* bred on the fell would *fail* to cope with a situation!

They seem to want to go places; through water or across a ghyll. Whereas other ponies, because they're not born and bred up there - if they're kept in a field and never been across a river - it's quite a daunting thing I suppose.

I once went on a ride, a pleasure ride, and the day before I'd ridden on the Dales 'President's Ride' with Charlie Parker, and we did some miles... and the very next day I took the same pony - and it had never ever been trained or anything for it like, it was just out of the field - and that same pony went on that pleasure ride, it had got be to twenty something mile again. And we came to this river, and everybody got stopped. Then, well my pony was knackered I suppose - it was head down and waddled through this water and everybody else had to follow... So I suppose because they're used to crossing these streams and ghylls and everything else, they seem to cope rather better than those that's never seen anything. (Thomas Capstick)

Talking about foaling the Peepings mares, Derrick Byas adds: '...if it brings a foal home with it, then it's a Fell pony.' If it doesn't, it isn't! Only wise and clever ponies rear foals successfully on the fell. There is no place either on the fell for a rider who thinks he knows best all the time, because the fell-bred pony has vastly more experience in its own habitat.

If you go up the fell and give a horse its head, it won't go through a soft place; you maybe want to send it one way, but if you give it its head it'll find its own way through - it is more intelligent than you. They won't go through something where there's danger and they can smell danger. (Barry Mallinson)

They wouldn't take you into a soft place if you were riding a one. And I have been out on the fell on a pony and the mist's come in, and I haven't had a clue which way I wanted to be. So I more or less gave it its head and let it find its own way and it's landed up at home. We might have gone quite a long way round-by, but I just couldn't say that; it was mist down to home. I thought well, it's a better knowledge of the fell than I have! (Chris Thompson)

The hill-bred Fell will cope with steep ground, but it will avoid what it considers unnecessarily difficult going. Derrick Byas led a FPS Pleasure Ride from Dufton one year and his rather stony choice of route was almost over-ruled by the mare he chose to ride!

I took old Moss Rose, and she'd be eleven or twelve at the time, bred on that fell; and the folks that were on the pleasure ride, their ponies were just following the Pennine Way, which is like a beck-bottom, rough. But old Moss was on one sheep trod, then she was on another sheep trod; you couldn't get her to follow the Pennine Way, there was no way would she walk on that stony stuff - she knew where the trods were and she weaved backwards and forrards, she took me and the rest followed on the track - you more or less just kept her pointed towards Dufton. Which is quite amazing really, to see how the natural pony actually works on its home ground knowing its routes. (Derrick Byas

Mrs Dargue told a story showing how easily ponies or horses who have not been reared on the fell will walk into danger without realising it.

[High Cup Nick and the fell round Dufton] it isn't a good place for ponies just to go... Jos wouldn't take anybody else - or advise them go... it was too boggy. We were once up there and there was two men riding hunters, and one of them

got bogged. And they couldn't make anything of it - it was still in when we came away. It likely got out all right eventually, but it was well and truly stuck. (Mrs Elsie Dargue)

Pony wisdom about the nature of terrain is not innate, however; it's not instinctive, but learnt. If a Fell pony, born elsewhere, is not taught by its dam about the nature of the fell, even one whose immediate ancestors have been bred and reared there can run into trouble:

They haven't the same instinct when they get to the fell, haven't the 'field ponies.' I know I sold a Fell pony mare and she was in foal; the man said would I take the foal back and I said, 'yes I will do,' and it wasn't turned out [on the fell] until it was a yearling. And about Easter Sunday, some people who'd been walking on the fell came and said there was this pony stuck in a bog; and there just was the head there when we got there. It's a lot softer round those places than you realise. So we pulled it out of the bog. What it had done, it had gone to where there was some nice green grass round the bog and it had gone too far and couldn't get out. We were lucky; it could have been buried and we'd have known nowt about it. I never let it go back. (Chris Thompson)

Glenis Cockbain gives a similar account of her Dales ponies which run with the Fells on her allotment. One of them, High House Tilly, is well aware of the dangers on wet fell land, but Glenis's other Dales mare was inexperienced and so got stuck in a bog.

Tilly is a wise old bird because she came from Sarge's, but the other Dales mare got bogged on the allotment one

January and had to be pulled out. She was chest deep and it took two and a half hours to get her out. Even though she has good broad feet, she knew nothing about bogs. (Glenis Cockbain)

If ponies do get bogged, we have to winch them out... we use three posts and ropes. Once you have done it you could do it again... I could show you, but it's hard to explain! They would never get out by themselves though. If ponies get bogged it does something to their brains. They would go straight back in. We never put them to the fell again. (Christine Morton)

If it comes a hard frost, they'll ga onto all t' boggy spots and eat mosses, seems as if they grow on them wet spots first. And if they're not so fit, in March, they can get bogged. There's three bloody bad patches. If I's yan short I always go right to them - I know where to go! I did loss a pony - no, I've lost two - and never did find them. And I've lost two cows and all. I never did find cows or ponies. (Bill Potter)

Some breed characteristics are unusual and perhaps only found in certain bloodlines or learnt from certain environments. For instance, the fells around Dufton and the northern end of the Pennines have been mined for centuries for lead, silver and other minerals. Is the ponies' knowledge of the nature of undermined ground the source of the behaviour described below?

The one thing I can say about Peepings ponies, having broken a few others, is that just about all the Peepings ponies I've broken to drive, could tell you where every drain was on t'roads, and yet ponies I've had from other places never showed any bother at all. I've had ponies I've had to coax to go over the mine down at Long Marton there because they've got to the edge of it - clonk! - 'bugger, I'm not going any further!' And you've to get off cart and MAKE them go across, and they've been sort of quaking in their boots - 'there's summat under here that isn't right!' One of the first I ever broke - Tim - bloody near jumped every drain in the road when he first started. He'd be going full trot and it was hellish on the cart, played hell with my back. After a bit I realised it was wherever a drain went under t'road, that hoss knew; whether it was running water or he could sense summat different in the ground. It doesn't happen with other folks's hosses. I would say most of that came about because they were born and bred up there and so it selectively bred itself. It's a trait that's developed in them because of where they live. (Derrick Byas)

The capacity to weigh up a situation and decide instantly (and usually correctly) whether or not it's necessary to react is found quite commonly in most breeds of native ponies. There have been four or five incidents this year where my gelding would be going along a narrow road, then prick his ears, move over onto a layby, and stop; and I'd say, 'Get on!' - and at that point a car would come into view. I hadn't heard it, but he had, and from experience he knew what to do about it.

Because low flying aircraft are common in the Lake

District, which is a training area for the Royal Air Force, fell-bred ponies are usually unbothered by such assaults on their senses as fast fighter jets howling over their heads or even through the valleys below them. Road or farm traffic is normally no problem to them either; most ponies are unflappable, whether or not they have encountered a particular hazard before. The close passing of an express train caused no stress to my driving Fells, even in the early stages of their education. If they were standing, they simply stood, while if we were trotting they dithered once, read the situation, decided there was nothing dangerous in it despite the noise and speed, and went on as before.

Fells quickly learn the consequences of actions and situations, which makes them easy to train. But the 'placidity' noted by Thomas Capstick does not mean that Fell ponies are lazy, or stupid; I have never met a stupid one. A stupid pony on the fell would not last long enough to breed. A stupid pony on the farm would not be worth working or riding and again, it would certainly not be bred from. As for lazy ponies, Bob Charlton says it depends on the situation whether a pony behaves lazily or not!

It's what I call in old fashioned terms the fact that they're intelligent, and they're mettle-y and they're not fat black slugs, or most of them aren't. We've got dull ponies here to ride at home which do Riding for the Disabled (RDA) and all the rest of it, but you take them out into other circumstances and they wake up and GO. Beauty, she is the dullest, doziest thing when you walk back from the grouse moor;

she's done RDA which we ran here for fourteen years till this year; she plods round there. But go with two or three other people riding up the hill and she's the one that really wants to go like hell. She actually can't travel to keep herself warm; some of the more Linnel type ponies can beat her hands down; but I like that sort of old fashioned guts that they've got. (Bob Charlton)

Jos [Dargue] always wanted a pony with a bit of go about it. That's what he always said. You shouldn't have to feed it to make it go. You just feed it to make it go faster. (Derrick Byas)

Trainability is a major characteristic of Fells, stemming from their ability to understand a situation and its consequences. The word often used is 'docile'. This has come to have connotations of slow-witted submissiveness, as if they know no better than to do what they are told; but it really means 'teachable and co-operative'. Mrs Newall says: 'On the whole the ponies were very good natured. They still are, once they get their faith in you. They accepted everything. I've rarely had a pony that wouldn't settle to whatever it was asked to do.' Fells do indeed learn very fast and seldom need telling twice what a job entails. The operative word there, in case you have not seen it, is 'job'.

1948 we went to live at Fell End, and Mr Willie Preston, that was auctioneer at Sedbergh, he had the farm rented [Green Hollins] and my Dad was farm manager up there. That winter, me and my brother Ernest, we didn't know a lot about job but we yoked a pony up and we were pulling tree branches for a bonfire, with this Fell pony. They called it Uldale Dinah II. It would be like four year old... (Bill Potter)

I can give an example of the speed with which Fells learn with my present mare's behaviour. Bought on 1st August as a mature mare 'backed and ridden away', but not broken to harness, Ruby started her training to drive on the 2nd. She behaved like an old hand at the job and was driving quietly and safely down the road by the 5th, revelling in her own trotting speed while remaining totally biddable. It helped that she already knew a common stock of commands expressed in exactly the same words, but also she is extremely inquisitive and sweet natured and clearly loves to learn. You could see her joy at fitting the new task into the jigsaw of commands she already knew. She sulked a little when she was bored, when the job was obviously just repetition for repetition's sake, with nothing new in it and no purpose that she could see - after all, she had learnt already how to pull the cart along that stretch of road, so why do it again? Yet it took only quiet insistence to get her co-operation.

They're very intelligent is a horse. But the human has to know when it's right. And that can't be put there. A lot of people think they know and they can come into horses at any time, 'oh it's just a horse... be all right' - no. A horse knows, soon as you get on, whether you can ride or you can't ride. But every horse'll try it on [test you], it doesn't matter what breed it is. You've got to know when he's trying it on and when he's not trying it on. (Barry Mallinson)

While most of the breeders interviewed commented on the general niceness of Fells and the quickness of their understanding, they also remarked that the ponies will size you up and decide whether to trust you or not.

I think Fells, like some other ponies, when they were used on the farm, the whole time, they would be suckling a foal, and that's why I think the ponies used to be so easily broken, because it was in-built - once they got their trust in you they would do anything for you. (Mrs Newall)

Craig had his first horse when he was born; a filly, one of the best I'd ever bred, the only one at the time I'd had a champion. I could whistle on her, and she would come from a mile away. She was great. You could put him on it, and she was three year old, without a halter on, and she would follow you down t'field with him riding it, like a lamb. Then Tracey went to get on to ride it, and she was there; all there ready. Normally all my horses have been very very quiet natured. You could take them anywhere, ride them anywhere, they always give you 100%. I've always found they're very very trusting. And they're all sure footed. And they'll give their heart out, a lot of them; they're good to handle. (Barry Mallinson)

This nice nature is just as evident in the near-wild pony as in the one that is accustomed to humans.

Temperament, I think. Aye. They're bad to get away from, there's good and bad 'uns in everything but it doesn't matter, the wildest of ponies seem as if you handle them quietly, they

75

come in very very quiet. They trust you whole heartedly. *(Bill Potter)*

One or two people have commented to me over the years that they think brown ponies are slightly more cautious; more restless and alert when in the herd. But when I asked the breeders they didn't agree.

There's no real difference between the brown and the black. A lot is how you handle them; very much how you handle them. You can go among wild 'uns in a building, you can walk through among them and they don't bother. So long as you don't touch them with your hands. Rub and shove in and everything, but so long as you don't make a sudden move, you can get up to them, they're all right; you can go and talk to them like, they're no bother.

Bishopdale Duke... he's just come back from the Artificial Insemination Centre... They said they'd been 'entertained' because he'd never been handled much before; he'd never had anybody handle him but me, he was only used to myself. Took them an hour the first time. They said they wished they'd had a video camera, cause they had to be very very gentle with him; but he come in that quiet with them, they were sorry to see him go. They said he was a little gentleman.

I lunged this horse last year; we were just getting him going. We'd got to exercise him somehow, being indoors all winter; that was his first winter in, he'd never been indoors before. I was on lambing, there was a lot of lambs about, so I had to exercise him somehow under control. There was some big logs, and Tracey's kids were sitting on

them playing. So, I was lunging, and my lunge rope broke. And, he WENT... And me and Tracey we just looked at one another. I thought - if we shout, kids'll move - and do you know, he stopped DEAD - smelt them kids, and walked round them, and off again. (Barry Mallinson)*

The ability of a trained pony to gauge the competence of its handler is very clear; gentle respect is given to tiny children, wheelchair users and people on crutches. I have seen small children come up and hug the knee of a Fell because it was the highest bit they could reach, and the pony, rooted to the spot, just reached down and softly touched them with its nose. An injured owner told me how her pony matched its stride to hers even amid the excitement of going out to the field after being cooped up in a stable. An able-bodied carriage driver related how her RDA Fell pony stood firm, clearly demanding intelligent help, when the adapted carriage carrying a wheelchair-bound client ran into difficulties out on the road.

But good nature extends only so far, and those who 'take liberties' are apt to be put in their place.

I think they're a pony that takes everything in and sums you up very quickly. And that includes many of the people I've had here supposedly knowing how to look after them. They sum up their riders...

I've sold ponies to a girl who kept a small trekking centre. She kept all the ponies outside, but she had a big barn and brought them in before people turned up to ride. She had people who hadn't ridden before. And I do think, the genuine people who can't ride, they take care of them. She found that. And then the ones that think they can ride, and they're going to trot when they're not supposed to trot, the ponies think, 'I've got a fool on my back, I'll GO!'

Some like showing, and they show off, 'I am here to win!' And I have had one pony who if she didn't get a red rosette, she sulked. She really knew the colours. Even if she'd got a second: 'I'm not going to bother any more...' They are very thinking ponies. (Mrs Ailie Newall)

The need to work on the farm and to do it safely and thoroughly, meant that any really wicked ponies were weeded out - and that meant slaughtered, not just sold away. Frank Wales illustrates this. Over a very long career he has encountered only two ponies who were unsafe, but the sentence upon them was final.

If they're good natured, that's t' main job with a Fell pony; they're good natured. You can get odd 'uns, only twice, I've had ones that weren't good natured. But they went for fat [slaughter]. Christine tumbled off one and it came back to kick her, so it went for fat. (Frank Wales)

'Going for fat' implies sale at auction to 'the meat man' whose job is to buy horseflesh for European tables.

How the wicked ponies were dealt with varied from place to place. The most certain alternative to sale by auction is to 'be sent to' the local hunt kennels. The hunt staff routinely dispose of 'fallen' (badly injured or dead) and otherwise unsaleable livestock. They put the animal down humanely, take the carcase away, and feed the flesh to the hounds. Such was the fate of any horse or pony who was dangerous:

My husband used to ride round the stock you see, and one day [the stallion] came over a wall and attacked him and the pony, and broke the saddle. He just got him in, ordered the kennels up, and that was the end of him. [This is recorded in the Stud Book; the entry has a note below it: 'This stallion died on 21 May 1952.'] (Mrs Ailie Newall)

Decisive actions such as this, down the centuries in which the ponies have been used, must have ensured that only nice natured Fells were allowed to breed. A Fell that was not safe to work may sometimes have survived, but there was no outside pressure to retain and breed from a nasty tempered animal for the sake, for instance, of its speed on a racetrack.

Although in England there is a historic reluctance to eat horse meat and a kind-hearted dislike of ponies going for either human or dog food, 'meat' sales of unwanted, substandard and bad tempered animals at least created a bottom line for market prices and got rid of the poorest stock. Thomas Capstick reminds me that when trade was poor, 'Quite a few years, colt foals would go to the meat man.' The main area of concern with such sales is that ponies and horses should not be exported live over long distances; they should be humanely slaughtered at the nearest possible location and exported 'on the hook' not 'on the hoof'.

Intelligence

IT is very tempting to praise these ponies' intelligence, and to cite it as a breed attribute. Certainly there are some ponies who appear to have 'been here before,' as knowing grandmothers say of confident babies. One breeder said that she liked a particular bloodline of Fell ponies who were 'bold as brass, wide awake and totally on the ball. I just love them like that.' But opinions differ about how far one can make assertions about the quality of intelligence throughout the breed:

I've always found different ponies have different intelligence, same as any other horse. Heltondale Prince was very intelligent, for a pony that had never been handled much; he knew what was going on! Exactly! And some of his descendants were, as well, but they varied a bit like any other really. I wouldn't say they're all more intelligent. (Ted Benson)

They're not intelligent, not any horse. It's not intelligence, it's something else. It's the bonding, how they bond to you. It's like the stallion, he's bonded to me where if Craig went in he would kick him. He's playful with me, and he knows how far to go. And it's just getting that bonding. Once he's bonded with you that's it. I think that's what a lot of it is, if they bond and trust you. They live with you, and it's how you treat them. (Barry Mallinson)

Peter Robinson, for whom I worked in the early 1970s, owned Sleddale Angus, a big dark-bay gelding. Peter was lame in one leg from a wartime injury, but he had often led the treks in the early years of the business, when he and Angus always appeared to be contemplating a wild cavalry charge up the fell! When later he gave the job up to Betty Walker, she always rode Angus at the back of the trek in order to oversee the whole ride. He was considered too strong and keen to be ridden by unwary customers in the trekking string because he would jog, and if you let him, the jog would escalate into the very big, fast trot that qualified him for endurance rides. You could see how restraint bored the 'Old Lad'; his ears were always out sideways, when he was not at the front where he loved to be. But when Peter rode him, Angus's delight was obvious. The bored ears sprang forward as though on elastic bands and nearly touched at the tips, and the hoofs danced in anticipation of another cavalry charge.

On odd occasions, though, bonding can work too strongly. Eddie McDonough tells of Mowcop Bess whom he bought from Robert Clegg. Bess was unbroken, but Eddie and Robert agreed a price to include training.

A few weeks later we came and picked Bess up. She loaded without any problems and travelled well all the way home. The following day the fun started. Bess would not let me get the head collar on her. She was standing far back in her stall. She had her teeth bared and her ears pinned... she was one confused and angry pony, quite capable of doing me harm. I knew if I walked away, she would have won and it would only get worse. So I kept at it. Eventually I got the head collar on and brought her out of the box.

Over the next few days this became one evil pony, a real witch… Finally, I had a chat with Robert… he could not believe the problems I was having with Bess. After an hour of both Robert and I going over everything together, Bess was working in her normal way.

The following day I was still thinking about what had set her off. It occurred to me that Bess had a strong bond with Robert. She trusted him and so he had earned her respect.

I also realised Bess was used to Robert speaking to her in a Westmorland dialect. I gave it my best imitation of a Westmorland dialect while working her, and guess what? She responded immediately.

(Eddie MacDonough, *Bess - a Working Man's Pony* by permission of the author and the Fell Pony Journal [Summer 2004])

Bess's story is an extreme example of bonding. It was compounded by the fact that her temperament is also very sharp. She likes to work and 'can be a real pain when she has nothing to do.' She is 'one of those ponies' as Eddie puts it, 'who would overpower a child or a timid adult and take command in the blink of an eye.' Bossy ponies may not be as common in the breed as gentle, friendly ones, but they are not rare either.

A lot of it, it's in the breeding; I have one, even as a two year old, she was bossy; and I've a yearling now, it's same, it likes to be boss. She likes to be in there, but she just likes to be that bit independent. Like the brown mare; if she wants to be caught, she'll be caught; if she doesn't want to be caught, there's no chance. (Barry Mallinson)

Fell mares have to rear and educate their foals outdoors, living naturally in the herd on the fell, so responsibility is bred in them. The strongest charactered mare will look after the herd, too: Frank Wales says: 'On the fell they're just wild. They still display a herd behaviour. One o't mares is boss.' Small wonder then a Fell mare may treat a diffident owner as an inferior pony, and decide that the safest thing is to take charge, as she would of a herd! From her point of view this is a positive behaviour and it should not be seen as wicked or domineering. Ponies don't understand right or wrong, just whether it 'profits them' or not (Tom Roberts, 1985, *Horse Control: The Young Horse*).

Actual wildness is quite different from the nastiness that the Wales family dealt with so promptly. As Bill Potter remarked, a wild pony will learn to trust and will behave quietly. David Trotter explained that in the ponies he broke in 'there was nowt evil in them, just they were frightened of human beings, they were just like wild deer you see.'

However, Barry Mallinson describes the caution needed when you move a wild pony to an unfamiliar place:

Take them away from their own environment, they are deadly. I found that out at Hawes horse sale once. For ten year I'd shoved up again' that horse, among another dozen or twenty, in a building; never bothered, and she knew me. But at Hawes she didn't have her mates with her, she just had her foal with her in the ring. She came backwards at me, both back feet; she got me right on my shoulder and side; I was black right down my arm. (Barry Mallinson)

Typical phrases that come out about Fells are 'it was kind', 'it had no badness in it.' Mrs Bell told how Granda Bell, and Jimmy, biked all the way down from Wigton to Adamthwaite one Sunday to see a colt they were thinking of buying. 'He was such a grand little feller was Adamthwaite Lucky Star. He had some good shoulders on him. A real pony. He hadn't had any training but he was kind, he had no badness in him at all.'

One major topic that has not been mentioned here is Fell ponies' attitude to food. In *A Lifetime with Ponies*, Mr Charlton asks: 'What does a pony worry about most on earth? Food!' Glenis Cockbain's Fell and Dales mares run together on the same ground. Though she sees no difference in how well the two breeds cope with winter weather she does say that her Fell mares are more bossy and forward.

In the group, when we worm the mares, the Fells eat their little bit of hard feed so fast they will choke themselves, in an effort to get it down before the others can boss them off it. (Glenis Cockbain)

The topic of food is so important that it has a chapter to itself: the next one, which will explore the Fell pony's eating preferences, and the traditions of feeding and keeping Fells.

FEEDING IN PAST AND PRESENT

Breeders of ponies on the fell know where to find their ponies under varying conditions, and they can deduce, from the locations and the herbage, what the ponies like to eat. Short sweet grasses are favoured; heather land is avoided. However, few breeders have time to observe closely what the ponies choose for themselves between those two extremes.

> Mr Charlton lectured to the pupils of the Cumberland and Westmorland Farm School, near Penrith:
> …Mares roamed on the mountains and moors all the year round; but, if he were to be critical, he thought this hardening was perhaps a little bit overdone. He could not see how a bite of hay would do the slightest harm, and some of the mares one could see, with a foal, a yearling, and perhaps a two-year-old trailing behind, did look a wee-bit thin at Easter. *Livestock Journal,*
> date unknown but probably before 1927.

David Murray, a freelance conservation scientist, writer and explorer, is currently conducting research into their eating habits both on the fell and in pastureland with the aim of recommending their use in conservation grazing projects. To date, twenty-two Cumbrian and eighteen other British Fell pony breeders have given him information about the ponies' grazing habits. Sixteen herds live on common grazing, nine

Heltondale Lady on the Howgills,
photograph courtesy of Thomas Capstick.

Copyhill Suzanne, FP2681, aka 'Ruby' at her first
carriage driving event.

Fell pony mares at Fell End, near Sedbergh.

Above, Lunesdale mares and foals, June 2004: close to home for service.

Below, Murthwaite mare and foal on the fell, photograph courtesy of Laura Hart.

*Thomas Capstick's champion mare Heltondale Misty IV,
photograph courtesy of Laura Hart.*

Below, Fell Pony Stallion Show at Dalemain

of them on heather moorland, and several herds graze on Sites of Special Scientific Interest (SSSIs). They will browse prickly shrubs such as hawthorn, gorse and bramble, and regularly eat coarse grasses, rushes and a variety of herbs (Murray, Royal Geographical Society International Geographical Congress, Glasgow 2004), but their main preference is fine, sweet grass, whether growing or saved as hay or silage. If they get that, they will do well. Contrary to Mr Charlton's remarks, the breeders who use the fell say that those ponies who forage for themselves do better than the ones that stay around the edges of the fell expecting to be fed. An important reason for feeding ponies, however, is to stop them being a nuisance when other people fodder their stock on the fell.

I always used to bring the ponies home, or they always used to come home, for winter. I used to go and get them if they didn't come home. I'd fetch them to take the foals off. I suppose I always wintered them in-bye because a lot of farms fothered their sheep on the fell in winter, including our own, and we didn't like them going and robbing the sheep. But when I was feeding them - both ponies and sheep - I always fothered my ponies on the fell bottom, and the sheep up the fell, usually out of sight, and the ponies got to know that, so they used to come down, and the sheep used to stop up there. And if the ponies weren't down in the morning, I used to go up and bring them down with the [quad] bike; so it worked quite well. Nowadays very very few people do winter their sheep on the fell; myself included. Just this last

three or four years I've sent my sheep away down to Preston so that hasn't been a problem. But there is a lot of ponies don't come home all winter. Out on the middle of the fells, those ponies'll winter as well if not better than those ponies that come home, who're coming home and they're getting as much as they'll eat, but then they're just going back on the same upper ground every day. (Thomas Capstick).

They got no feed while they were out; no, they just used to scran for theirselves. And they used to scran better as well. We used to have some that just hung about Tebay, so while they were out, they got hay. You found that they just hung about the gate, waiting. These, they were wintering on the same bit, you see. But they never wintered as well, as those that were out scranning, that were out Longdale Bottoms or on Fair Mile; they always wintered better. They were scranning all the time and moving on to fresh pasture. (David Trotter)

Ponies will nibble at bracken, but they don't seem to take a lot and this can scarcely be called 'feeding'. But breeders observe that they very seldom eat heather, because they don't go onto that kind of wet peaty ground if they can help it. 'It didn't matter how much snow there was, you hardly ever see them on heather,' says Bill Potter. 'They like white, dry, benty grass rather than heather.'

Ponies will readily eat seaves (rushes) which grow in the wet patches on the fellside. Pauline Robson remembers her father Jos Dargue saying that the ponies survived the 1947 winter by eating the seaves which, growing taller, were easier to reach than the short fell grasses under the snow. They got no supplementary feeding from the farm.

Just grass. That's all. They eat seaves o' winter. One o't best things; they get rid of seaves, does horses. You know that field of Stan's down Tebay road, how seavy that was – horses did away with it. Thistles? I've seen them take odd-'uns. Mine eat the tops but mostly after I've cut them; they'll eat them once they're cut. Maybe my grass is too good! But this last year or so I've been feeding big bale haylage again t'motorway bridge at Colville's; they just go and help themselves. (Barry Mallinson)

I tell you where they did best on, very good clean pasture, that down the Fair Mile. In winter if it got long, the grass you know got a bit benty, but there'd always be little shoots coming through, protected with the longer grass. And occasionally they would have a go at a seave bed and clean that off; more perhaps in winter. Whether there was summat in it, perhaps a mineral of some sort that their bodies needed, that they got off the seave; but every now and again you'd come across a seave bed and they'd just about clocked it like. With living naturally you see, they'd find out... You'd see them occasionally eat a bit of bracken. Not often, but every now and again; if they're going through a bracken bed, they'll happen just have a chomp at it. But not a lot, just a little bit, as though their bodies needed just that little bit of something out of it. (David Trotter)

You didn't feed them, even on your own fell where nobody else had any stock, unless they come. If once you started feeding them at yard gate they were there every day. But if you didn't start, they used to go off looking and never come. It would take a real clashy night to bring them home. 'Weather's gonna change, hosses've all landed.' And if you fed them, that was it, they stopped till spring. (Bill Potter)

All the time I've been at Drybarrows, if they've been at the fell, I've liked them to come to the gate, and just give them a bite of hay each morning - to let them know where home is. Then they're not bothering anybody that's wanting to feed the sheep either. When I was farming on my own I used to let them in to a little paddock, and shut them in, because I was there and I saw what came and such like; and then I could go and feed my own sheep and other people got theirs fed, and after I came back I let them out. I probably held them till two or three o'clock in the afternoon. But they always knew to come home the next morning. They're really knowledgeable. (Chris Thompson)

On lower ground, Fell ponies will nibble at nettles after the stinging hairs have died back in late summer, and also if they are dried in hay. Yellow 'sow thistle', dandelions and other milky-sapped composites are eaten if the ponies get the chance, although on the fell these rather coarse, weedy plants are not commonly part of the local vegetation. Lowland pasture herbs such as plantains (white man's foot) seem to attract them too, but many other flowering plants are ignored especially if the leaves smell strongly. Unfortunately, ponies do not seem to eat docks, those pests of disturbed ground, although the plants spring up readily where ponies have churned-up the soil in winter!

It's hard to tell, we don't have the time to spend observing them on the fell... but in the last couple of years I have noticed the mares seem to be nibbling the nice soft green shoots of gorse, just picking the tips off the bushes. There were fewer stock in general on the fell until quite recently - but now the numbers of sheep are down since foot and mouth so there is more grass on the fell. (Margaret Wilson)

Working farm ponies used to be fed conservatively. Until fifty years ago, on the fell farms even cattle and sheep did not receive much in the way of extra feeding; calves got hay and oatmeal in winter, and cattle and sheep only hay. Cattle cake, sheep 'nuts' and 'mixes', and the making of silage are relatively new concepts. Silage in particular has been extremely useful in this area of high rainfall. It enables a good crop to be taken in a couple of dry days, though the technique did not become popular until big-baling came along and tough air-tight membranes such as polythene sheeting and bale wrap were available. If the farm did not have a silage clamp there was no alternative to spending an uncertain week, or more, trying to save it as hay.

Frank: Wasn't much problems with working them, they were very hardy. In winter they were laid in [stabled], but in summer they weren't laid in. Just in a field. You just had to catch them in the morning. They got a bit of hard feed;

oats, in them days. Mashed haver, yard-mashed haver - rolled oats. I can never mind us giving salt. But later on when I farmed I used to buy rock salt for lots of things.

Christine: Minerals and additives seem to be a modern day concept. I would say, since the sixties.

Frank: We didn't use minerals, no.

Christine: Just grass really. They like short sweet grass. We never feed hard feed in winter on the fell: too much kicking.

Frank: Unless it comes a lot of hard frost and snow they don't want any feed. Fell ponies that's been bred at fell, they lay a lot of layers of fat on for winter. They can eat barer than a sheep can't they... where a sheep can't get it, they'll get it, will a Fell pony. They've had hay three times this winter, but they're very fit, they're in terrible fit condition. (Frank Wales and Christine Morton)

Ivan Alexander: They like sweet grass! Aye, sweetest grass on t'fell, they knew where that was.

Henry Harrison: No, they like summat good does ponies.

Ivan Alexander: T'only hard feed my grandfather's got was in hay time. Not in winter. In hay time. But if they were carting muck and that in winter, he used to put them in; it was no good leading till dark and letting a sweating horse off, so they were stabled up; well one was stabled up, all winter. We used to ride to field houses and stuff with it. They just got hay and watter - but it was still a la-al fat thing.

Henry Harrison: I remember hosses getting some hard

feed. Bran... They just got hay really. Aye they wouldn't get owt else I don't think.

Ivan Alexander: They wouldn't get hay till they come home for it, would they? They used to know when weather was coming bad, they would come home. I know Stan Mawson's used to, on Tebay Fell; they seemed to know from one year to another where to get the fother at. They only got hay really. They never used to get supplements.

Henry Harrison: There was a hogghouse and when the hay was cleaned up, what hoggs had left was thrown over the wall for the horses; but they got other hay besides like. But they were sweeper-ups! We had one or two used to go and bother other people's sheep, kind of thing; they maybe were a bit of a nuisance; but I've cut mine down last few years, maybe eight and ten year ago. *(Henry Harrison and Ivan Alexander)*

I bought me first black 'n which was Heltondale Sonny Boy's full brother, and I sold him to Walter Tuer to go to the Isle of Man. I dunno what year that would be. I nearly lost him; had him in slings for about six weeks. Couldn't stand. He come round - t'was just malnutrition mair than owt else, you know, in them days they didn't believe in feeding them, they didn't get any supplements at all. The stock numbers on the fell weren't as high. *(Bill Potter)*

I've a feeling since foot and mouth there haven't been as many sheep on the fell and the mares have sucked the foals better. Mine seem to have grown better these last two or three years - whether it is that I've been taking them off - but then, they were taken off before that! And handled inside; they're getting a better start I think now. It stands to reason if there's more for the mothers to graze at, you know, they're getting plenty of grass and that. *(Chris Thompson)*

I have often seen ponies in the field eat big spiny 'spear' thistles. They eat them particularly in springtime when the rosettes are succulent and taste sweet and slightly nutty, but also at flowering and at other times of the year. Some ponies deal with prickly foods like gorse or thorn bushes by stamping on them, but thistles definitely go straight down.

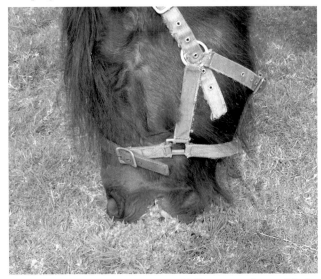

Fell pony eating a thistle.

How they manage to eat those leaves - half inch spines and all - I still can't fathom, although I've watched and photographed it happening time after time, as well as the bare patch that is revealed by its disappearance! Ponies will eat the flowers off creeping thistle in July, which smell very sweet.

Ivan: You know, if you put them in a paster, they would eat around cow clap where cow wadn't eat; and they would eat weeds around gateway where cow wadn't.

Henry: They sometimes do, aye.

Ivan: They seem as though, it's like owt else, mixed farming works better. Same as if you put a horse in a field; I notice, just in corners, horses aren't eating it, cause they've put all their business in there and they won't eat after themselves, will they? But put some cows in, they'll eat it off, and vice versa. (Henry Harrison and Ivan Alexander)

They certainly are better if they have a mixture of stock with them. It keeps the grass more even, because they leave these horrid patches of stuff they don't like. They wintered out with the cattle, before we had all the big sheds for housing the cattle; they stayed out. One lot stayed up on the top there with a bull, and the other lot stayed down the far end of the farm, which is a 50 acre field and has its own water; and they got turnips; they ate them with the cattle. The cattle just got turnips outside, but they don't feed turnips now, they only get hay. (Mrs Ailie Newall)

Ponies that were working got fed oats, bran and turnips

as extras to the main diet of hay. They were sometimes given salt, either as a lump of rock salt or in a bran mash. Some local farmers at least must have added cod-liver oil powder (CLOP) to their cattle and horse feeds, because the Fell Pony Museum at Dalemain has a big old earthenware pot with the letters emblazoned on it; while Fred Todd, a horseman from Levens, told me that he always fed 'blood salts' to his horses. So adding minerals to horse feed was not a totally foreign concept, but they do seem to have been less commonly used than they are today.

They got hay in the winter time, and in the summer time they were brought down to these fields. And if we were riding them and going long distances, we had them in and they got an oats feed - oats and a mixture of bran and, just like the hunters, they got a mash every so often with salt in it. (Mrs Ailie Newall)

I can remember as a kid Fell ponies being worked. They were just fed as any other working animal. Bran and oats and rock salt. That was the only mineral they got. Everybody fed rock salt; they used to put a piece of rock salt in the manger. And turnips; they used to get whole turnips in the winter, 'to play with'. That's what they used to get, oats, bran and turnips. And a little bit of boiled linseed; they didn't give it every day; twice a week maybe, for horses that were working hard, you know. (Bert Morland)

All the fell breeders emphasised the naturalness of the ponies' feeding patterns. Grass is expected to be the mainstay for them, either as high fell pasture in summer, or upland hay in winter. When Cumbrian farmers talk of ponies getting 'good hay', they do not mean what the race-horse men mean, such as hard, first year seeds or rye grass hay; it is usually meadow grass, sweet, fine and soft and not stalky. Being married to a hay and straw merchant, I have had perforce to try quite a lot of variety in the hays my ponies have been offered, as on the principle of 'the shoe-maker's children always have holes in their shoes' my ponies had to have whatever did not sell. Although they will eat anything fibrous they much prefer the lighter, finer grasses. I have had, at times when we had sold all our hay, to feed the ponies in winter on wheat straw with an under-sown grass mixed through it. I wouldn't recommend straw as a permanent forage, but they ate that mixture readily and did pretty well on it. They probably coped better with the low-protein, bulky, fibrous straw than they would have done on a high protein diet, and in any case I could not afford to feed my ponies heavily on concentrates. Certainly the adult fell-bred, fell-going pony will not be getting concentrates as a regular, frequent addition to its diet.

Only time my mares get any feed is to catch them, and when they're going in the show ring and they have to stand all day. So they get wet beet pulp and Sheep Mixture, just mixed up; night before and that morning, so they've some-thing inside them when they stand all day. (Barry Mallinson)

Digesting grass and fibrous food, however, takes a lot of storage space. You can parallel the Fell and other Mountain and Moorland ponies with the British cattle breeds such as Herefords that are traditionally reared and fattened on grass.

They are designed to cope with constant, fibrous, rela-tively low protein intake. That needs a large belly. So, no pony will look sleek and trim without work. A pony fed a lot of grain needs a great deal of work to use it up and must still have hay to keep its gut working properly. However, what a Fell considers 'a great deal of work' is not what most people these days have time to ask of him, so his body con-dition and behaviour must be the guides to how much food is really needed.

THE FELL YEAR: THE NEXT GENERATION

It is tempting to think of the typical Fell herd as being a wild group of mares, foals and young stock, led and defended by an attendant stallion on a remote, wind-swept hillside. However attractive this view may be, the truth of the matter is much more prosaic. It is the boss mare who leads the herd; there are very few true fells where the stallion is allowed to run with the mares; and very few ponies are truly free to choose a mate. Breeding for the semi-feral herd is actively managed, just as it is on a lowland farm.

Even on the highest and harshest mountain land, breeding a foal begins with the owner's matching of mare and stallion. A new breeder will have invested cash in a mare. An established breeder will have kept a filly from one of his own mares for three or often four years until she is mature enough to breed safely. These investments of cash and time may be made for one or many reasons.

All the breeders I spoke to wanted some foals to perpetuate their existing bloodlines; these are not intended, in the first instance, to be for sale. If the foal does not match up to expectations, then it may be sold, but the hope is that it will remain in the herd, and be an improvement on its parents. They take care to choose a stallion that will match the mare's qualities - good temperament, hardiness, vigour, breed type - and that will improve any faults she has; sometimes a rather plain mare can produce good offspring to a stallion that suits her. He will certainly not have faults that might degrade future generations. A pony with poor, narrow feet or upright pasterns; light bone, 'round' joints at fetlock, hock or knee; straight shoulders, a narrow chest or quarters; a big coarse head, big ears, or droopy lips, will not have got to maturity with his assets intact!

After the need to breed a select few replacements, breeders want a foal to sell. The breeders interviewed, for various reasons, are wary of commenting on whether breeding Fells is actually profitable. In a lot of years I suspect it has not been, because everyone told me that there have been lean times when surplus Fell stock were virtually given away, especially colt foals, because they were worth nothing.

At the other end of the scale, where examples of 'exotic' breeds have been imported to a new country, the expense involved in transport gives an imported animal a 'cost' value that may be out of all proportion to its breed value. It doesn't guarantee that they or their offspring are any good. The Fell is classed as a rare breed by the RBST because the breed has fewer than 500 breeding mares. When animals are rare, for whatever reason, it can be difficult to ensure healthy genetic variation without losing the breed type. Some people who go in for 'breeding rare breeds', whether sheep, goats, parrots or what-have-you, appear to do so in order to become big fish in the rare breed pond. With others, despite the sentimental statements they make about their stock, their behaviour often reveals one interest, the bottom line of the balance sheet. Sadly, the reverse is often also true, that the ones who do try to keep rare breed animals in a responsible manner spend an awful lot of money on their hobby. A friend of mine who bred various rare and primitive sheep got a lot of fun and satisfaction out of it, but never made any profit in all the years I knew her; in fact, 'a smaller loss' was cause for celebration!

Overseas, I see examples where all the young Fell ponies are sold by their breeder early in their lives. It's impossible to know if sire and dam are a 'good nick' until the foal is growing up, but in some cases, all the expected foals are contracted to buyers before they hit the straw - sometimes before conception. If the foal is sold before birth even a good one cannot be kept by the breeder. Isn't that short-sighted? Something must be kept at home to provide future sires and especially dams. It's notable that the Fell breeders I have spoken to like to keep a filly out of every mare, and even under pressure from a keen buyer they take very good care not to sell away everything from a line they mean to maintain.

In British conditions, the increase in sale value of young stock per year does not offset the cost of keeping them (especially on limited lowland grazing) to the age of four years old. They take up space that might be more profitably used for the sheep and cattle whose offspring find a ready market at under a year old, and for every year you keep them, there is another crop of foals being born. Let's say you envisage keeping ten mares. If you keep progeny till they are four or five and sell them as trained stock, you can ask higher prices, but if you do you'll have fifty or sixty mouths to feed, not to mention the cost of passports, vaccinations, worming, hoof trimming, any veterinary care needed, and the biggest cost - gelding the colts. A filly foal may sell for £500 to £800 at the autumn sales and colt foals and yearling geldings rather less despite their larger outlay, while the same animal at four years old needs to sell at £2,500 to £3,000 to cover the costs incurred in that time and the 'hole' in profits if any are lost. And that is without calculating the investment in training that is needed if nobody in the family is fit, active, interested and skilled in such work. This helps to explain why most of the Fell breeders make use of the extensive grazing on the fell, why they keep only a selection of their foals, and why few do much breaking of young ponies.

Some breeders, but not all, have favourite stallions. Breeders will describe a foal as 'by X'; but it is the good mare lines that they keep and value and assume you know about. A stallion that is used exclusively on a herd may well be sold or leased after four years when he will be coming back to his own daughters, but all the breeders I spoke to have favourite mare lines that they have preserved, which can often be traced back in family ownership to the early years of the 20th century and beyond.

Amid the rustle of old pedigree certificates, Mrs Dargue and her daughter and grand-daughter talk about the ponies their family has bred, and Derrick Byas reads off the names like a roll of honour:

SEASON 1934.

War Office Premium Fell Pony Stallion

"Peepings Swell," (1880)

Bred by and the property of Messrs. DARGUE.
Bow Hall, Dufton.

Sire—Mountain Jester (1409).
Dam—Sally Grey (6569), by Blencathra.
Gt-Dam—Nancy Grey (2263), by Union Jack.
G G Dam—Fanny Grey, by Mexican Joe.
G G G Dam—Doll, by Minstrel Boy.
G G G G Dam—Murton Lass, Telegraph.

"PEEPINGS SWELL" (1880), black, three years old, will travel the Appleby District, and meet mares by appointment.

Terms—Fell Pony Mares 15/- each and 2/6 Groom's Fee due at time of service.

The Owners will not be responsible for any damage through trying or serving mares, but every care will be taken.

Mares tried by this horse and served by another, sold, exchanged, or given away, will be charged the full season's fees.

"PEEPINGS SWELL" holds the Ministry of Agriculture Certificate for soundness.

Further particulars may be obtained from the Secretary—

Mr. R. B. CHARLTON, The Linnels, Hexham.

J. Whitehead & Son, Printers, Appleby.

Derrick Byas: You've got the original registration for Peepings Swell here: out of the Nancy Grey line. Peepings Swell is actually in Jos's current line. His grand-dam was Sally Grey by Blencathra who was brown; she was out of Nancy Grey who was by Union Jack who was bay; and her dam was Fanny Grey who was by Mexican Joe, which was a bright bay. And Fanny Grey came out of Doll, a grey by Minstrel Boy who was black. And Doll came out of Murton Lass who was a grey by Telegraph. So that takes you right back to the original dowry when Jos's [grand]father married Miss Shepherd. And in 1931 Sally Grey produced Peepings Swell by Mountain Jester and Peepings Swell was sire to the line we still have. (Mrs Dargue and family)

This produces a line like this:

Peepings Swell
  { Sally Grey
      { Nancy Grey
          { Fanny Grey
              { Doll   {Telegraph
                  { Murton Lass

It is nearly always the tail female (mare) line that is traced; very seldom is the stallion line rolled out in the same way. 'If you haven't got a female line, you haven't got a line,' says Derrick.

Very very rare we selt [sold] a filly. I've had some good ones - very first line I ever started, 'twas old Greenholme Glory would be like third generation, now I've another three, four generations; and by, I bloody near selt last 'un not lang sin, and when I realised what it was I said 'Whooo!' I said, 'I'll keep that'n!' Else they'd been all gone. (Bill Potter)

I like to keep a filly foal out of every mare. I usually sell the mares when they come to nine, ten year old; when they're broken and that. I think there's two seem to have got to thirteen… One's not haltered so she isn't worth anything to anybody, and t'other mare's my brown mare that Stan [Mawson] gave me as a foal; I never will sell her. (Barry Mallinson)

Jenny, that's the bloodline that we still have, Pearl and all them. Her mother was a Waverhead mare [that Shuttleworths, of Barbondale, bought] and then they gave us two fillies back, Barbondale Pearl and Barbondale Petal. (Mrs Frances Bell)

One of the first ones in the black book is a Sleddale Daisy, isn't it? I suppose if you got one mare, well you could breed up off her. They'd be mainly Fell bred up here before they started keeping records in 1898. (Ivan Alexander talking with Henry Harrison)

Although breeders aim to produce what pleases their eye, the stamp of pony that they produce is generally determined by the mares that they keep. Henry Harrison's mostly brown/bay Sleddale herd is an obvious case in point. If you mention a pony without naming it and say it is bay, most breeders will ask, 'Is it a Sleddale?' Yet the Sleddale stud has mostly used black stallions. The colour is maintained by the mares.

Grandfather had favourite lines; because he probably would have three, four or five of the same line. There was a 'Fern' line; all beginning with F, anyway; they were very very good; then there was a jewellery line, Pearl, Opal, Sapphire. (Bob Charlton)

Bert Morland who writes extensively of his stock in his book, *A Lifetime in the Fells*, traces the lines of both stallions and mares, and talks of those he has retained. For instance, Adamthwaite Dawn 12944 was a daughter of Heltondale Princess 12135, whom Bert considered the best Fell mare of her era. Dawn's daughter L. Grey Dawn 17847 was the dam of the highly successful Lunesdale Lucky Lady FP1327. Other ponies he bought were sold if they 'proved disappointing as brood mares'. Some breeders who decide that a pony is disappointing will sell it without papers, so that if it later breeds other poor quality ponies, the offspring cannot be registered as Fells.

All the breeders interviewed expected mares to foal every year, but they did not foal them younger than four years old, and sometimes even five. The main reason for this is the toughness of the environment on the fell, which is a challenge to the development of bone structure and its 'furnishing', its covering of muscle.

Frank: Well my Dad said, 'Right - we don't put a mare with the stallion till it's over four. Because,' he says, 'if you do it hasn't furnished, it hasn't fully developed. And instead of having a lot of foals it'll maybe have six or seven and

*then be finished if you foaled it too young.' Now we foal
them at four. But then, you wouldn't have foaled them till
they were five. (Wales family)*

*I don't serve any mares until they're four year old. When
they have to exist up there, and specially if they're not coming home all winter, they just need an extra year to furnish.
(Thomas Capstick)*

Mares for service have to be managed, just as ewes are
managed ready for tupping time. Mares should be rather thin
at foaling time and service. They then put on fat over the
summer, and go into winter in good condition. It is normal

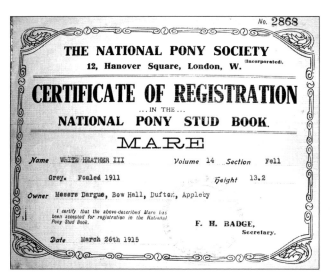

No. **2868**

THE NATIONAL PONY SOCIETY

12, Hanover Square, London, W. (Incorporated).

CERTIFICATE OF REGISTRATION

...IN THE...

NATIONAL PONY STUD BOOK.

MARE

Name WHITE HEATHER III   *Volume* 14 *Section* Fell

Grey.   Foaled 1911   *Height* 13.2

Owner Messrs Dargue, Bow Hall, Dufton, Appleby

*I certify that the above-described Mare has
been accepted for registration in the National
Pony Stud Book.*

F. H. BADGE,
Secretary.

Date March 26th 1915

for them to lose that during the bad weather, and be lean
again at foaling time. Letting the mares live freely on the
fell is the easiest way to achieve this. Carole Morland noted
that a geld mare who is too fat from living on lush grazing
or doing no work is a problem to get in foal in the first
place, and Barbara Bell said the same: 'When they get
mature it takes getting off them. I've tried and tried all summer. She's returned and returned. They scanned her and
examined her, and couldn't find anything really wrong with
her, so it must have been that she was just too fat.'

Taking off the foals by Christmas is a common activity
with most breeders who use the fell. Some trust the mares to
wean their offspring themselves when they feel 'enough is
enough,' and they like the foals to stay as long as possible
with their mothers, to learn where shelter is from any wind
direction, and use the fell to its best advantage. However, a
mare who is still willing to suckle a foal late in the year in
bad weather, or is on poor grazing, may reabsorb the foetus
she is carrying. Some textbooks on foaling in lowland conditions recommend that mares should foal only every other
year, saying that this is less taxing on them than foaling annually. None of the Fell breeders even considered this option.
Although they accepted that mares might not foal every year,
or might lose a foal some years, most would eventually sell
off a mare that didn't breed annually, or would put her to
work under saddle or harness. Henry Harrison and Ivan
Alexander, David Trotter, and the Dargue family, all pointed out that, if a mare is in foal, she does better at the fell in

winter; 'a breeding mare kept her flesh better in winter than a mare that was geld.' 'It was just as if they thrived on breeding.' 'If it was in foal every time, it would do a damn sight better than one that was geld.' In their observation, it is less stressful for a mare to be in foal. If she was not doing well, it actually helped to put her to the stallion; 'it was as if she thrived for the foal.'

Christine Morton observes, though, that this only holds good for mature mares who are used to being in foal, not for the youngest who have only just begun to breed.

Stallions

THERE have always been people in the Fell breed working their stallions, walking them long distances to serve mares, riding and driving them, showing them and doing odd jobs such as light logging. Over the years, stallions have been ridden out hunting, or driven in harness; one, Lingcropper, spent twelve years of his life working to deliver the mail. The nice nature of the Fell is a strong factor in being able to use stallions, but it is also to the good of any breed to test temperament in both the male and female breeding lines by work. Otherwise it may take a generation or more to find out any faults.

The stallions' chief moment of glory, the Stallion Show, is nearly a century old in its various forms. The mares and geldings get a chance to shine at the Breed Show, but that only started in 1970, while the Southern Show is even more recent. By contrast, a Stallion Show has been held almost every year since 1912, before the FPS itself was founded. In that year and for eleven years afterwards, there were five shows, one in each of the stallion districts (Appleby, Keswick, Kirkby Stephen, Middleton-in-Teesdale, and Shap). These were held between mid April and the beginning of May. By 1924 they were replaced with one main show held in conjunction with the Penrith Agricultural Society's Stallion and Colt show. In 1927 classes were introduced for younger stock, although five £80 premiums were still given by the War Office for the stallions to travel the districts. The Fell Pony Stallion Show has been variously held on the Foundry Field in Penrith; on a field on the Lowther estate; and for the last two decades, at Dalemain, Ullswater.

On the second or third Saturday in May all ages of male stock, from yearlings to senior stallions, are paraded in front of a knowledgeable crowd in the parkland. There are classes for ridden and driven stallions too. It's very good publicity for a breed when stallions can be shown to be as useful and good-natured as the mares. The would-be breeder's challenge then is to choose a stallion that will be 'a good nick' with his own mares.

He wasn't terrific looking but he got good stock; well for me he did, he suited my mares. You have to think very carefully; you could have two brilliant ponies, a sire and a dam, who'd won everything in the country and been top of everything, and put them together, and they will not necessarily have a good foal or even have a foal. (Mrs Ailie Newall)

Henry: I wanted one I thought would suit my mares really! I just looked at stallion - a bit of both [pedigree and stallion] but mostly stallion.

Ivan: I think if you were going to look beyond stallion you would look at its parents rather than pedigree -

Henry: Aye, that's right. See what mare's mother was like.

Ivan: I always think a stallion's rather like a woman: you want a good legged 'un, don't you!

Henry: You want yan with a good temper!

Ivan: You want yan without a temper!

Henry: Does the mare or the stallion have more influence? I would probably say t'mare like; quite often they take after their mother.

Ivan: It's more of a 'trying to knit 'em together', than 'picking two good 'uns'. You've to try and find summat that'll suit what you've got. Mind, having said that, you want summat that you like, cause if you don't like it to start with you'll never like it, will you? (Henry Harrison and Ivan Alexander)

People think, they're putting the best to the best, but it doesn't always work. They want to look what to improve. I look at the actual quality of the ponies. You're just trying to breed better each time as you go along. And it can go wrong. It can throw back to its grandparents and you're nearly back to step one again. (Barry Mallinson)

Romany Boy very rarely won a top prize in his life. And yet he was Ponies of Britain Champion for all progeny of all the nine Native breeds three years running, for Ailie Newall. So the best looker doesn't always get the best stock, and vice versa. (Bob Charlton)

> …it was not a good policy to breed from a stallion and mare that shared the same faults… a stallion will… almost always pass on tight narrow feet, round bone and a long back. It is therefore imperative to look for a stallion with good round feet, flat bone, a well laid shoulder and short back... I have found it is possible to breed well from a plain mare provided that she has good breeding on her maternal side. (Bert Morland, *A Lifetime in the Fells*)

At the Stallion Show the yearling classes are usually well filled, but the numbers dwindle through the age groups as unwanted characteristics show up in the maturing youngsters.

The entries in the catalogue for the 2004 Stallion Show are evidence of this:

Age group	Numbers	(average per year of age)
Yearlings	17	(17)
2 year olds	6	(6)
3 and 4 year olds	9	(4.5)
5 to 9 year olds	13	(2.5)
Over 10 years	3	(< 1)

…there would be quite a lot of yearlings there at Stallion show, but there was never more than maybe four or five

good uns. Quite a lot of them went somewhere before next year because there was always fourteen or fifteen yearlings but maybe four or five two year olds. (Ted Benson)

One by one, the young stock are gelded until only the best remain. Nobody will keep a colt entire if it isn't worth the trouble it will cause, and on a lot of farms colts are either sold off early or gelded, because of the difficulties of keeping them away from mares. Mr Roy Charlton mentioned these difficulties when he lectured at the Cumberland & Westmorland Farm School, around 1927:

> Encouraged by War Office Premiums, and also by the keen rivalry of the past few years, breeders are now retaining their best colts entire. This, of course, involves a good deal of extra trouble, for, whereas young [female] stock may ordinarily roam the fells with their dams - a mare may be found with three of her offspring at foot - a young entire has to be cared for inland.
>
> *Livestock Journal* c. 1927.

This extra work probably accounts for some colts getting foals at an early age; by putting a precocious colt in with a couple of senior mares, not only can they teach him his manners, but his stock-getting potential can be evaluated against what the mares have produced before, and if he doesn't pass-on what's wanted, he can be gelded while still relatively young. Quite a few working geldings were stallions up to the age of five or six, my own included.

So what do breeders look for in their stallions? As one example, at Townend, six colts and nine fillies were registered in 1977, got by three different stallions: the homebred favourite Townend Flash II 5278, Lunesdale Lucky Jim 6525, and Heltondale Black Magic 5862. Just as there must have been a lot of thought behind Eddie Wilson's choice of stallions, certainly every breeder had a clear idea of what was wanted and was quite fussy about which stallion would suit his own mares and which ones were better passed over.

For a stallion we wanted one with fine hair, and a good nature; it's difficult to judge their nature. A good eye - a kind eye. Mostly how it was made; with a bit of bone, and a good chest. A broad face rather than a narrow one and not too big a head.

Storm Boy [2288], we had him during the War, and he was black. Dad took it off Joe Baxter and kept it for him because of the War [food and animal feed rationing], and we used him. It was a good horse. We never used a Dales stallion; but we have selt a stallion to go onto Dales. (Frank Wales)

The main difficulty is in picking the right stallion. Just 'the one down the road' or what a neighbour recommends, is not good enough.

Ivan: You can get five people looking at same horse and they'll not all five like it. You've got to use what you like, and what you think'll suit your horses.

Henry: We've mostly just used our own stallion; just, sometimes, used a fresh 'un. I like a good 'un! It wants a bit of bone, and feather.

Townend Flash II 5278 and Glenis Cockbain, nee Wilson.

Ivan: You want one with a bit of timber in him, don't you? A la'al slender 'un's no good - you want summat with a bit of stuffing in him, don't you? (Henry Harrison and Ivan Alexander)

For a stallion I wanted a nice little head and little ears, and a bit of nice bone - flat bone. I wasn't bothered about colour; or a bit of white. One or two had bits of white on the back foot, but it didn't really matter if it was black, bay, brown or what it was, as long as it was a nice sort, and specially a pony. (Bill Potter)

I look for a short back - a nice head, a nice outlook; flat bone; and short coupled; nice free action, a bit of lift in the hock as well as the front end. Good heart room. I don't like

these long backed, lanky things with big ears. I know some of mine have got rather big ears; but that stallion down there [Dene Rebel FP50721C], he's got small ears, he's got a pony head. (Mrs Ailie Newall)

Thomas Capstick is one of the few breeders whose family have not been wholeheartedly behind his activities with ponies. His parents were not in favour of the addition of a stallion to the herd, although later, as the stock improved, they were pleased by the successes in the show ring.

I know when I bought my first stallion, off Henry Harrison, Sleddale Bertie, I was in the doghouse over that! I was asked, 'How many mares do you have!' I maybe only had four or five, but I intended to have more I suppose! At first, we used to go to Ted Benson's Heltondale Prince and Mountain Roamer. I used to take my mares to Bill Potter's; to Lowthwaite... always trying to improve your stock by using a good stallion. No, I don't really go back in the pedigree at all; I just chose stallions that had been proven to get the type that I like. (Thomas Capstick)

We wanted what's put down in the breed standard. Storm Boy [2288] was the only real traditional pony [then] that fitted the breed standard. One of the stallions Ted Benson and I picked was Heltondale Sonny Boy [4473]; and he had four brilliant legs, but he was far from being correct.

Storm Boy was loaded with feather. And - unless there was one or two stragglers up on Heltondale, that nobody saw - he was the only traditional Fell that was registered, properly registered. *There might have been others registered, but there was nothing came up to his standard. (Bert Morland)*

Storm Boy was a favourite with Joe Baxter's grand-daughter Eileen, who was a neighbour when we lived in Shap. I asked her once to describe him, and I can still remember the expression of glee on her face when she said, 'He was a reet black un!'

Given the stallion's ability to influence a generation, breeders need to have an eye both for what is correct and which Fell type is suitable for their herd.

Rambler was our stud horse for 25 years, and Prince is 22 now. After Rambler went we would use a few other stallions - but we weren't just too happy with what they got. Rambler seemed to click right every time and it was just a job to follow on. (Barbara Bell)

There is a difficulty in finding unrelated stallions. Mrs Newall, Chris Thompson and Bert Morland all remarked on the difficulty of finding 'a right stallion.' Given these comments by experienced breeders it may be worth considering a scheme such as the Highland Pony Society have recently brought in, where colts with unusual bloodlines can be run-on to adulthood on a large secure allotment (*The Ark*, Rare Breeds Survival Trust, November 2004). This scheme gives a bit of breathing space for evaluation of their potential during adolescence.

I've to use all my own stock because I'm a stickler for movement; if they don't move I don't want to know. (Bert Morland)

Legs, head and feet. Temperament is a lot as well; normally, that's the best. Feet isn't as much as the bone, and the head, cause my mares have very good feet; I can stand one bad point. (Barry Mallinson)

> ...if your goal is ultimately to breed the perfect specimen of any breed it is no good being unrealistic, and faults, when they exist, must be acknowledged and considered when choosing a mate. (Bert Morland, *A Lifetime in the Fells*)

It's which 'clicks'. Four or five foals and you might think none of them were related; one gets both riding and show quality, one gets one, one gets the other. So you've got to breed three or four to get the real good 'un. And to see whether they can breed the real good 'un. (Bob Charlton)

Mare lines, as we have seen, tend to stay in family ownership so the 'type' of each stud is most often influenced by them, while stallions are more likely to be passed on from stud to stud, either by sale or loan. When selecting a stallion, breeders look at the offspring he gets, and perhaps his immediate parents, but not his extended pedigree. Breeders mentioned the quality of stock got by stallions such as Heltondale Black Prince III FP188C, Lunesdale Jerry 6841 and Tebay Campbellton Victor 6641.

Foaled in 1976, Victor was by Lownthwaite Star Dust 5965 (a full brother to 15144 Lownthwaite Star Trek, see chapter on *What makes a Fell unique?*), out of 15877 Tebay Brandy. Victor's name appears in three different forms due to typographical variations in the Stud Book: Campbell Ton, Campbelltown and Campbellton. The form given here, 'Campbellton' is what his breeder has always insisted it should be. (See photograph in the *Ideal Ponies* chapter).

We'd Heltondale Laddie [4848], the first one I bought with the two mares; then we got Heather Lad [5493], off Sarge around 1970. In 1973 we had Heltondale Lucky Boy [5851]. We didn't have so many browns though. Then of course we bred Victor. We perhaps over-used him, but he was so good. The quality came out.

You know, it didn't matter how common a pony he served, he threw that quality to it. Very true to type. If they come in, you could pick 'em out: what were his, and what were Heather Lad's. Same as Victor, they were like peas in a pod. He transmitted it, like the majority of stallions don't. You know, they'll get one or two. But every one of Victor's you could tell when they come in as yearlings and two year olds; that silky feather right from the back of the knee.

His father was good, one of Wales's; he was good, he was nice; he was their top mare's full brother. So the quality was there. (David Trotter)

Tebay Campbellton Victor 6641
{ 15877 Tebay Brandy
  { 15036 Tebay Queeny (B)
    { 13454 Heltondale Mary II (A)
     {Heltondale Mary (I.S.)
      { High House Dolly

Heltondale Mary (I.S) was by Heltondale Star Boy 4854. As early as 1916, mares were inspected for 'Fell Pony type' before they were served by a Premium Fell stallion. The inspection scheme was set up in 1940; on application, two FPS officers would visit an owner to check that a mare was of Fell type, and then she could be registered, with 'I.S.' following her name. Her fillies could be bred, but her colts had to be gelded. In March 1962 the sections were defined in the Stud Book: first generation offspring of I.S. mares were registered as Section (A) and second generation stock as Section (B); the descendants of (B) fillies were registered in the main section. Inspected stock were not necessarily of completely unknown pedigree, but perhaps had been sold without their papers or never registered with the society. The inspected section closed in 1970, and there will be very few Section B ponies left now. Entry to the Fell Pony Stud Book is limited to foals bred from registered stock.

There were some good ponies that Handley [Haygarth Farm] used to breed - we had to get a mare of theirs inspected, that we'd bought. She was top quality but there was no papers; I asked some of them lads and nobody knew where the papers had gone to. I said to Peggy [Crossland], 'it's a wonder there weren't papers,' but we just had to set off and get the mares inspected and just breed them up. So two judges came to inspect her. There was three when they came for a stallion inspection, but just two for a mare. We kept putting the fillies to a pedigree Fell pony stallion. After we'd got three generations, they were considered pure Fell. (David Trotter)

Some of the ponies that were inspected were probably being registered for a second time, often because of lost or mislaid papers. Not all were mares; keen newcomers to Fells sometimes had geldings inspected and registered (eg in Stud Book Volumes XXXIV and XXXV in the mid 1960s) to be able to show them in Mountain and Moorland classes. Inspected colts, of course, had to be gelded before they could be registered, as did Section A and Section B colts.

For inspection, all they needed was to look Fell type. Flicka [a newly purchased filly] went to Adamthwaite, and they came and inspected her, so that we could breed off her. There was one or two more came there; Rex Stott would have a few inspected as well. So they were given a certificate of inspection. (Thomas Capstick)

Cross-breeding

ALTHOUGH the Stud Book is closed, it does not mean that Fells can't be used in other breeding programmes. For instance, before I bought him my gelding was used, while still entire of course, with a herd of unregistered Fell mares near Sedbergh. Cross-breeding is neither supported nor penalised by the Fell Pony Society though there is a strong feeling that mares should be bred pure because of their more limited numerical input to the breed compared with stallions. In the early years of the 20th century a Premium stallion was required to serve 'only mares of Fell Pony type, approved by representatives of the Fell Pony Committee'.

FPS does not run a part bred register itself. In a sense, this is a similar attitude to that of breeders of Rough Fell or Swaledale hill sheep. The meat trade wants a swift-growing, large-framed meaty lamb, so many farmers cross hill-bred ewes with a Leicester ram to produce the Mule or Greyface. The Mule female sells at a good price to the lowland farms that can support a prolific flock. She will usually produce two, three or even more fat lambs when crossed with a Texel or Suffolk ram. Her brothers, who will not be breeding stock, fatten well. However, in order to produce the Mule, the hill sheep must continue to be bred pure to provide the base for that top cross with the Leicester. The Leicester itself has no direct influence on the Rough Fell or the Swaledale. Similarly, the early registrations of hill-bred ponies were intended to keep them pure, partly in order to provide a continuing foundation stock for crossing and partly in recognition of their intrinsic value. This is an argument against the myth of the Friesian horse being much involved in the 'creation' of the early Fell type: if the market demanded it, a 'foreign x local' cross may well have been made, but most of the saleable offspring would go on to work and not to breed, so the local stock would still be of the same foundation blood.

Putting the two together

SO, to breed you chose a mare from a line that you liked, and a stallion that threw stock that you liked and which you thought would complement your mare or correct her faults.

How then did you get mare and stallion together to produce your perfect foal? I asked breeders about the ways in which stallions were kept and used.

There has been, and still is, a considerable difference in Fell breeding practices. There are stallions kept in doors and led out under control to serve mares 'in hand'; stallions kept alone outdoors, with mares just being let into the allotment for a month or two for service; and there are stallions being run almost all the time with their mares and foals. Even in one family the practices can vary; although the Charltons, for instance, prefer to keep a stallion with his herd if possible, there have been occasions when that was unwise, and then they served mares in-hand. And as we shall see, there used to be the 'travelling stallions'.

There were a few descriptions of stallions being let out on the fell, but where more than one herd runs on the common land this practice is mostly not allowed. It can cause a lot of ill feeling if a stallion is put out among other people's ponies, and even an accidental escape can escalate into a court-case.

No you couldn't put a stallion out - you hadn't to put a stallion or a tup or anything out. You weren't supposed to - but some did. (Mrs Dargue)

Maybe someone else's stallion serves your mares; or a filly is served who is too young, or whom the owner wants to show next year or wants to sell without being in-foal; or maybe a stallion gets in with yours and starts a fight, or injures a mare. There is no guarantee either that a stallion on the fell would be a Fell, or if he was, that he would have a licence! The actions taken to discourage farmers from turning entire males on a shared fell have sometimes been very decisive indeed.

Frank: We've never kept stallions out on the fell. No, never. Just kept them in a field at home. Once a feller put a bull to't fell and the other farmers castrated it. In my time.

Christine: You can't. Our fell isn't like an enclosed allotment. You're sharing it with everybody else. (Wales Family)

We ran the stallion out on the fell with the ponies in them days. A rule come and we got into bother for having a stallion on t'common.

They were run from Ullock Bank in them days, and then when we come here [Stoney Gill], Uncle Kit always had a black and white stallion here, well he used to keep him inside [in a field] through t'summer because a lot of mares used to come tull him; but he didn't like it when our stallions were on t'fell because they used to rush t'wall you see. He used to ring up and say, 'Come and git yer stallion!!' So we'd to go and get him back. (Bill Potter)

In those rare cases where a stallion was allowed to live 'at' the fell, it was usual to remove him to in-bye land for the winter and especially during February, March and April. This prevents mares being served too early if they have slipped a foal, or have not conceived during the preceding year. Removing the stallion from the fell prevents foals arriving at an inappropriate time. The effect of day-length on the mare's oestrus cycle is not certain enough to prevent conception, particularly in very young or very old mares whose hormones may be unpredictable and permit them to foal in, say, December or January, when the weather is far too bad for a young one up on the tops. But this regulation of the foaling season, described by all the breeders, does not seem to have been true for all the fell areas; there is a faint air of criticism in Bill Potter's comment on a lack of management on Crosby Ravensworth Fell, which was later cleared of horses.

...stallion on Crosby Fell, he was never picked up, he was there all the time, so as soon as a mare foaled... I've seen Stan [Mawson] buy a mare, in October, he'd put it out on fell and then it would foal next September... (Bill Potter)

Though some stallions remained relatively local, I recall Sarge Noble telling me a story about one who was known to have travelled nine miles upwind into Kentmere to serve a mare, returning to his regular beat on Askham Fell the following day.

There was rights to let the stallion go out in the breeding season - well I do now, put the stallion out [on Askham Fell]. Probably bring him back at the end of July, beginning of August, on account of the driving trials [Lowther] - well they go out on that side of the fell you see, and there's sometimes these sponsored rides as well. So it isn't wise to have him out then. I think in the old rules there was a right to put out a stallion in the breeding season: beginning of June to just into August; then I'd keep him in-bye at home.

But you see Sarge had one or two stallions out at the fell and my mares were out there so I didn't have to bother very much! When I got, you know, seven or eight mares I thought about getting my own stallion. (Chris Thompson)

The FPS newsletter of 1968 announced that, 'It was agreed that in the near future all stallions should be licenced. This is not entirely easy, as some breeders with ponies living in their wild state do not like to handle them at all, as they lose their natural ability to fend for themselves and keep out of the way of strangers.' It is natural to have a stallion with a group of mares; they put him in his place very firmly. It is easy enough to keep a group of geldings, or a group of mares, or mixed mares and geldings, always provided you have room, and the make-up of the herd stays the same. They squabble, but once they establish their order of dominance there is not too much risk of ponies being injured or 'rushed' over fences or walls. It is much more difficult to keep more than one stallion handy on a farm without shutting them up securely in a building of some kind, especially if the in-bye land is needed for sheep and cattle and so safely-enclosed grazing is at a premium. Their competitive behaviour in spring and summer can be hard to contain.

One time, about foal time, old Romany Boy was in the bull pens and we were putting him out with the mares. I went up and I put a halter on, and father-in-law said, 'What are you doing that for?' I said, 'Taking him to the mares....' He said, 'You won't get there!' And he got in the car and he drove off round to the gate. *I promise you I hadn't got twenty yards and Romany Boy just ducked his head out, everything came off, and he was gone. We couldn't keep a head collar on him. We used to call him Old Little Ears because you could plait the mane in, anything... in fact he got loose at the stallion show once...(Sarah Charlton)*

Baldersdale Hero used to barge down walls to get to where he wanted to be, if he was put in the field. (Margaret Wilson)

We sold Model as a yearling, and we bought him back at eleven year old, after Rambler went, because we'd tried different ones a few year and we just were getting things we didn't like. This place where he went, they were all stone walls, but they were down. And he got into crammling over

Baldersdale Hero.

the walls, and we had a job trying to hold him. He just used to go over the top and off. (Barbara Bell)

My daughter Jen was once knocked off her pony by a big Dale type stallion who was pastured with mares on a nearby allotment and jumped out over the wall to attack her pony. Jen was only bruised and shaken, and the pony just had a few cuts from running into the stone wall, but a year later the same stallion jumped out to attack another passing horse, and this time he injured its rider. Mrs Newall told of a similar incident (see chapter on *What Makes a Fell Unique?*). The horses attacked were not rivals; just mares or geldings passing by. Thomas Capstick observes, 'I know of a woman who keeps four or five stallions together; but they were just a bit marked-up so they obviously didn't agree all the time.' 'Didn't agree all the time' is a typically understated remark. Farmers are always aware of the battles that may occur at service time between, say, stock bulls or tups, no matter how good-natured they may be for the rest of the year. In autumn one sometimes sees rams fastened together with a short length of chain between their horns, to prevent them getting far enough apart to batter each other in that touchy period before the tupping season starts; tups have killed newly-purchased rivals for the flock before now. Equally, stallions have to be handled with common sense and an awareness of the rivalries that may flare in springtime. And although most Fells are nice natured, if one stallion does not 'get on' with other horses, he may have to be kept apart for the safety of all concerned.

The Travelling Stallion

AN old method of breeding ponies and farm horses, which avoided such troubles, was to use the 'travelling stallion'. Stud cards were his 'local advertising'. John Gate, who grew up around Caldbeck and farmed in Mosedale and then at Friarbiggin, Orton, recalls, 'When we were boys we used to kind o' collect them, y'know, when they come round wi't stallions, they used to give you a card. Like you used to collect cigarette cards, we used to collect stud cards.' If the mare was consistently not in season on the day of the week when the stallion came round, she had to go to him when she was, or miss a year. But in the times when few farmers had their own transport, this could be inconvenient, and not always satisfactory.

Mrs Dargue's collection of family papers includes cards advertising Fell and Dale stallions: Blencathra, Heather Boy Again, Kirkdale Hero, and their own Peepings Swell. Among them is a registration application for Daybreak in the Fell Section of the Mountain and Moorland NPS Stud Book. He was foaled in 1925 and like his sire, Sporting Times II 1328, he was piebald; his dam was a grey 'pure Fell pony' and he appears to have been named after an older Daybreak who was the sire of Sporting Times II's mother. It is unlikely that this application was ever sent, because the paper is still in the Dargue family's possession (see opposite page) and the name is not in the compiled Stud Book.

The War Office, requiring sturdy ponies for Army pack work, supported British native breeds financially up to

SEASON, 1920.

THAT WELL-BRED FELL PONY STALLION,

KIRKDALE HERO,

(968),

The Property of J. B. RICHARDSON,
Wythwaite, Newbiggin, Carlisle,
Will serve a limited number of Mares on the following Terms :

£1 when Mare proves in Foal.   Groom's Fee 2/6,
due at first service.

Kirkdale Hero (968),
Bred by Mr. T. D. HUTCHINSON,
The Flash, Newbiggin, Carlisle.
sire, BLACK BOY.
g sire, SIR HARRY.
dam by LITTLE JOHN.
g dam by JOLLY SIR JOHN.
g g dam by Mr BRAMWELL'S HORSE.

KIRKDALE HERO (968, Volume 16),
Is a good dark brown with the best of feet and legs and nice hair. Standing 14 hands high, and is a right typical Fell Pony.

All mares tried by this horse and either sold, exchanged, or given away will be charged full season's Fee, except by consent of the Owner.

KIRKDALE HERO will travel locally and meet mares by appointment.

For further particulars apply Owner and Groom,
J. B. RICHARDSON.

1932. Each year the society held stallion shows, and awarded premiums to the best ponies. In 1916 a premium was £40, plus 2s 6d per foal, so it was well worth having. Five stallions were chosen, one to travel each of the districts of Appleby, Keswick, Kirkby Stephen, Middleton-in-Teesdale, and Shap.

The stud cards in the Fell Pony Museum, which were found on a beam in the stable of Mr J Graham of Caldbeck, include a card for Mountain Hero 2nd, who was advertised

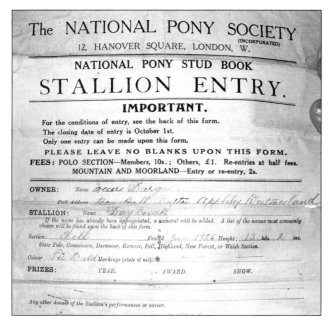

in 1900 as 'a rich bay Highland pony'. He stood 13.2 hh at three years old, and had 'spectacular action'. Hero's dam was Black Bess by FitzGeorge; she was a Fell. Mountain Hero 2nd was himself registered two years later as Fell number 250 in Polo Pony Stud Book Vol VII.

> At the Fell Pony Society's Stallion Show at Penrith on 24th April, 1928, Mountain Jester was awarded the £80 War Office Premium to travel Kirkby Stephen district.
>
> Mountain Jester is a typical Fell Pony, built upon true pony lines, and possesses great strength and activity. He has wonderful legs and feet and goes with that great dash which is so valuable in Fell ponies. His size and weight makes him a very suitable pony to cross with the smaller mares of Ravenstonedale, Kirkby Stephen and Stainmore districts.
>
> Mountain Ranger, the sire of the Premium Pony is acknowledged to be one of the greatest prize winning Fell ponies of the age. His type, size and style of moving, was simply perfect. He was a great prize winner in his home country and also at the London Pony Shows.

Frank W Garnett, in his Fell Pony Committee Report for 1914, pointed out that of the five stallions awarded premiums to travel the districts, all traced back to Blooming Heather (325) and 'the time is fast approaching when the question of introducing fresh blood must be faced.' He went so far as to recommend selecting 'the very best and purest blacks or browns' of the Highland breed to put onto

Fell mares. Mountain Hero 2nd may be an example, as cited by Garnett, of 'the interchange of stallions between the two districts in which they are bred' which had been 'continuous from time out of mind', although there is very little acknowledgement of Highland blood in the early registrations as there is of Dales and Norfolk Cob blood. Here is the wording of Mountain Hero 2nd's Stud Card:

'It can be seen from the breeding of Mountain Hero 2nd that he is bred from two of the best breeds of ponies that England can produce. Being bred and brought up on fell land, he cannot fail but produce a healthy stock.'

{ Ling Cropper
{ Highland Laddie
{ Rob Roy
{ Old Mountain Hero
{ Young Mountain Hero (owned by J Bell of Caldbeck)
Mountain Hero 2nd
{ Fitzgeorge
{ Black Bess
{Grey mare 13-1, by Jack's Delight, brown 13-2

'Will Serve Mares at 15s each, and heath-going Ponies at 12s 6d each, with 2s 6d Groom Fee in each case. The Groom Fee to be paid at time of service, and all other demands at the end of the season.'

Heltondale Victor, a stallion travelling in 1912, had his own poem on his stud card, and again action is a prized quality.

Here comes Heltondale Victor,
We know him by his walk,
This is the horse that goes so well,
And makes the people talk.

Look at his head, his neck, his eyes,
Mark well his shape and size,
Superior action he displays,
Amazing strength likewise.

1920
PREMIUM
FELL PONY STALLION
"Heltondale Victor,"
No. 938.
The Property of
Mr. JOHN METCALFE,
Dale Foot,
Rumpton,
Penrith.

Heltondale Victor.

Here comes Heltondale Victor,
We know him by his walk.
This is the horse that goes so well
And makes the people talk.
Look at his head, his neck, his eyes,
Mark well his shape and size;
Superior action he displays,
Amazing strength likewise.

Fertility varied a lot, despite the stallions' long weeks of purposeful walking which kept them fit. The percentage of live foals to the number of mares served by premium stallions was recorded by the Fell Pony Committee as noted on the next page.

The committee, which in 1913 had not yet become a society, reported that the 'percentage of living foals to mares served must be considered fair' in comparison to other breeds of horses at that time. The table does not give any clues to the condition of the mares, at what period in their cycle they were served, how they were kept, or what work they were doing. Yet these travelling pony stallions were doing nearly as well as any today; the average foaling percentage in horses is still around 65% in modern times.

One point that is of interest is that the Board of Agriculture, who oversaw the use of stallions at that time, raised an 'important matter… which will require careful consideration by the Committee… the question of inserting a clause in the conditions precluding the award of a premium to a pony to travel the same district for more than four consecutive seasons.' This would be in order to prevent a filly being served by her sire, thus preventing a narrowing of the genetic material of the breed.

The travelling stallion is still remembered in Cumbria. Although in the following two instances he was not a Fell, the respect paid to the horse by his handler comes through.

Tom Dargue, he travelled a Clydesdale stallion till he was over 90 - walking, they used to walk for miles. They

1913	Mares	Barren	Live foals	Slipped foals	Dead mare	% fertility
Dalesman	50	10	37	3	-	74.0
Highland Fashion	38	9	24	-	2	63.1
Mountain Ranger	29	11	17	-	1	58.6
Dreadnought	42	-	21	-	-	50.0
Blooming Heather II	35	16	17	-	1	48.5

Overall live foaling averages			
Year	Average	Year	Average
1913	59.7	1916	55.9
1914	58.8	1917	51.3
1915	55.3	1918	43.0

Me and father - father used to work at Shap Granite, and then come home and have his tea - and at half past five, we would start to walk from Ullock Bank to Sedbergh; of a night, with stallion, on travelling like. We used to go down t' Fair Mile, and call at all them farms all t' way down to Sedbergh. We used to call at Bob Nicholson at Intake, and by, he'd some good ponies, what a shame like when they all went away.

And would be half past nine, quarter to ten when we left Sedbergh to come back at night. I used to say to me father, coming back along Fair Mile, 'Let's have a ride Father! I'm tired!' Whoa, he wouldn't let us on its back, no way! You walked! (Bill Potter)

came from somewhere about How Hill - The Flatt, they called the farm. I know they sent a stallion up to Bow Hall; I think just for his last years; they didn't want to put him down. I remember Jos used to say he was a real nuisance! He knocked walls down, and if there was any mares in season he used to create an awful racket. He didn't do anything; he didn't serve, travelling or anything like that - he was just sort of in retirement. (Mrs Elsie Dargue)

I can remember, like when Uncle Kit had a black and white stallion, Fell ponies weren't as popular. Rennie Watson from Roe Busk fetched five Fell pony mares to t' stallion. Quite a few used to fetch them to try and breed colour, you see, black and white 'uns. He was bought in 1945 for 45 quid. Top priced foal in Kirkby Stephen.

Fair Mile was the first Roman road in this area, but is now a relatively quiet unfenced byway. Taking a nearly straight line south from Borrow Bridge Fort in the Lune Gorge, it meets the Sedbergh road round the southern flanks of the Howgills. From Ullock Bank to Sedbergh and back is about 20 miles; a tough walk at the end of a working day, with the stallion to control; and it must have been a tired boy who trudged home with his father in the long midsummer twilight. But the old stallion men walked huge weekly mileages, and having to walk to a place was not seen as a problem, at any time of year.

You'll have read about Jos's father walking across [from

GENERAL PRIDE (641).
is a beautiful black, foaled 1906
Bred by Mr John Swinburn, Gowbarrow Hall, Penrith
Sire: Lothian Prince
Dam: by Old Mountain Hero
Gr. dam: by Sir George

GENERAL PRIDE is a horse of class and character. His class of bone, hair, his legs, feet and pasterns, and his general appearance at once denote a breeding horse; in fact, he is admitted by competent judges to be a perfect model of the breed; and as regards his action, a single glance at the same will convince anyone that he is, without a doubt, the finest stepping pony in existence.

His sire, Lothian Prince, has travelled the Penrith District for sixteen years, and has left a grand stock. [Lothian Prince was by the Clydesdale Royal Lothian reg 6991 CHSB and so was ineligible himself for any Fell Pony Society premiums.]

His dam, the property of Mr Stephenson, Bowscar, Penrith, was the winner of a great number of first prizes.

His dam was by Old Mountain Hero, the property of Mr Cannon, of Borrowdale. He left the best stock, and the most of them, of any pony in Cumberland. He travelled until he was 30 years old. His gr. dam by Sir George, the property of C. Wilson, Esq., of Rigmaden, won eight first prizes at the Royal, and had an unbeaten record.

With breeding like this, and himself a perfect model of grand pony type, he cannot be beaten.

Dufton to St John's Chapel, Weardale, on the other side of the Pennines] to judge the Dales stallion show in the snow. He couldn't open the gates so he rolled over them. He was well over seventy then. But they just used to set off and go where they wanted! My grandfather, he used to open lead mines out, he used to go to about Coniston, and then near Appleby; then he opened the mines near Alston. They had a little farm as well. He just used to set off and walk to wherever he went to. (Mrs Elsie Dargue)

Joe Baxter was the Guardhouse man. He'd a Mountain pony as well did Joe Baxter, cause he used to come round my grandfather's, travelling, with that 'un; before my day. (Ivan Alexander talking with Henry Harrison)

The 'Mountain pony' was Mountain Ranger (see chapter 4). His stud card in the Fell Pony and Countryside Museum at Dalemain shows that his handler walked a minimum of 88 miles per week during the covering season (May to August). He left Guardhouse on a Monday and did not return till Saturday evening:

Season 1923
BOARD OF AGRICULTURE
PREMIUM FELL PONY STALLION
District B. - Shap
'MOUNTAIN RANGER' No. 598
The Property of Mr J Baxter of Threlkeld, having been awarded the £60 Premium, will cover Fell Pony Mares at 15/- each, with 2/6 Groom's Fee, due at time of service.

ROUTE

Commencing May 7th, 1923.

Monday: Leave by Gill Head to Dacre and Askham.

Tuesday: Helton, Bampton, to Mr Holme, Thrimby.

Wednesday: Shap, Orton, Tebay.

Thursday: Bretherdale and District.

Friday: Howtown and Martindale.

Saturday: Pooley Bridge, Watermillock, and home over Sunday.

'Mountain Ranger' is black, foaled 1906, and stands 13.3 high. His sire is Park End King and his dam is Scoredale Queen by Blooming Heather (325).

He will travel with the Board of Agriculture Certificate of Soundness, which is open to inspection.

Mr Baxter will not be answerable for any loss or damage through the trying or serving of mares, but every care will be taken.

All Mares tried by this horse and served by another, or sold, exchanged, or given away will be charged full price.

Joe would walk beside the stallion, with his coat strapped to the surcingle together with a 'bait-bag' containing oats and the day's food for himself, and maybe a few 'bare necessities' in the coat pockets for the night's stopover. People I spoke to remembered him clearly, 'not a very big man', 'a naughty old monkey', 'a real old character'. Grace Teasdale of Longlands, quoted by Clive Richardson (1990),

said that Joe was 'unfailingly cheerful, patient and skilled in the work.' Mrs Frances Bell remembers that he used to come round to Waver Head every other Friday 'and from here he would walk back to Threlkeld.' Stallion walking seems to have promoted longevity in handler as well as horses; Tom Dargue, who travelled a Clydesdale, lived to be 90 and Joe Baxter to the great age of 96.

It was the late Mrs Hasell-McCosh who drew my attention to Joe Baxter in 1982 by asking me to paint a panel to illustrate a travelling Fell stallion for the Fell Pony Museum. She wanted to show him still providing a useful service long after its demise in general use. She remarked

Joe Baxter & Master John as illustrated in the Fell Pony News, Vol. V. The date given of 1932 is an error as Master John was foaled in 1946!

though that when Joe travelled Master John, it was hardly safe for him to do so. The traffic was increasing on the roads, and he was an old man, so if the stallion played up, he was becoming too frail to control it.

The stallion running with his mares

Sarah: Well it's natural, isn't it? Anyway, that's how I like to do it. I just feel they're much happier, and then much easier to handle. Do you find many people cover their mares in-hand? We very rarely do (B: we've given up) because the stallion gets rather sweet with us too. When we did, on the whole, Bob would handle the stallion when we were covering a mare and I would handle it otherwise, so as soon as Bob came with a bridle the stallion would say, 'AHA!'
Bob: I think we used Foxy [Linnel Reynard] in-hand quite a bit because Foxy was young - Foxy used to get hell belted out of him by some of the older mares and I think we used to try and be kind to him. Now he's much wiser; how to handle the mares. (Bob and Sarah Charlton)

Margaret Wilson said that when stallions were being used to serve in-hand at Townend they were kept indoors, but others ran with their mares during the season; after which they were either brought in, or remained outside with an in-foal mare for company. Then when the mares returned from the fell to foal in the fields, the stallions were brought indoors.

I didn't like a strange one to come if the stallion's with the mares. He chased it into the herd; and the herd chased

it out. If someone brought a new mare, you brought stallion in and hungered it, you didn't give it anything to eat, and then put it out day after. It wasn't so keen - it was hungry. (Frank Wales)

If just one stallion is used on all the mares throughout a stud, then his filly foals that are kept will need a different stallion. This must have been one reason why Heltondale Black Prince III - four times Stallion Show champion - was sold at the height of his career to go to Mrs Muller in Germany. It was the only reason for David Trotter selling Tebay Campbellton Victor to Sarge Noble. Few owners would want to line breed fillies back to their sire. Looking at the Stud Book you can see that stallions are moved from breeder to breeder through their careers. Sometimes a breeder on a harsh fell will lend his stallion in early summer to another with a kinder environment, who wants foals earlier in the year; then he will bring him home to serve his own mares.

The stallion was with them all the time. And then we used to swap him for Roy Charlton's stallion; he used to get a loan of mine for the summer, and I used to get a loan of his. (Mrs Ailie Newall)

Derrick Byas: Normally when you borrowed a stallion it would be July and you hoped to get rid of it by mid August, late August - depending on whose you'd borrowed and what excuses he could come up with for not getting it back - which is how things happen occasionally. (Dargue Family)

Linnel Reynard, photograph courtesy of Laura Hart.

Ted Benson comments on the breeding season at Adamthwaite and the mares being turned in to the stallion's enclosure:

We used to get them in when breeding season came round; I used to run stallion on a bit of rough ground next to the allotment; it was interesting, but it was a darned nuisance, a lot of extra work. People used to bring mares; I've seen thirty two or three in; not all registered. That was the problem; people you knew, friends, they used to want to bring them or send them; and you couldn't very well refuse them. Oh, maybe half of them that was in to t'stallion, they weren't registered ponies. (Ted Benson)

Owners might find it hard to refuse friends, but the stallion had the final say on which mares he would serve!

The grey one, now he was rather funny with his mares; he would maybe dislike one. He wouldn't have it. That's the only one I've had any bother with. He wasn't any bother really; he would maybe chase it off for two or three days, but it would end up in foal! (Ted Benson)

Stallions can refuse mares, and they can mark them up very very badly. Chase them out of field; I've had two this year. They don't seem to want to, whether they're in season or not. It can be mares that have been pets, not used to running with other ponies.   (Thomas Capstick)

The Enclosure Scheme

THE Breeding Enclosure Scheme was begun in 1945, when the travelling stallion system began to fall out of use. The society took the rent of a piece of rough allotment at The Nettles, Berrier, west of Penrith, and ran a selected stallion on it during the breeding season. This proved so successful that another enclosure was organised at High Arnside in the southern part of the Lakes. During the period when two enclosures were available, not more than 20 pedigree mares were to be allowed in either; this was partly so there were not too many mares for the stallion, and partly to save the grazing; in the hot dry summer in 1949 The Nettles had proved insufficient for the 37 mares who had been served there.

They used to vote on them at the Stallion Show. Yes. I

can remember them doing that. Mr Bell and Mr Wilson used to tell them to bring the nominated stallions, and then they used to vote on them and it was the one that got the most votes. It would be when Mrs McCosh was secretary. I think if you were a member [of FPS] and you were going to send a mare you would have a vote. (Mrs Elsie Dargue)

At that time, it was considered that there were two different types of Fell, the heavier 'Cumberland' pony and a lighter 'riding' type. To accommodate this, two different types of stallions were chosen. In 1950 Linnel Osprey ran in the Berrier Enclosure; Rowland Boy, whom Chris Thompson considered one of the best his father ever had, was the heavier type who ran that year in the Arnside Enclosure. In 1951 Berrier held William Winder's Mountain Model 12884, and Arnside had J J Taylor's Park House Victor 2850. These same stallions ran in the enclosures at Berrier and Crook, Windermere, for the next two years. This was evidently popular but genetically unwise, because both were of Storm Boy 2288 breeding, and too many of the mares were also of this breeding. In 1953 the council decided that, to try to get different blood for 1954, a committee of five mare owners would pick the stallions regardless of which ones had been winners at the stallion show. A similar situation occurred in 1966-68 when Waverhead Rambler 4101 (by Black Grouse 3733 who traced back to Storm Boy, x 8886 Jenny O' The Hill) stood for three consecutive years at the Caldbeck Enclosure, while Heltondale Sonny Boy 4473 (by Heltondale Star Boy

3854 x 11658 Fusedale Black Bess of Heltondale) stood at the one in Wet Sleddale.

[Jos] used to go to Berrier. Rosebud used to go in the tractor-and-trailer and soon as you got within a couple of miles she used to know - she started to be restive because she knew where she was going, to this wide open place! It wasn't a trailer like you have nowadays - it was home made where you could look out! You wouldn't be allowed to do that nowadays, you'd be in jail accused of cruelty. (Mrs Elsie Dargue)

The enclosure moved to several different locations over time: The Height, and Snow Hill, both at Caldbeck; Wet Sleddale, Shap; Dowthwaite Head, between Troutbeck and Ullswater. The scheme was discontinued in 1976 owing to the difficulty of finding suitable secure land, which was probably exacerbated by the tendency of some owners to leave their mares beyond the agreed date of August 1st. It certainly annoyed the farmers at Crook and at Berrier. Mrs Dargue explained that there was another problem too, 'There got to be too many people popping mares in - it didn't matter what - and scooting off with them before anybody came!'

In-Hand

SO much for the management that involves letting the mare and stallion into a field together. It takes minimal manpower. However, serving mares 'in-hand' is also quite usual, particularly mares who are strangers to the herd, or maiden mares. One handler holds the mare, and another leads the stallion up. I was spared any discussion of the process by the breeders but one lady owner of a maiden mare (name withheld to protect the innocent!) gave me a ribald description of the neighbouring farmers who turned up as spectators to the service. Her images of a romantic 'candle lit dinner for two' followed by 'a tryst with a handsome black stallion on a wind-swept hilltop' were rudely dashed when the stallion owner asked her if she wanted to 'hold the front end' or 'handle the tail' and guide the stallion in. She chose the front and was a little embarrassed to find that all the 'old boys' remained at the back to cheer the stallion on. 'And at the end of the service the stallion let out the most enormous fart I've ever heard!'

Service in-hand gives a degree of control if the mare is uncertain of the job, and it ensures she has actually been covered. That can be difficult to guarantee out in the field with others, where the new mare is the outsider and may be bullied by those in the established herd. Of course even service in-hand cannot mean that every breeder who puts a mare to the stallion will get a foal from her every year. Some mares don't like the stallion you want to use; even in-hand, they may behave so badly that they actually endanger him.

A horse that's not had a foal, I'll serve it in-hand. I just served a four year old today that's never seen a stallion before. I served her in-hand and then let her go. But if it's an older mare, all depends if we're in any big a rush. Last year I'd one, she went to two stallions elsewhere and never did get served. She was lucky, she got served with me, she got served 1st of August. But kick! She could kick standing on one leg! And in season! Otherwise, I put the mares in with the stallion. Take them out once they're served, if I get too many about. (Barry Mallinson)

In Cumbria, despite what the breeders have said about not knowing where to go for a stallion, there is at least always some choice of animals locally. This for many years has meant that there has been no need and no attempt to use artificial insemination methods; in fact until very recently there were no FPS regulations for registering a foal conceived by AI. However, with the Rare Breeds Survival Trust having recognised the breed as endangered, frozen semen is now being stored from Fell stallions under the Trust's 'ReGENEration' scheme. Surprisingly for such a hardy breed, the post-thaw qualities vary between stallions. At the time of writing however, the RBST scheme is only an insurance against difficult times ahead. It is not a replacement for natural breeding; AI is still very uncommon in Fell breeding in Britain. Fell foals produced by embryo transfer are not eligible for registration.

Mare behaviour

Ivan: Say, if such as Richard [Whitfield] borrowed a stallion for a day or two, maybe before you used him, mares on t'fell would go up into that area. Them that was coming in season, they knew - if you put a stallion in the field next to t'fell, they'd land like. It's just nature, they seemed to know he was there.

Henry: Yes, most of my ponies were out on the fell most

of the time. I just brought them in to t'stallion; June, July.

Ivan: - Twice through, sort of. (Henry Harrison and Ivan Alexander)

Derrick: Mares know when it's stallion time anyway. Because that's one of the times when you can go and get em off fell, because they hang towards t'Front. And if they're nowhere in sight you can put a stallion in the allotment and you can guarantee that in two or three days they were there at the fell wall waiting to come in. (Dargue family)

David Trotter's Heltondale Heather Lad had a range on a northerly section of the Howgills, and again, one by one as the mares came into season they made their way to him.

Henry: Most of them, they were foaled again following year at same spot. [time of year].

Ivan: It would all depend - if she was first to foal, she would maybe miss t'foal pride. And if she missed foal pride she foaled at month end. Roughly they used to come in a week into June, 6th, 7th, 8th, summat o' that. That was time you lowsed stallion and they were wanting to come in. Then they weren't too soon. You'd to regulate 'em with stallion. (Henry Harrison and Ivan Alexander)

Mares ovulate on a 21 day cycle, so a mare who has been visiting the stallion stays three or four weeks. The stallion man travelling his weekly route would call again, and the stallion in the allotment with the fell herd is left with them for six weeks; all to be sure that the served mare 'holds' and does not come back into season.

So long as all is well, she can go home, or back to the fell, and await the arrival of the new foal.

THE FELL YEAR: FOALING

Birth in a rural community is regular, keenly anticipated, expected yet routine. It is not feared, in the way it sometimes seems to be in more sophisticated settings. As a personal example, I clearly recall my husband telling me that, if we were snowed in and unable to get to hospital from Shap when our February daughter decided to arrive, he had calved cows and lambed sheep and farrowed sows, so he didn't doubt he could handle the situation if necessary. At the time, I can't say I was reassured. I know better now!

All the breeders in this book are farmers. They deal with foaling the way they deal with lambing and calving; as a natural event and part of the annual rhythm. They time it for when the spring grass is sprouting, earlier in the lowland areas, later on the harder hill ground. It always follows lambing time.

Breeders manage the date of foaling, exactly as they manage lambing and calving, by keeping male and females apart until after a certain date in the year. However, unlike sheep (whose gestation period is ~150 days) and cattle (~282 days), the timing is much more critical; a mare foals at ~340 days, so there is only a window of 25 days to get her served to foal at the same time for next year. If she misses that, her foaling will get later and later as the years go by until she misses a year. Breeders on the whole expect every mare to breed every year.

She could have a year off... but the mare that didn't consistently breed, you wouldn't bother keeping. Just same as with cows and sheep. (Christine Morton)

But if you didn't get the stallion there; or if they didn't hold to service; that would be it. (Mrs Elsie Dargue)

I missed [serving them] in foot and mouth year; and they're getting older now, yan or two missed this time. (Henry Harrison)

'Foot and mouth year' is a phrase regularly used in Cumbria, as no doubt in Devon, Northumberland, and other areas which suffered from the disease, to indicate the year 2001. The countryside was more or less closed down for eight months under disease regulations. There were restrictions on all livestock movement, and the preventive culls, in which all cloven-hoofed animals were destroyed on farms adjoining places that suffered from the disease, had deep emotional effects: frustration, anger and despair which still show at times, even four years later. In these siege-like conditions it was impossible to gather open fell to bring mares down because they shared the grazing with the sheep; even where mares were in-bye, it was difficult to take them to the stallion after foaling, or to bring back a stallion that had been out on loan. The result was that fewer Fell foals were born in 2002.

Breeders in an ordinary year would not want foals before April. Partly this is because the sheep take up everyone's time at lambing due to sheer numbers. But also the mare needs to be able to find good grazing, and the grass doesn't get going on the high land till early May. The majority of Fell studs aim to foal the mares in the latter part of May, and sometimes later, from coverings around the middle of June. At Waver Head, the Bell family used to foal in April 'and the foals seemed to get bigger. But we're foaling in May now. You think when you're foaling later and there's more grass and that, they'll 'get away', but they don't just seem to catch up.'

My brown mare always used to foal 25th or 26th of April - t' only mare I know always foals dead to 11 month. The others tend to go over into May, 11 month and fortnight normally. It's normally May time; I like May foals; they get a good start for t' back-end sales. (Barry Mallinson)

May is the time when the grass starts to grow fast on the fell. Ted Benson says of the Howgills, 'By 20th of May if there isn't a bit o' grass showing it's a bad year.'

Mares foal middle of May onward. I always used to foal them on the fell. I suppose I just didn't have room to bring them in, because I had suckler cows you see, and there were always plenty of sheep. But since I've sold the suckler cows I bring them in now to foal. You still get your problems; but at least you don't have to go up to find them. (Thomas Capstick)

Bill Potter's land above Shap lies around 1,000 feet above sea level and is a wet, treeless, north-facing fell: his ponies foal later, in June. However, he now runs some ponies on the Howgill fells which are higher but offer a bigger range of shelter and grazing, and he considers that they will be able to foal successfully a little earlier than on Birkbeck. The Peepings ponies, which run on the fell not far from Lownthwaite, are also managed to foal in June.

...we get our foals about 9th of June, Appleby Fair week, usually. I'm going to try and get them a little bit earlier on t' Howgills because it's a better fell, mair shelter. (Bill Potter)

Jos wasn't actually that keen on them foaling before June, because fell wasn't good enough. You weren't putting yows and lambs out till beginning of June. On the whole you go up mid June and they either have a foal running at foot, or shortly after, they foal. They weren't brought in to foal as such. (Derrick Byas & Dargue family)

Of course if you had mares that 'broke', it would be later. The latest I ever had, was the 29th of September. We didn't realise she was in foal. (Mrs Ailie Newall)

A most important point is that none of the breeders interviewed likes to foal the mares actually indoors, in a stable. None of them have enough boxes to spare to house a herd separately, one mare and foal to a box. Frank Wales says, 'They always used to foal at the fell, and that was that.' When breeders say they bring mares 'in' or 'inside' they mean, 'into a field', from the fell; they never mean 'in' a building.

It can be hard to decide exactly when to move the mares off the fell: if you want to bring in the in-foal mares but you leave it a few days too late, you may have to wait three or four weeks until they have all foaled and the foals are old enough to travel a long distance without stress.

Well we went to fetch Thomas's mares [off the Howgills], thinking 'is it wise to chase pregnant mares, or wise to chase babby foals?' And we didn't know what to do, so we went and had a look. And there was one foal nobbut only two-three hours old, so we'd to leave them. And next time we went there would be another eight had foaled, and we thought, 'Well, what do we do?' Cos as soon as you get behind them on quads, they come like hell right down to George Winder's, and so we didn't know what to do. Anyway, I said, 'I think we'll leave them another week', and we went back and there was only one that hadn't foaled. So we fetched them. (Bill Potter)

Those who foal their mares out on the fell, bring them in after foaling, and let them into the field with the stallion when they come in season. However, on some fells, bringing in the mares is a relatively recent development:

When we first started, they just were left. We never even used to fetch them in, we just let stallion out. It was a lot easier. Fetching foals in fast - they can soon get a chill. Last time on t' Howgills when we got them in I did twenty eight [miles] on my quad. It is a long way! Bloody twenty eight mile up and down, so if bike did it, hosses had to do twenty at least! Well it's a lot for a foal, only a week old. But touch wood, we haven't had any disasters. (Bill Potter)

As can be seen from these remarks, the Fell breeder differs markedly from the small lowland horse breeder and the commercial thoroughbred breeder who will have a mare stabled in the foaling box for six weeks before the birth to let her accustom herself to, and develop immunity to, the indoor bacterial 'flora', perhaps even under surveillance from closed circuit TV cameras.

No, we didn't bring them down to foal. Just used to leave them. Yep. Look after theirselves. If they were handy, then we used to put 'em in Cocklake, or we had that field down at Lune's Bridge there. I think leaving them out on the fell is better. It's sort of natural. I mean, obviously if you've got them inside you can keep your eye on them and if summat goes wrong you're there aren't you? But they seem to foal naturally; we used to go out nearly every weekend on horse-back, just to look round 'em, you see, and you'd go and you could tell how they were bagging up, and you'd go next week and she'd be foaled and cleansed. (David Trotter)

Let me repeat: to the Fell breeders, 'inside' means in a handy field rather than on the fell, not 'indoors' as in a building. They all treat their mares as self sufficient animals, and allow them to foal where they choose, outdoors. Breeders commented that mares on allotment land will choose a similar location year after year. Although they acknowledge that sometimes other ponies can get too involved with the foaling mare, and some prefer that the mare foals in a field, they looked at me in astonishment when I asked if they ever foaled under cover or sat up watching for this normally swift event.

I really like to foal them in a field. One or two would have foaled earlier than we expected and foaled on the fell. I like to handle the foals while they're small, in the first week. (Margaret Wilson)

Bob: Normally they foal when you're asleep!

Sarah: I foal in a separate field; occasionally you get it wrong. It's more likely the other mares, jealous mares - or mares that are about to foal and think they have foaled, and that's their foal - so they try and pinch it. We thought that had happened last year; there was a mare that hadn't cleansed and I went out to get her, and I saw the other mare standing with a foal. And I thought, Oh you've pinched that foal! and of course it wasn't - she'd had one in the last hour.

Bob: Clean as a whistle. No sign. Just, plonk!

Sarah: The brown mare foaled up in that field one day and I had an awful problem with Sleddale Ruth who was trying to pinch the foal - and within five hours SHE foaled, and that's why she was trying to pinch it. (Bob and Sarah Charlton)

I asked all the breeders about interference by other ponies, and specifically about how the stallion behaves with foals. Those who had observed his behaviour said it was protective of the foals.

Well if our stallion doesn't behave with the foals, he wouldn't be here very long. If he abused any foal or any mare, that would be him 'had it'. It's not tolerated at all. (Christine Morton)

We foal out in the fields. That foal out there was born with the stallion; he was standing guard over her. She was dry and licked, and no problems. (Mrs Ailie Newall)

Keeping stallions apart from the mares? It isn't natural is it? You never saw him chase a foal or owt. (Bill Potter)

Sarah: You occasionally hear of a stallion savaging a mare or a foal, but it's unusual. And I've never had a mare foal in the field and the stallion's been a problem.

Bob: The mare is usually the boss!

Sarah: Rusty is a very wise stallion; he looks after himself very well. OK, if the foal gets in between, he'll say 'Out of my way!'

Bob: If they're foaling we'll take him out for an hour or two. (Bob and Sarah Charlton)

Surprisingly few of the breeders had seen their mares foal; and of those who had, they had seen only one or two do so. Considering the numbers of ponies and people, and the span of years we are talking about, this is really a remarkable fact. It is mainly to do with the custom of leaving mares at the fell, or in a field, to deal with birth themselves.

Henry: They foaled at fell, and just come in to stallion. I don't think we ever had any took any harm.

Ivan: I've never seen one foal. They just say there's a couple of pushes and it's there. (Henry Harrison talking with Ivan Alexander)

Well, they seemingly just have one violent pain, don't they, throw the whole lot out at once; anyway she did; we just turned stallion away and there was a lump and foal was there like. (David Trotter)

I have very seldom seen a mare foal. Although I have two nights ago, I saw one foal, but it's a very rare occurrence ....Bill [Potter] tells a tale, when he was a boy at school, his Dad let him stop off school to watch this mare foal. And he sat out there all day, and at four o'clock, tea time, he went in for his tea, and whilst he was in for his tea his father come home and his father asked him how long that mare had been foaled. He said, 'It hasn't foaled.' And Dad said, 'Oh yes it has!'

So it doesn't take them long either, they're not like a cow, they don't faff on for hours. And they foal of a night when you're not there. It's not because they're unsociable or shy or whatever; if they were a shy animal - like a wild animal - you could understand it. (Thomas Capstick)

Some even go so far as to say it's unlucky to get to see a mare foal, in the sense that if you do, it is probably because there's something going wrong with the birth.

My grandfather always reckoned, right or wrong, that it was unlucky to see a mare foaling. There was summat wrong if you saw her. (Ivan Alexander)

Glenis Cockbain, Eddie Wilson's daughter, says the same, 'Dad used to say it was bad luck to see a foaling - the odd ones you did see had problems!'

Of course, there can be problems with foaling, just as there are with any births of livestock. Some breeders noted in particular the losses of foals born on beck sides, which slid into the running water and were swept away and drowned.

Sometimes if they foaled near the stream, it fell in. They always seemed to want to foal where there was water. (Frank Wales)

We lost one foal down at Lune's Bridge. We brought her in to foal, and she was on the far side in that little bit where they have all them hen huts. We never found the foal. Just assumed that she'd foaled it and it had slithered down that bank and into t'river. (David Trotter)

I never brought them down near home; just once I brought Stella down into a little garth near t' road side. She went and foaled next to t' beck and it fell in and drowned. Beck runs down bottom of this paddock, I never thought about it. If she'd foaled at t'other side of t' beck, ground sloped away and it would probably have worked itself away from t' beck, but t'other side it sloped down to t' beck; I think it would wriggle about and slide in like. I think they've a habit of foaling near a beck, but I just lost two all t'time we were there with that. Stella, that was her seventh filly foal. I should have left her at fell. Foaling on the allotment was the best place. (Ted Benson)

After I had heard four such stories on the trot I began to ask the breeders if they had ever lost a foal that way! The rest had categorically never lost one by drowning, but did have mares come in off the fell, which they knew to have been served, without a foal. These losses are taken philosophically, as are all farming troubles, 'Aye well, it happens.' Some of them consider that losing the occasional foal is a form of natural selection.

Another thing Jos always said was, if you took a mare to the stallion, you turned it to t'fell, and if it comes in with a foal it's worth having. If it comes in geld, or it lost the foal it wasn't worth having anyway - you got natural selection. Just the odd occasion: there's a mare come in this time and she hasn't brought a foal with her and I'm certain she's foaled. It's her first foal. What's happened I don't know. It maybe didn't get out of sack - or it wasn't worth having. (Derrick Byas)

Most also expressed the opinion that foaling indoors can be a cause of problems that would not occur outdoors. They seemed surprised that anyone would bother foaling indoors when the mare can manage perfectly well by herself most of the time.

We never foal inside [in a stable]. Never. I don't know what happens down country. They're all squirting their navels and that; out in a good clean field it shouldn't be a problem. I've never known any problems. So, they're better outside, Nature's way. (Barry Mallinson)

After the birth, the membranes and placenta have to come away cleanly; in horses, cattle and sheep this is referred to as 'cleansing'. Several breeders commented on mares holding the cleansing past its usual time. If it is not removed within twelve hours, the tissues begin to decay and can cause infection which quickly spreads through the bloodstream; if it is left untreated beyond 24 hours, the toxic result can be fatal for the mare.

The only problems I've ever had have been with the mares not cleansing. And that's just come more in the last few years. They never seemed to have that trouble before. And that is a

Heltondale Lucky XII (May) and Bamptonfair Flora in the first hour after Flora's arrival. Looking on, Blackberry, an unregistered Fell gelding. (He is subject to sweet itch, and wears a protective mesh blanket to keep off the midges.) Photograph courtesy of John Keen.

Above, a young Greenholme filly on the fell.

Opposite, top, Duke of Edinburgh driving HM the Queen's Fell team at Lowther HDT in 2004.

Opposite, below, Glenis Cockbain's Carrock Pollyanna and foal at Sizergh Show, June 2004.

Below, Lunesdale Honey at Lowther Show 2004.

Photographs, clockwise from above:
Swindale Rose at Lowther 2004.

A foal picks at its mother's droppings, which populates the gut with bacteria that will help to digest grass.

Swindale Rose at Daw Bank,
photograph courtesy of Mrs E Williams.

bother. Otherwise, touch wood… (Mrs Ailie Newall)

Occasionally one held its cleansing; well, we'd bring it back home; just occasionally. And very often what I used to do, if the cleansing was hanging from her, I would just get hold of it; not pull it, just hold it. And then as she walked away, just gently, if you were very careful with it, it would very often just slither out of itself. And you'd lay it out and make sure it was all there. It had to be like a sack with two horns on it. If there was one horn missing well we would bring her home then and get the vet to her. (David Trotter)

Now, there seems to be more things go wrong with them when they foal, than they used to. Some don't clean, and foals get a bit of scour maybe. I don't know if it's because

> They are brought down from the fell at different times of year, namely the mares at foaling time and to be brought to the stallion… I arrange that none of the foals are born before 20th May as in this part of the country the April weather can be unkind and the grass can still be in short supply, which makes producing enough milk a difficult task for the mares. Once a mare has foaled, the foal's navel has been treated with iodine and I am satisfied that mare and foal are well, they are returned to the fell, where it is a marvellous sight on summer evenings to see the mares peacefully grazing on the fellside while the foals form large schools in which much racing, mock 'fighting' and mutual grooming takes place
>
> (Bert Morland: *A Lifetime in the Fells*, p23.)

we're foaling inside [in a field]. (Frank Wales)

After foaling, it's important that the foals get the first milk or colostrum, and that they know how to suck efficiently. But in the fell situation, there can be very little control over this.

…four year olds foal, and maybe don't let them suck, and just turn up without a foal. And you don't know if foal's dead born, or just starved to death or what's happened. (Bill Potter)

I've never had any problems. The only problem that I've had, is when they haven't sucked. That's the problem, getting it sucked. (Henry Harrison)

Some breeders, for example those who bring mares in-bye to foal, like to treat foals' navels, while they are still wet, with iodine to ward off infection. Most breeders however rely on the mare choosing a clean place on the fell and don't expect to have to handle a foal until it's up and running. Other accidents happen of course, as they do to any young animal even in carefully supervised conditions.

I leave the mares out on the fell. They're all on the fell, and I seem as if I have the best luck [foaling] on the fell as well. In fields where there's cows and calves the foal'll be trampled on or something. I just leave them to their own devices, and they do pretty well. I have no problems with foalings, not on the fell. It's my own opinion that you feed them a bit through winter, not too hard, but you're giving them a bite of hay every day and they go away - well mine have been gone about a month now, middle of March - and they lose condition; and they seem as if they have no problems foaling, for they're not too fat. And when the young grass starts to come the foals are able to take the extra milk. At two or three weeks old, well, I suppose they do scour off certain times when the mare comes in season, but it isn't a thing that seems to bother them at all. As long as you can keep them on the fell I think the mother's used to the type of grazing and that and it isn't a big problem for the foal to handle the milk side of the job. In bye, yes, I've had foals trampled on, and probably mares foaled where there's been cows and calves and my cows just wouldn't leave it alone. Whether it is because it isn't on its feet properly at the start (but they'll be up as soon as a calf) I've finally decided the fell was the best place for them, and left them there.

I've had no problems with mares foaling in awkward places. I'll have lost an occasional foal, as I have had mares which I thought have been in foal, and they've come in without a one. And I've had mares come in foaled, to the stallion, and gone back and lost an odd one; but not of any consequence, just the odd one you don't worry about. I think the less you have to do with them at foaling, the better they are. You see some people are not as lucky as us to have the fell... They're not a pony that wants a lot of interference when they're foaling. (Chris Thompson)

...one other filly; it was a brown, to Prince; at two days old I found it in a well, drowned; a very deep well; I don't know how deep this well is, but halfway down there's a big beam through it, and it has to be very dry weather before this beam shows. But this foal, I went up one evening, and it wasn't there, and this mare was hanging about this well, and when I looked in the water was dirty, so it was obvious there was summat in - and all I could see was its ears sticking out above the water. But this didn't foal it into the well - it was two days old. (Thomas Capstick)

I was surprised that the question of the Fell Pony Foal Syndrome seldom arose in conversation. There cannot be any Fell breeder in Britain who is unaware of this disease. The foal which suffers from it weakens, usually around one month old but sometimes later; it develops a range of infections, and dies before the age of six months. The problem has been under investigation by research teams in Britain since 1993 and more recently at Cornell University in the United States. It is discussed in more detail in the chapter on *The Low Maintenance Pony*.

A normal foal will learn to drink milk; will follow its dam; will pick at her droppings to gain the gut bacteria that will help it digest grass; will bounce and play, eat and sleep in rapid succession in the same charming way that all young things do. It will go back out with its dam when it is a month or so old, to spend the rest of summer in the herd, learning about life on the fell, racing and mock-fighting and grooming with the other foals. Just a chosen few out of the many will stay around the farm and be halter-trained because they are being taken to shows.

The Fell Year: Growing Up

Breeders who choose to keep young Fell ponies to adulthood are certainly doing it for love, not money. It costs time and keep to evaluate the potential of breeding stock. This is a particularly serious consideration if 'added value' is to be put onto the stock by good training for riding or driving. A breeder starting out with this philosophy is tying up money that won't give a return, even if he's lucky, till the first foals are four years old or more, out in the world, performing and showing their quality. And he'll have to wait even longer before his reputation brings in serious money. He's got to be ready to stand some initial figures in the red to get to the point where he has a product ready to sell.

However, Fell ponies have been around in the background of Cumbrian farming for so long that in many cases they seem to be taken for granted. The established breeders in Britain already have enough years behind them; they have access to extensive fell land on which to rear stock, they have an established reputation, and they will have kept a foal or two every year who are growing into promising young ponies. Their problem is not so much having to wait but having too little time, in between farming responsibilities, to put the final polish and value onto the stock. This chapter and the next will look at those growing years between foaling and serious work.

The first chills of winter are touching the hills. The sun is lower and paler, the blue of the sky is more distant, and the clouds racing before the sharp winds often bring rain, sleet or snow. The fine sweet hill grasses are growing more and more slowly and their oldest tufts are fading almost to white in the brisk air. The bracken has first turned fox-red with the frosts, and then darkened with drenching rain. The stiffly upright stems and arched fronds fall and wither back, to remain as mere scraps of tan and soft brown across the tracts they claimed in summer. Only the seaves stand tall, and rattle in the wind.

Babyhood is over; the foals who have been running with the herd on the fell are strong and independent, and it is time

Lownthwaite Fable, photograph courtesy of Christine Morton.

for them all to leave their dams. December is the month most breeders mention as the time to wean foals.

If they're stopping, I just leave them sucking till Christmas and I take them off then, or just into New Year. I've always tooken them off, cause the mares are in foal, and they're not getting a lot, it pulls them down, and they re-absorb. You loss them. A lot of things got kin-bred on the fells - the mares that went further and further away and foals were left on, and you would get two-year-old colts, serving their mams. (Barry Mallinson)

We never used to spean them at all - we let the mother say when she'd had enough. But young mares, if they didn't stop the foal sucking, say December, January time, they would loss the other foal that they were carrying. It's a funny thing in Nature, if you didn't stop one, you lost the other. And so we started and thought; well, they were just having a foal every other year then, so we said, well, once we did away with cows, we'd take all the foals off, have them all off for Christmas. (Bill Potter)

We take foals off in December. I don't think they did well if they left the foals with them; they didn't foal every year; probably foal twice in three years, something like that. They seem as if - well it's Nature isn't it - that's what it is. If they can't carry it, discard it. (Chris Thompson)

Notice that they make no comments about any fuss that the foals make at weaning time. On a farm, it's the norm that weaning is done when lambs and calves are capable of living and thriving without milk, and before winter sets in; and it has to be done abruptly. Because of the large numbers involved, there can be no period of gradual adjustment; there is no slack in the system to allow it. They bellow for their mothers for a couple of days, but with secure housing or good fences, and good feeding, they soon get used to being separated from them, and turn to the company of their peers for security. Foals are treated the same. They are not accustomed gradually to being separated, as they might have been on farms in earlier times, when the mares worked after foaling and the foals had to be shut in for a period each day without them.

The foals, the first winter when they're weaned, they come in and they live in the big hemmel. We keep them in all together for about a fortnight or three weeks till they've all quietened down, colts and fillies. Then the stallion and the mares are put back up on The Fell (it's called The Fell; that bit of high ground). Then the foals are let out by day and brought in by night. But they're just run down into the field. And gradually we used to handle them and get them so we could lead them in turn down to the field. But you see I haven't had a girl for a number of years now who could do that; and so we've just run them out and run them back in at night, and they get a bit of a hard feed and hay in the hemmel. The other young ones, these yearlings, they'll stay out all winter. (Mrs Ailie Newall)

However, there are some breeders who do not take the foals off at all; or not till quite late.

You'll get some breeders will take the foals off at back-end – yet Jos's [Peepings ponies] always run on till next spring. They never actually got officially weaned. If it was a colt it had to be off the fell by the time it was a two year old; if it was a filly, mother spained it when she was ready. It wasn't a case of taking them off in October and boxing them and feeding them. Yet you won't find a much harder fell than ours. (Derrick Byas)

Weaning is the time when all the foals get some handling. Breeders separate them off and keep them indoors for a time. To begin with, this is as much to prevent accidents with wild foals trying to get back to their mothers as anything else; but it also gets them used to eating hay and hard feed, and to being handled on a regular basis.

I used to bring foals in and leave them loose (in a building) for maybe a month and then I would start and tie them up and handle them then. More so than what I do now. One job that we used to do, I used to earmark, and Sarge earmarked his; he punched the ears, and I had a little piece out of the nearside ear about an inch from the top. It was very good to see and always solved any problems really. (Chris Thompson)

Foals are often microchipped to enable quick identification; this is also done in autumn. Where possible, groups of owners get together and bring their foals to one farm to meet the vet and ensure his time is not wasted.

Until 1992, it was possible to register a pony with the society at any age. In past times, often a Fell mare and a youngster were registered together. This meant that many fell-born foals might hardly be handled at all. Then FPS reduced the age to one year, or 18 months in the case of 'heath-bred' ponies who run 'above the fell gate'. The paperwork for the new 'horse passports', which have replaced the original FPS certificates, demands quite a detailed description including the foal's sex, colour, whorls in the hair, and white markings. To comply with these recent EU regulations, all foals have to be registered in their year of birth and there is no dispensation any more for those who run their ponies on the fell. This means that even fell-bred foals now have to be handled early, which was not the case in former years. Late registration is very expensive,

Gareth Thomas checking the chip on Charltons' stallion, Drybarrows Rusty.

involving DNA sampling of both parents and the foal.

I ear mark the foals when they're fairly young. Now, I ear mark them and get my whorls off within the first week if I can, because they show up best, and I can still hold them and handle them myself to ear mark them. (Thomas Capstick)

The amount of handling the foals get has always depended on the ability and age of the breeders and the time they have to spare from other kinds of farm work. Some, when asked what training the foals get, just say NONE! Many of the Fell breeders are 'getting a bit of age about them' and admit they do less with the youngsters than they used to. When you ask who used to deal with them, they say it used to be the farmer and the farm men; but nowadays it may be just the farmer himself, and on the higher hill farms the income is such that he may no longer be able to afford a farm man to help him. The son of the farm has probably taken work in a quarry, or building, driving a wagon, or perhaps working on a bigger lowland farm which can afford his wage. The daughter will be working in a shop or office. Doing rough work like handling wild stock now requires detailed pre-arrangements with all the working members of the family, which even then may be let down by bad weather! So, the time of year for weaning varies according to the working pattern of the owners, and of the farm.

Frank: The foals don't get training; just haltered.

Christine: And we don't do imprinting - good heavens no.

Frank: No, we sell them as foals now; I'm getting ower old and girls is busy.

Frank Wales and Lownthwaite foals.

Christine: We're all living scattered and I've to gather the troops... if you're going to halter foals you have to get a time when I can do it and Dad has got to come, Frances has got to come; when there's a few of you. We don't muck out the shed. We like a deep layer of muck and bedding for when we're haltering the foals; then if they fall down, they fall soft. If you don't sell the colts, you keep them over the winter and then geld them and chase them back to the fell.

Frank: It costs £100 just to geld one - it's a lot.

Christine: We sold them at home, at Wigton, at Penrith - anywhere. To anyone who wants to buy them. Just the same with fillies. (Wales family)

And then we worm t' mare and let it ga back out, and fetch t' foals home, and tie t' foals up like cows [usually two to a stall], for about six weeks. And hopefully I can stroke them all ower, and make them quiet, and put them all out in twos and threes into t' boxes. It hods ten does t' byre, and if there's mair than ten we just do them twice, put the ten out and put another ten in and tie them up like. It helps them for later life, being tied up and stood; you can, when you come to halter them, you can ho'd them. You've just got to be quiet, and I can git him on t' halter, and follow him up t' yard and you've cracked it in two or three times, they don't go back up and down and hurt themselves. (Bill Potter)

The need today to record the hair-whorls and markings in order to register foals and apply for their passports before December 31st means that they are handled much earlier than they used to be. While this is not done as early as the

'imprinting' recommended by some schools of thought, it must convince the foals very early on that humans are in control. 'I remember Margaret Raines (a former vice-chairman of the Fell Pony Society now living in France) being surprised and delighted when the foals all left their mothers and gathered around us for a 'chat'.' (Margaret Wilson in *Native Pony*, April/May 2004.) Barry Mallinson's 2004-born foals do the same and have done from birth, but he considers that unusual:

I've two foals there and since they were born they'll come right up to you for a stroke. As long as I've had horses, I've never had a foal that would come right up from the word Go. And they come up now and they lean at you, to be petted. They'll leave their mams, and come. And they'd left their mams that morning, when they were born, to come. I've never known it, it's unreal, the nature that this stallion's got is unbelievable. (Barry Mallinson)

Some of them'll never have been handled; I've two four-year-olds that have come in to the stallion; they've never been pulled-off, they've been haltered and probably tied up but never actually led. Yearlings'll be turned out and running wild. They travel about, and there's a lot of people think, because you have, you know, twenty ponies on a fell, that they stick in a herd, but they don't; usually ages; I suppose because you winter your yearlings inside, they go out and they tend to stick in a little group. Otherwise they would stay with their mothers. (Thomas Capstick)

133

I used to go out and sit on a bucket, or lie in't field, and all t'foals used to come round me. I still do it with my own foals, to get them to come. They'll come, and sniff about, and nudge you, and their mothers wouldn't bother; mothers would come and have a smell, and that was it; it was t'easiest way to see them. Curiosity. It gets them used to people and they don't bother people t'same, they're not bothered, they know what people are then. Just sort of move a hand nearer and nearer; that's how you've got to do it. It's like when I get a wild mare. I bought one coming three year old, she'd never been touched. In that building, I took both doors off the pens, and I've an alleyway in front; I sat on a bucket, and she just walked back and forward, and she'd stop and have a smell. She was haltered and leading in no time. If you're quiet with them, talk to them, no rushing, take it easy, with any of the wild horses, they'll come. And when they come in off the fells, they're all excited and everything, it just takes them a week or two to settle down. (Barry Mallinson)

The young ones I have in-bye at present; well since foot and mouth, I took allotment ground for them and kept them off the fell and just let the mares with the foals at the fell. (Chris Thompson)

We would go out at the spring time of the year and try and get the colts off. We'd put the colts in the building and tie them up to those rings. I used to like to bring them in on a Saturday - or say Sunday - and then I'd spend all day -

just tie 'em up and spend all day just walking from one to t'other, talking to them and stroking them. There was nowt evil in them, just they were frightened of human beings, they were just like wild deer you see; but once they got used, and you would perhaps have four or five tied up, and the next day you would go in and you could tell by one's mannerisms, as soon as you went in, that he'd accepted you. He would prick his ears and give a little snicker. One or two might give in even that day; and then you always had the older one, who was boss of the others; it might take him two or three days. The art of breaking them in is, when you have a herd animal like that, you've got to be the stallion; those lower down the chain, they would give in first. (David Trotter)

David remarks on the stock handling ability of other farmers he knew, for instance, John Winder of Gaisgill Row, who was not a breeder but helped his father George, and David, with their ponies at times. John was killed tragically young in an accident with a silage trailer on the farm.

John Winder, if you were bringing a lot in, he would help sort 'em out. Bit lost after he died. He'd no fear of them. Like me, he could go in among them wild 'uns and put a halter on 'em. Bring 'em in the building, get a halter on 'em and tie em up; and show no fear. Your job was half done then.

Thomas was like that, Thomas Noble; more so than Sarge. When they used to sell those wild horses up at Wigton, and somebody would come [to the pen] and say, 'That's mine,' Thomas would go in among them, but Sarge

Prizewinning colt foal Lunesdale I'm the Man at Roundthwaite during the winter of 2003-2004.

never. Thomas was more the horseman to go among them. But if you'd someone working at arm's length, and jittery, well it just made the ponies worse like. (David Trotter)

Halter breaking foals, we would do first time maybe just before they were turned away to fell, after they'd been with stallion again; about end of June, July. Just quiet, not to be really severe on them - just put a halter on, get them outside, let them bounce about till they realised they were stuck. I never believed in this 'pulling them off'; give them time to realise what was going on, and it was surprising how soon they set off to walk with you. (Ted Benson)

I used to bring foals in and leave them loose for maybe a month and then I would start and tie them up and handle them then. More so than what I do now. And if I was working in the yard and leading muck out with a tractor and spreader I used to tie them up round the yard and they got used to machinery and tractors, which they don't get now! It's what you have time for and if you can do it! I think it would be those that were pulling me now, not me be pulling them! (Chris Thompson)

Early on, most of the foals got no handling. Odd ones that went to shows would be halter broken. Most of the foals went to Wigton Sales; they were driven, walking, to Wigton, like the cattle were. (Margaret Wilson)

Ivan: We used to halter break them - odd 'uns got broken in to ride, but -

Henry: We'd tie 'em up; quite often.

Ivan: They might as well take stuffing out of a tree than you, mightn't they? Be a hard job holding one all day like a tree does. I think they have to learn to be held before you do anything.

Henry: Learn what they can do. Like with young bulls. A thing comes on back of tractor frame like - you can put three a-back of it - then they can't get off you see. Once they get off they'll try it again.

Ivan: Happen learn them the first winter they're in, as foals. You needn't trail 'em about all day - half an hour and put 'em back; it'll do as much good as trailing about all day.

Henry: Our foals used to go right to t'auction. We never had time to halter most of them. Maybe a few fillies if we were keeping an odd 'un or two. (Henry Harrison and Ivan Alexander)

I very seldom had anybody to give me a hand with them. I used to tie them all up by myself, and suchlike; an odd time if I'd a one that somebody had bought and wanted a bit more handling, I'd ask one of my brothers to come and give me a hand for an afternoon or so, but not very much. And now I have like a door that fits on the tractor, on the hydraulics, and I've three shackles to it and I put them to the shackles and let them stand and do their pulling there; and then probably somebody'll get on the tractor and I'll walk in behind and get them to leading that way. It solves one problem, you don't get pulled about a lot, but it doesn't get them any road sense or anything like that. We don't see

anything you see; just our own tractors, and there's a lot to be said for it. (Chris Thompson)

They're tied up. There's difference of them. Some of them I've shown all the time are handled right from the word Go. Others, I just bring them off a fortnight before; bring them down, into the building, and just bring them in with mares and tie foals up for an hour; then start walking them out with mothers; and then take them off, and take mothers away, and give them a little bit of feed and play about with them. But I do have a post specially made in the building, so - telegraph pole, two foot into ground and bolted through beam that goes at top. It can take anything - it

Jim Bell with Waverhead Mayflower - champion at Kinsley Show 1969. Photograph courtesy of Anthony Barber, who bred Fells under the prefix Crossfell, and of Mrs Bell.

Greenholme foals at Stoney Ghyll, gathered up ready to go by trailer to spring grazing.

can take a six year old Welsh cob pulling.

Craig helps at times, yeah. Nine times out of ten I'd rather do it on my own. I can manage better on my own. Trouble is I'm not getting any younger!

It's surprising how fast I can halter them. If I can get there I can click it with a rope halter in no time. If I can just get there over the mare's back it doesn't know it's been haltered. And then Craig helps me after that, to get them tied up and to pull them off and that. (Barry Mallinson)

The young ones, specially if they were colts, we had got a bit on the Border hills, up near where the reservoir is now, Keilder, out that way - and we took them up; we had a farm

cattle lorry of our own. You got them into the lorry, and just let them out on this bit of land, which was looked by a farmer up there, and he used to have them down in the yard when we went to collect them in the autumn. (Mrs Ailie Newall)

We used to sell any colts that weren't going to be kept entire, at Kirkby Stephen in October. I would maybe keep on the yearlings to see how they were going to make out; if we weren't going to be keeping them, they would go to Cowper Day at Kirkby Stephen. (Ted Benson)

We'd bring the colts in as two-year-olds. Jos only ever kept two or three mares, so it wasn't a big bunch of colts together. They'd either get selt at two-year-old entire; or we'd do quite well keeping them on and selling them as four-year-old broken. I would be breaking them... keep them away from mares till their third or fourth year and get them sold on. Let somebody else have the expense of gelding them. (Derrick Byas)

Halter-breaking, weaning and worming are enough pony-handling to fit in round the other duties of the farm. Also, the years from foal to useful life at five are expensive and take up a lot of pasture, so it makes a lot of sense to let someone else have the trouble of gelding and educating the youngsters, especially when your main income is really from cattle and sheep farming. Prices for broken ponies at the autumn sales are often very cheap compared to the prices paid for foals. The top price there for a riding mare

137

tends to be from 1100 guineas (£1150) to 1500 guineas (£1575), while a well-bred filly foal can make 800 guineas. It doesn't take a rocket scientist to see that the extra years of keep and care, and especially training, that the ridden pony will have had, will not really pay off as a sale through the auction ring at five years old or more. From the breeder's point of view, if there is little time to spare and no young, strong, skilled people within the family interested in doing the job, most of their ponies should be sold as foals.

When such skills and interest are available, some ponies will be kept on and broken in where they were bred. A fairer value for a nice young pony 'backed and ridden away' and sold at home would then be upwards of £2,500; and a show win or two will help breeders to profit from hard work and extra training.

MATURITY AND TRAINING

RB Charlton wrote in his 1952 book: 'It is most remarkable, but quite true, that very few Fell pony breeders of today possess a saddle. They are pony breeders and have good eyes for a pony but they are not horsemen.' A good many of the breeders I spoke to either never rode, or usually rode bareback; so there was no need for an expensive leather saddle which most of the time would be stored in a building suffering from dust, mould and mouse nibbles! Mr Charlton's remark is perhaps better interpreted as 'they are not showmen'; and even then, the Wales, Bell, Wilson and Morland families would give the lie to this statement. What Mr Charlton omitted to mention is that then, as now, the pony breeders were farmers first, whose main priority was to get the farm work done, and that most of them didn't have time to spend on pony-breaking. Another reason many of them never had rideable ponies for sale was because mares were in foal and suckling a foal, the fillies were too young for either breeding or riding, and they had no colts because they had been sold at weaning.

Ivan: You didn't break them but you got them broken; Lib was broken to ride.

Henry: We showed them mostly in hand.

Ivan: You once showed Rose IX under saddle at Penrith; t'black 'un. Celia Robinson, she rode it.

Henry: Aye, she showed it that day. T'only time it was

ever ridden; I never bothered.

Ivan: They were just there to look at.

Henry: That's right. You hadn't time a lot to laik with 'em when you were farming. They were only a hobby sort of thing really. If we hadn't all the rest to do, I suppose we'd have spent more time with them. (Henry Harrison and Ivan Alexander)

Sarge used to come on to me, if he had a customer come, cause Sarge never had any broken ponies. He would give us a ring and say, 'Have you got anything? I've a customer wants a gelding, broken to ride and drive.' I used to sell them to Sarge then for I think about five hundred and he used to get seven or eight, sometimes a thousand, for them. But he hadn't anything like that on, you see. Foals, and mares and suchlike, but he never had any geldings. (David Trotter)

Some appear to have regarded breaking as rather a game; if the stallion, or a three year old gelding or filly was hanging about with nothing to do, then when there was time to spare from the real business of the farm, those who were 'lish enough' would do a bit of breaking in.

Our Jeff was a good hand at breaking in. Uncle Kit always kept us right. Wasn't any saddles - just jump on - a decent bridle, one hanging up now on byre door - that thick a leather [indicating an inch wide or more] - but an old fashioned thing - just a lump of rope for reins - nowt posh - a straight bit in t' riding bridle, but breaking bit, a key bit,

was a wooden 'un.

We broke in Heltondale Ranger II, we'd done chain harrowing and all sorts, so we said, 'Oh we'll put him in t' cart', so we put him in t' cart and done everything right, right along to St Ruth's [about 400 yards up the road], turned round, come back, and Roy Wilson'd walked down from Eskew Head. T'was a flat cart and he just sat on t' side wid us like. I think there was four on us on t' cart, and with that bit extra weight, when britching started to catch him he started to buck. He bucked about a hundred yards down t' road, then he took to t' grass and tipped us all off! (Bill Potter)

Of course, there were other farms on which breaking in was more scientific. Mrs Newall, whose ponies were notable for their excellent manners and show ring performance, tells of the methods used with her ponies in the 1950s and 60s:

The first thing was of course when they were yearlings or two year olds you tied them up in a box, and they would have a halter on, strong rope, and a collar; and they were just left to pull, and pull and pull. And that got them handled. And the colts were usually lassoed and pulled over. Of course the stable yard then was grass. It was penned, but it was grassy. Then they were taken out into the field and do the same thing. Give them the length of the rope and pull them over. It was, you know, rather rough.

We started on them at two; and we mouthed them - of course it was only done in the summer - when they were three. *We got front shoes put on, just plates, and by then they were handle-able, you could tie them up. Actually, the very good girl I had in the sixties, she had been in a big riding stable in the south, in the Chilterns. She was top class at producing a pony, and she broke the young ones; she always said, you must feed them as much feed as you can, and then you know that you've got the pony when it's at its wildest and not half dead coming in off grass. (Mrs Newall)*

Time and again I have heard breeders say that the less handling ponies get before breaking, the better. Although this is partly because they do not have the time or inclination to pet and indulge their young stock, it's also that they are very much aware of how easy it is to spoil a young animal by weak handling, no matter how well-intentioned. If the handler does not set firm boundaries, any horse or pony will take advantage of the uncertainties that occur. Then if the opportunity presents itself again, it will try the same behaviour because it profited from the first attempt.

Those that have been spoiled are hard work. So no, they're not handled very much, at all. (Thomas Capstick)

'Swinging' a foal, to teach it to follow a rope, photographs courtesy of Gwendy Byas

I'd rather have a wild horse come in; it'll come in better than a quiet horse that's been spoiled. You can not break a spoiled horse. They've no respect what so ever. A wild horse it comes to you and you go to it; you're meeting halfway. A spoiled horse you're keeping it off. It'll buck you off as soon as look at you. Where a wild horse it'll just go on, as and when you ask it. You ask it, and if it's very trusting with you, it's gained your trust, it'll do whatever you want. A spoiled horse won't! It'll fight you. (Barry Mallinson)

The foals were best handled when they got to about two year old. They came in off the fell as wild as hell and you made a better pony of them breaking them than if you had a pet that was nowt but a damn nuisance - and we've had experience of that. They might get swung as a yearling - that is, halter on, tied to a post and fight with that overnight, we'll drag you off next morning and if you follow t'rope for a few feet that'll do and away you go then. That was it. Then they'd be two or three year old, we'd bring them and and we'd start on them. And some of them we've had - they don't get a lot of handling. (Derrick Byas)

I thought I might be able to break one or two but I'm always full time working! I was gapping walls yesterday all afternoon, and I don't know, there's other jobs you can do I suppose but I never got any chance to get any in and break them! It's just like a dog, you've got to carry on day after day at them until you do get them broken.

If I'd a sale at home, well I could have a sale at home, and if not at home it would go to Wigton. If you can sell them half handled it's a big difference to one that's had nothing done with it. But you've got to have time to start. If you're going to break a one you've got to be at it every day and be the boss in due course.

If I did break a one, and I wanted it onto the road, it was when the girls were big enough, I would take them down to the road, and then I would go in front with Land Rover and trailer and they would ride behind, and if there was anything coming at a speed well they had to slow down; I pulled into middle o't road and looked after number one! (Chris Thompson)

We used to break them in to ride and drive. What I used to do, while I had them in, that first fortnight; mouth them, and laik on with 'em; then after I'd finished mouthing them and got them long reined and that; I'd get the vet in and we'd cut 'em. Then put them out in the field and just keep my eye on them, and from then on they were to sell sort of thing. (David Trotter)

It is worth noting that David Trotter did not start breaking ponies until he could arrange his days to give plenty of time to them. Mouthing, in his case, involves putting an old leather bridle headpiece and a bit onto the young pony, which is then left to stand in the box and chew on the new experience. His straight bar mouthing bit is an old Liverpool driving bit, made of nickel, that has had the lower cheeks cut back to the rings, leaving nothing to project and catch on anything. The mouthpiece is loose on the cheeks and can be played with. It is left in for half an hour or so the first day, an hour on the second day, and then increasing by an hour at a time until the pony wears the bit for almost a whole day. It has hay and water, but in order to eat and drink it has to learn to deal with the bit.

Derrick Byas: Used to tie them up in t'hull there at back of building, git 'em quiet then get 'em pulled off; then we'd mouth them for weeks on end - Jos always said you couldn't get a mouth on a hoss in less than six week. We were on with breaking bit for ten minutes each end of the day to start with and build it up, build it up; you got them mouthed and you long reined them for bloody miles! Then you sort of built up from there till you started pulling a log, and you built up from pulling a log to putting them into a pair of shafts and seeing what happened in a nice confined space, so if it did owt daft it couldn't just make a run for freedom.

Folks keep commenting about, 'Why do you use a lump of rope for reins?' 'Well because we actually had a lump of rope...' you know! Well somebody give us a pair of reins and they just felt numb and horrible and unusable compared to two bits of nice cord that you were used to.

We didn't really have much of a budget for buying tackle, so they had to start in a breast collar because we hadn't got an English collar. I lighted on that one there and it cost us fifteen quid - I mean - hell of an expense! It was just mainly cobbled together. Jos went to great expense and bought me a new breaking bit. A NEW 'un! Yes a brand new breaking bit - he did job right! But main thing was the time you spent doing it, and the product you had at the end wasn't the tackle that you put on it, it was the end result.

We used just whatever we could beg steal borrow and scrounge, and knock together ourselves. One of the best things I ever had for actually getting them to pull was a pallet with a deck chair nailed to it, which caused mass hilarity in Dufton. 'What the hell's that pallet got a deck chair nailed on it for?' 'Well we sit on it behind hoss and howk thistles up as we go along!' It got more sophisticated - we put a couple of posts underneath deckchair to make it slide a bit better... it wasn't just the flat pallet... it had runners!

***Derrick Byas and Alice Robson backing Peepings Double H,
photograph courtesy of Gwendy Byas***

And then eventually it was one of those steel tube deckchairs and it sort of folded up on us one night when we hit a big bump.

Mrs Dargue: And if a bit of string or binder twine would do, you didn't go for anything expensive when you had something else. We'd to start on our own after we sold up you see. Well all our money went on sheep!

Glenis Cockbain would start basic work with her father Eddie Wilson's ponies quite early:

We would mouth them at two and a half. The longer they chewed on the bit, the better. We'd lunge them and long rein them, and back them. We were riding them in shows at three - you could show them ridden at three then; it's only in the last twenty years or so that the rule has come in that ponies have to be four years old to be shown in ridden classes. Maydew went hunting when she was three and a half. (Glenis Cockbain)

Ivan Alexander explains how farm horses could be taught basic manners while working:

I remember when he was leading muck, he put a young horse in t'cart once; he fastened reins back to t'cart, and then he lowsed shoulder chains, till he would load t'muck. I thought, what's he doing? He said, 'It'll not take off, cause it'll have to pull cart with its mouth.' So it had to stand; it couldn't go back for t'middin. Couldn't go forward because reins tightened; reins weren't tight but if it moved forward they would tighten. It could waddle back and sideways a bit but it had to stand! That was where they learnt them. You

couldn't say it was cruel, because it just stood there. You had to be like gentle giants rather - quiet with them but firm. (Ivan Alexander)

Equipment was plain and serviceable.

Frank: When we drove them we used ordinary trap harness, leather. Straw collars. I rid bareback; and then I got a saddle. Bridles, they were leather; bits, we all just used plain snaffles, the one that's broken in the middle. We don't know any other kinds. But we had all sorts of bits for driving; Liverpools and Wilsons. For mouthing them there was one that had some keys in it.

Christine: Quite thick - they all seemed to be substantial. Bridles without nose bands, what we would call hunter bridles. And nickel snaffles - we liked nickel, still do; it's not as cold as steel. (Wales family)

We would start work at two; and get them really well handled, and at three we would put a mouthing bit on them - just bring them in each day and put the mouthing bit on them in a box, and leave them just to play with it. Just put on a head collar and tied the bit onto the head collar, a mouthing bit with keys, and they just played with it for half an hour or a little longer, and they soon got totally used to it. Eventually we'd put a roller on and put some side reins on, and lunge it from the cavesson, not touching the bit; and then it was long reins, and then attaching the reins to the bit; and you got a lovely mouth. And then it was a case of putting a saddle on it, and attaching bits of paper and that

143

on the side of the saddle, that flapped when it was lunged, all that sort of thing, that hung down; then the stirrups were tied under its tummy; and then they were left to flap; and so on. And they got shoes on their front feet. It all took time, and dedication. I mean there was always me and the girl, two of us; someone to lead the pony to get it to go round on the lunge, that sort of thing. (Mrs Ailie Newall)

There is a patient, and often decidedly frugal, approach to training. Most of the breeders are busy farming and because they have young ponies coming on all the time, there is no hurry to get any particular pony going to show. There are spells throughout the farm year when there is time to 'laik on', followed by spells when everyone is busy, and so the ponies can relax and think over their learning. Breakers with long experience of Fells all indicate that once a young pony has accepted a task and does it quietly, it is time to turn it away again to grow and mature. They know that although Fells do pick things up fast, like any young horse they may be sickened by too much early work, and 'lose heart.' A 'stroppy teenager' attitude induced by doing too much too soon can be enough to discourage a new or inexperienced owner and a pony ends up being sold on again which if it had just been handled more patiently might have turned out well. An Australian horsebreaker, Danny Fitzgerald, is quoted by Tom Roberts, 'Don't hurry - you'll take longer!' (Roberts, 1974, *Horse Control - The Young Horse*). The market wants a made, sound, fit, ready-to-ride horse or pony, but it is skilled work rearing young stock to

adulthood without spoiling their tempers, and a spoilt pony is a menace, no matter how expensive it was to buy.

Barry Mallinson says, 'A Fell doesn't mature till it's six year old.' All horses and ponies mature more slowly than the racehorse industry leads people to believe; British Native ponies, in this case Fells, mature particularly slowly. It is hugely tempting for the newcomer to start serious work with a young pony if it looks mature. Young Fells, the big roomy sorts in particular, may look less leggy and much broader than the frame of young light hotblooded horses, but the general feeling among breeders is that they really don't mature till quite a late age. They will live and work honestly and breed to a great age if they are given time in the early stages, but they are not usefully mature until they are over five and some not until they are seven, eight or even older.

They differ, definitely, from Thoroughbreds, especially flat-bred Thoroughbreds, who if you look at them are probably mature by five. Whereas the Fells, they are probably seven or eight when they really have settled in and you think, 'I've got an adult horse.' I would say there is that much variation. You see some and you think, by eight, 'yes, they've got there'; some are there by six; but exactly what's dictating that I don't know, probably the strength of bone. Some of them look very gangly for quite a while, then suddenly they fill out and they mature. (Paul May, MRCVS)

Time allowed at the beginning of its life for the pony to 'furnish', and for its bones to complete their growth particularly in its knees, hocks, spine and shoulders, will be time gained at the other end, when it will still be working and sound at an advanced age. This self-restraint is explained very clearly by Frances and Barbara Bell when they talk about the age at which they usually start work with their ponies:

Mrs Bell: Mainly at three, but they weren't allowed to be ridden till they were four.

Barbara: We'd start mouthing them at three year old. I don't like this rushed job as if you can do it in such a short time. Longer the better, Dad always used to say: put the bit in for a short time, each day or every other day - it was never a rushed job. I don't think we've ever been on a one before it's four year old.

Mrs Bell: They're not mature.

Barbara: Their backs aren't strong enough till then. People break them in as two-year-olds, but it's too soon. Every year really we'd broken one - most of them were broken in. Nancy and I had one each to ride. (Mrs Frances Bell and Barbara Bell)

Chris Thompson says that for the pit dairy work, pulling milk carts, 'they didn't start to break them in till they were four year old.' Frank Wales also says, 'they never broke them in until they were four.' Ann Varley who used to breed Fell ponies with the Calgarth prefix, and was 'a doughty competitor' with her tandems of Welsh and British Riding ponies in horse driving trials, says of any horse, 'You can only 'bottom' them once. After that, they will never really try for you again.' With a young pony, however much heart it has, the bottom is much more quickly reached than in the more developed older pony. It is patience that avoids problems.

At a more mature age, Fells will accept new experiences not only quickly, but with evident relish. It is quite common to see 'novice ponies' in ridden Fell classes who are fourteen or fifteen years old. Often they are mares who have been broken early, then turned away to breed foals, and are now having a year out under saddle. It is a delight to see an adult Fell with riding experience step into a new role, say as a driving pony; handled carefully, within a few days it has the job 'off pat'.

QUIET TO RIDE AND DRIVE

The point of breeding any type of animal is first to maintain the stock. But even in the most diehard conservation scheme, once you have bred your replacements, the rest are to sell. Any horseman will tell you, 'You can't keep them all.' The sales help to keep the ones that are retained. Accordingly, most colt foals, and any fillies who duplicate lines or otherwise look unpromising, are taken to the autumn horse sales.

Ivan: They're not 'surplus to requirements' but they're like your calves. They're not a by product; they have got a use, so really they're part of your farm income, your crop. (Henry Harrison and Ivan Alexander)

Sales by Auction

TODAY the main Cumbrian sales are held at Wigton, Penrith, Hawes and Kirkby Stephen, but previously ponies have also been sold at Brough Hill, Rosley and Appleby Fairs. If mares are starting to find life too hard on the fell, or their progeny do not meet with the breeder's approval, they too are sent to the autumn sales, alongside the foals and young stock. Selling at such fairs used often to be very rough and ready and did not do justice to either the breeders or the ponies. Even now, breeders may not get the full value of what they breed unless they keep ponies for three or four years, then break and train them, for sale as adults.

Research done by the Agricultural Advisory Service for the New Forest breed 'shows the end consumer is looking for a 'ready to ride' pony.' (Hickman, 2004).

> Mr Charlton lectured to the pupils of the Cumberland and Westmorland Farm School, near Penrith: ...he thought the breeders did not make most of their selling chances. Droves of ponies, straight from the fells, unhaltered, were each year walloped up in a corner at Brough Hill Fair; the dealers bought them at low prices, and a few weeks later the same ponies, haltered and broken, were resold for double the price. *Livestock Journal* circa 1927

Les Thackeray told tales of Brough Hill and Kirkby Stephen sales:

Paul Metcalfe's father had a neighbour, that used to come and work with him cause he was interested in work hosses, he used to take staggs to Brough Hill Fair. In those days they were all wheeling and dealing... He said they were sitting at Brough Hill with these staggs, and a mate of his, he says, was sitting having his bait, with t'halter wound round his leg, and d'you know he said, hoss set off and off it went down t'field and took him with it, legs first, and his lug was just full of cow shit! (Les Thackeray)

In them days [1948] they used to send horses to Brough Hill, in October. I've seen me, we'd brought them in off fell, and they were three four-year-olds - and never been haltered.

Dad would put a cavesson on one. He used to make a halter out of Michael [baling twine], a big strong one, and he plaited that into the one's tail that had the cavesson on. That's how we took them to sell, with a cavesson; and I walked them. Going out of the front field, they fell over one another - you know what I mean! - but I had a long plough cord on the cavesson, and I kept in behind. And when I got down there on that road, there's a lady came in a motor car. I went one side, and the horses went t'other. And I ran over top o't bonnet. And she said 'STOP!' but I couldn't stop… I came up to Appleby fair with the three ponies - they led you - and when I got home, me shoes had holes in! I'd walked them through. I got £22 for two of the ponies. I sold two and the other I didn't. I rid the one I didn't sell; it had had a hard day and it was jiggered and I rode it home. That's how they used to take 'em - t'was mad, wasn't it! (Frank Wales)

At Wigton foals used to come in in droves, and it was 'Particulars at time of sale.' These little weeds used to come in - well how he knew which mare they were out of, or which way they were bred or anything else, I don't know! (Mrs Ailie Newall)

A lot of years ago, Edgar Metcalfe's uncle lived up Mallerstang, just at side of Pendragon Castle; and he kept ponies of all sorts, particularly in t'early days black and white uns, cause he got friendly wi't potters, with these Fair Hill chaps. Charlie was a signalman at Mallerstang. He used to drive them down into Kirkby. Those days we used to have a week's holiday, and we used to get a lift up and bring these yearlings in for him, because he was very bad with the rheumatics, bring 'em in - some he'd never seen for a year. We'd wash them up and learn them to lead and we'd take them into Kirkby to Cowper Day.

I was interested for what it was worth, but I wasn't keen like Edgar and them; he had some black and white 'uns of real quality, and he always had a lot of folk round him. Walter Tuer, he had fifty, sixty, maybe more and he'd take them all down, he wasn't very popular! They used to come on down into Kirkby, used to drive them in and drive them out. At top of Mallerstang, there used to be two brothers and they had a whole heap of horses, and they come right down t'dale; they would be riding maybe two or three and chasing t'others, and me and Edgar would be leading a couple on halters; and they got mixed up with another person's and what a carry-on there was! (Les Thackeray)

Judging only by the conversations about the old days, it's sometimes hard to tell what was a representative price for a pony, or whether some sales attracted bigger-spending buyers than others. In 1919 at Queen's Letch, Hexham, Mr R B Charlton held a dispersal sale of ponies. The six-year-old stallion Linnel Comet, Dales 841 (a great-grandson of the fast trotting cob, Comet) sold for the astonishing sum of 175 guineas; formerly he was registered as Lingcropper II, 768 Fell, perhaps because his grand-dam was a Fell. At this sale, which was mainly of Hackneys and Dales, a three-year-old dark brown Fell, Linnel Fellsman, made 89 guineas; for a gelding, this again was a remarkable price. Look at the difference in value though when you move forward to 1928 at the local auction mart:

He bought them this pony, Jenny, at Wigton Auction; that was six guineas in 1928, and that would be a lot of money. (Mrs Frances Bell)

Jenny's value would be equivalent to a farm man's yearly wage. Although the sums involved look very small to us now, in 1936 Frank Wales' father would sell young ponies for the equivalent of ten weeks' farm wages.

I've known my Dad go to Kirkby [Stephen], when I was a boy, and they were three pound each. Maybe two-year olds. In 1938 I bought a cow at neighbour's sale and it was six pound ten, in calf; but there wasn't any money in things. A married man had twelve shillings a week then. (Frank Wales)

Henry: We used to go to Cowper Day at Kirkby.

Ivan: Walt Tuer used to drive all his mares and foals in, put all his mares in a pen; it must have been in agreement with t'auction. He had to take mares to get foals there; they used to ride ponies to herd them. Then the mares went yam at night. It was a big thing in Kirkby - Walt used to come down street with all his horses and three or four of them on horseback, and then they would get in t'auction and sort all t'foals out into a pen; and what he didn't intend to sell would be put into a pen, to go back at night and onto t'fell I presume.

Henry: You couldn't get in t'ring sometimes for folk. But you get a wild bugger in, then that made them stand back! And when they got to closing in again you see, auctioneer would say, 'fetch another wild 'un in lads!!' (Henry Harrison talking with Ivan Alexander)

Frank Wales tells that a pony of theirs by Peepings Swell, 'would win at London quite a lot. In 1940s Dad got £40 for it.' That was a very good price for the time.

In the late 1940s there was another dip in the Fell population. 'Fells,' says Bert Morland, 'were in a sad state of affairs...' The late Mrs Sylvia Hasell-McCosh wrote an article, 'Out of the Ashes of War' in one of the first *Fell Pony Society News*, about the lack of purebred stock back in those days.

Lownthwaite Pony sired by Peepings Swell, photograph courtesy of the Wales family.

> When war ended in 1945 there were very few pure bred Fell ponies in the country. So many mares had been crossed with heavy horses to produce useful animals which could carry out farm and other essential work more easily... (Sylvia Hasell-McCosh)

...*when farming went flat, they couldn't give the Fell pony foals away; so what they did, they started crossing them with a blood horse to make a hunter, or perhaps a Clydesdale to make a stronger work horse or black and white 'uns for colour. (David Trotter)*

Despite increasing standards of living in the 1950s, prices were still low even for the 'better than average' pony: Bill Potter's first pony in 1954 cost £11; Bert Morland's in 1958, £14. Then there would be a spell when someone wealthy was wanting ponies, and prices for a short while would rise spectacularly. The classic example was the sale of the stallion Johnny Walker to the millionaire horse-breeder and racing enthusiast E P Taylor of Windfield Farms, Canada in 1966. Taylor had already bought a couple of Fells in 1947/48.

We took two stallions down to Ascot; we took Johnny Walker and a young un, a three year old; and I said to Dad, 'It isn't worth taking this.' 'No,' he says, 'take it, cos you're going.' Did we get £500 for Johnny Walker? It was record price for 1966, and we got £300 for t'other one. So we did well. (Frank Wales)

This was the Ponies of Britain Show, in 1966. Miss Peggy Crossland who was FPS Secretary arranged for a number of ponies to go to the show, at the request of Mr Taylor. Frank's daughter Christine travelled with the ponies, while Frank went by car later that day. She pointed out that Mr Taylor was not just buying Fells. 'He would buy a shipload. He bought A LOT of horses.'

But there were often long periods when the keeping of Fells was not really viable, when Fell colts were 'worth nothing' and it was common for them to be given away with a mare as 'luck' on a sale. Most of the long term breeders seem to have gone on keeping Fells out of pride, whether you call it 'a sense of tradition' - though they seldom use the word themselves - or just 'sheer bloody mindedness.' It has always been more worthwhile financially to keep a cow, or

Frank and Thomas Wales with Johnny Walker, photograph courtesy of FPS Archives.

sheep, than ponies. It is only on the fell that there is space to accommodate the ponies' preferences for the good grass alongside other faster-maturing livestock.

We used to call at Bob Nicholson at Intake, and by he'd some good ponies, what a shame like when they all went away. Nicholson lads bought them, from Tebay, and they just disappeared out of t'society. Same with Evelyn Milburn, when she was at Gill; they had some good Fell ponies there; I don't know whether they gave over registering them or what like, but when we were gaan to school there were Fell ponies and when she gave over farming, Nicholson lads just went with them and they disappeared. Naebody wanted them you see. There was a bad patch in there, wasn't there... It would be in 70s, early 70s, when I started picking them up from Sarge Noble's to go to kill. By, he got shot-of a lot of good ponies just after Thomas died, like naebody wanted them and they were gaan that far away from home and you'd just to gather them in and sell them...

They used to die, and slip, and come off top and break their necks... me and him have been for't lake side many a time to bury them. We used to bury them like Indians - with stones. Pile rocks ower them. You couldn't dig! Nowt to dig into! So we'd to just build a grave with stones, and bury them like that. (Bill Potter)

I went to Drybarrows in '61 so I think it would be '63. 41 years ago... there wasn't a great trade for them for quite a long time. Tractors were coming in; there just was the beef [slaughter] trade and there would be a lot would go that way in that time. I can remember them going to Wigton and 18, 20 pound and they were away; I would say anywhere from two to ten year old. (Chris Thompson)

The FPS newsletter for 1968 recorded the prices at three sales in the 1960s.

> Every autumn for the last ten years there has been a class for registered fell ponies alternately at the Cowper Day Sale at the end of September and held at Kirby Stephen, and at the Wigton Horse Sale held at the end of October. This class is now held each year at Wigton, eleven miles west of Carlisle. In 1960 at Kirkby Stephen the top price, which was for the first prize pony, was £52 for Frances of Heltondale, a two-year old filly, sired by Packway Royal. One-year old geldings 21 gns., 22 gns. Yearling fillies 29 and 35 gns.
>
> In 1967 the top price was £130 for Sugar & Spice, a black in foal mare, eleven years.
>
> In 1968 the top price was £145 for Winston Charm, black three-year old mare in foal, sire Master John. 82 gns., and 1st Prize Waverhead Flash, two-year old gelding, sire Waverhead Rambler. 72 gns., and second prize Guards Bob, two-year old black gelding sire Guards Model. 86 gns., Dunnerdale Romany, two-year old black gelding, sire P. Royal. Other prices for two-year old geldings 72 gns., 66 gns., 64 gns., 72 gns., and for yearling colts 65 gns., 52 gns., and 48 gns., and for colt foals 30 gns.

I bought a mare in foal, untouched, and Sarge threw yearling colt in for luck; which they did in them days [1972]; they were worth nothing. (Barry Mallinson)

But sometimes, specially colts, you used to think they weren't worth registering sometimes - for what it cost, for what they're worth. (Henry Harrison)

The cost of feeding and gelding, or alternatively the trouble involved with keeping an entire, put people off keeping a colt in spite of there being a market for mature, trained geldings. Many young colts were going to Europe just for meat. To counter this, for a while the FPS gave a premium for people to keep geldings to riding age.

In 1973 the Wales family took ten Lownthwaite ponies to the autumn Wigton Horse Sale. The prices had now risen, though they were still nowhere near the record-breaking sale achieved fifteen years earlier at Ascot: the eight foals averaged £62; a three-year-old filly, broken to ride, made 330 guineas, and a yearling filly made 340 guineas.

Mrs Bell sent me a page from the *Evening News and Star* of 15 October 1981, with the report of the Fell Pony Autumn Sale at Wigton that year. There was a show beforehand in a small field behind the main pens. Prices remained roughly the same as they had eight years earlier:

> The champion Fell pony, a five-year-old registered pedigree mare, Martindale Glencora, shown by R Rayson, of Tirril Lodge, Penrith, was withdrawn at 380 guineas... The first prize for a registered unbroken pony went to

> Waverhead Gwen II, shown by Mr Bell, of Waverhead, Wigton. This pony made 200 guineas. Barbara Bell won the colt class with Waverhead Rob II which brought 72 guineas. The prize for the best registered stallion went to T Noble and Sons, of High House, Butterwick, Penrith. The stallion went for 230 guineas.

At a sale organised by a breed society there are a lot of advantages for sellers. Because the sale only occurs once a year, buyers come long distances to look at the assembled stock. In recent years the ring has been packed at the sale; it's standing room only. I have seen people there from Kent, Cornwall and Scotland and in 1995, the year when Sarge Noble dispersed the Heltondale herd, you could hardly move for the crowd. In such a situation a buyer often cannot see who he is competing against, which makes for uninhibited bidding. Once your reserve is passed, the sale is guaranteed and the money, less the auctioneer's percentage, is paid by the auction on the day. Prices for filly foals in particular are often good at the autumn sales so if breeders have a lot of stock to sell each season, the time taking them to auction is well spent.

Small breeders selling one or two animals a year may possibly feel that it is easier and that they will find a 'better' home for their ponies to rely on individual sales conducted at home, but there are drawbacks. With an appointment made to view, sellers will spend time and effort getting the animal into a stable, clean and smartly turned out.

They put off other work to wait for the expected buyer's arrival, yet so often no-one turns up - a waste of time for all concerned. Also, sales made at home often have an interim period when the buyer has verbally agreed to buy, or has gone away to think it over, but the pony and the money have not changed hands; in the meantime perhaps another buyer will have to be put off, and even so, the first sale may not happen.

Sales at auction do at least mean the job is complete; and an underbidder on one animal may buy one of your other stock through the ring. Buyers too have the chance to choose between varied examples of the breed they fancy. But there's always the man who wants to beat the sale system, in order to get a pony that he likes below the market price, without having to bid against anyone!

I always remember Frank Wales, he said this feller come, wanting to buy - we were in t'auction at Appleby, right again t'railway - wanting to buy this horse; we were earwigging cause we were in t'next pen. Frank said, 'No, it's going through the ring,' he said, 'but I'll tell you what - you go in the ring, and keep waving at auctioneer, and you'll get it.' (Ivan Alexander talking to Henry Harrison)

Even at breed sales, there are tales of trickery, and often trickery that goes wrong. It's a risky business to ask a friend to bid your pony up to make sure of a good price. This practice is called 'running-up' or 'running' and it needs clever judgement on the part of the friend to drop out at the psychological moment and let the stranger buy at the inflated price.

Red House Brandy, the brown mare, Matty Brown's mother, went through the ring as a foal at Wigton at big money. A man from over that West Cumberland side, he bought it; but he wasn't supposed to buy it, he was supposed to just 'run' it! He got left with it. Then Tommy [Bainbridge] comes through into t'bar and he says, 'Eh, David, you'll never guess what I've bought! I bought that good foal.' I says, 'You're joking?' He said, 'I have!' I said, 'Bloody hell, you'll have paid something for it.' He said, 'Oh, I got it for less money than it went through the ring!' (David Trotter)

Tommy's unexpected purchase of Red House Brandy was obviously fair game for a resale, so David decided to make an offer. He had a little theatrical help in keeping the price down.

Bert would bring it back in his wagon; Tommy was with Stan Bracken. Anyway we finished up at String of Horses [now a private house at a crossroads between Wigton and Penrith] coming back, and Bert says, 'We've got Tommy along now; you buy me a ginger ale and we'll pretend I'm full of whisky.' Well he got to fooling about and flopping about; then he fell in t'toilet; so Tommy come back and said, 'They're not fit with that pony David, he'll smash that wagon will Bert, he shouldn't get drinking like that when he's ponies in!' Anyway, he was that worried, he sold me it, did Tommy.

Bert dropped it off at Lune's Bridge in that field I had. Bugger me, next morning la'al Tommy lands down. 'Did that pony get home?' 'Yes, it's all right!' 'We'd better go and see, we'd better make sure, you know what state he was in!' 'Aye yes!' So we went down, and as soon as he saw it was all right he wanted to buy it back off me! (David Trotter)

Uses over the centuries

I asked all the breeders about what uses the Fell ponies had in times past. Christine Morton talked of the changes that have passed over farming and society in general, and concluded, 'It's impossible to think now as then... Things have changed beyond all recognition, even in my lifetime.' Like most of the long-term breeders she and her family have seen horses and ponies change from being essential for working the land, to 'a hobby, a non-essential accessory.' Leisure time then was hard-won out of the working week, and it is now big business. As an example, Center Parcs' Oasis holiday village at Whinfell offers pony treks and horse-drawn carriage rides, supplied by Leacett Cottage. The dozens of horses and ponies are of all breeds and sizes, who have to be bought, fed, shod, insured, treated for ailments, trained if inexperienced, and provided with saddles, bridles, harness, carriages and rugs. The income from the tourist customers also pays the wages of more than a dozen horse staff, whose job in days gone by would more likely have been working heavy horses on a farm, milking cows, or tending sheep.

Small wonder that the role of the Fell pony has altered. It's still there, but the demands made upon it are quite different from those of earlier times. Likewise the value of the pony is now set by different criteria. Whereas formerly its value was the work it might do, now buyers value its pedigree and looks, which are far less practical.

[My grandfather] was selecting forward going ponies, yes very much; he wasn't breeding for the show ring, he was breeding to perform. And consequently rather similarly today, we do better, and more enjoy, ridden classes than in hand. Not totally - we enjoy both - but our aim is to finish up with a ridden pony, not just have one that looks pretty on the end of a rope. (Bob Charlton)

Yet there is as much need now, perhaps more, to pay attention to a pony's temperament as to its performance in shows and competitions, because the people handling it are less likely to be experienced with horses or to have any resources to overcome training difficulties.

Pack work

WE know that merchants in Roman times used pack horses and mules as well as two- and four-wheeled waggons; and after the troops left Britain and the roads were no longer kept in good repair, pack ponies would have continued to be the main means of transport. In Cumberland and Westmorland, just as in other parts of Britain, for centuries ponies were the main method of transporting goods: wool, cloth, lead, pottery, foodstuffs of all kinds, wines and spirits, spices, fuel, and slate for roofs. They walked long distances, from the north of England to London, from the west

Peggy Crossland training one of her home bred ponies for a reconstruction showing pack work, photograph courtesy of FPS Archives

coast ports to the smallest inland farms, from the Pennine lead mines to the east coast ports. Even after the arrival of metalled roads, and the fast coaches and railway trains of the 19th century, there was still a need for pack ponies on the narrow, steep and stony tracks of the Lake District. And what ponies were used? From the Lakes and from Southern Scotland, it would be the Galloway and the Fell, just as from Northumberland it would be the Dale. They were just

'always there.' They were probably all the same thing in essence; smallish, tough, and useful.

The ponies no longer work in pack trains, though cynics might say that pony trekking is hardly different except that the load can climb on and off by itself! In the 17th century, the risks were not only bad weather and injuries to the ponies; the ale houses of Roundthwaite and Greenholme, for instance, were frequented by highwaymen whose main aim was to get money from rich people using the toll road through Orton. The ancient lane between those ale houses, running or rather ambling past my front door, was the poor man's 'drove road' and pack trail, seeing slower, commercial transport. It probably didn't pay for the pack man to recognise the highwaymen; he would get the ponies to pass onward as quickly as he could and hope the highwaymen didn't want to find out if he had any cash in-hand along with their loads. Modern pack work is not so risky, and neither do ponies go any more into the potentially dangerous Army work that they did in the early years of the 20th century.

The Army bought some for packhorses. They had to be fine, silky haired. If they were strong haired, they wouldn't buy them. That would be on account of the puddle; so as the puddle didn't stick to the legs. (Frank Wales)

There have been some recent uses of Fell ponies to do leisure treks, using some as ridden and some as pack ponies. Bob Orrell, for instance, has written books on his excursions round the Lakes and Highlands. Peter Moor in Switzerland uses them too. Our local farrier has a military pack-saddle, complete with loading manual, that he has used himself and lent to others to do holiday treks. David Murray (chapter 6) has made well publicised walking tours of Britain using native breeds as pack ponies, including a Fell, Sleddale Black Prince.

Trotting races and endurance riding

THE Dargue family's grey Fells had the reputation of being great trotters. Amongst the adverts in *The Field* of 1865, two Fell ponies were advertised for sale, the property of Mr. J. Dargue of Bow Hall, Dufton. The first, a dark grey pony, five years old, 13.1 h.h., 'can trot a mile in three minutes and two seconds carrying twelve stone, goes well in harness.' Secondly, 'Spanker, dark grey pony - and as above.' Mrs Dargue recalls a tale of a grey mare called Strawberry Girl; in the ownership of Mr John Wilson of Liverpool, she won the Borough Stakes at Blackpool in 1882 which was worth £60, a huge sum for the time. A print of Strawberry Girl (see Chapter 4) shows that she was a lighter type with quite clean, unfeathered legs. One of their ponies, Nancy Grey, was descended in the female line from a horse called Telegraph, who is described in one stud book entry as a halfbred Arab.

From the 1880s to the 1940s the racing of trotting horses and ponies ranked alongside cock-fighting and Cumberland wrestling as a North Country spectator sport. It was far more popular than Thoroughbred horse racing, which was an aristocratic hobby. The distances were half a mile to a mile. Races took place at shepherds' meets and other farming gatherings and also at local sports in summer. There was a race course on the Central Lakeland fell top

Print by Thomas Allom, 1835, of a race taking place on Racecourse Hill, High Street, photograph courtesy of Kendal County Library.

known as High Street, where there is a stretch above Riggindale called Racecourse Hill; it was last used in the 1830s and an 1835 print by Thomas Allom records a shepherds' meet with a race taking place. Another course was the Fair Mile in the Howgill Fells near Tebay. Both places are Roman roads offering straight, relatively level going.

In 1880 Newbiggin (Ravenstonedale) Sports offered prizes for such contests as foot races and egg-and-spoon races. They had trotting races that were both Open and 'Confined to horses of the Parish' which offered the locals a chance despite hot opposition from further afield. The Open races seem to have been run in heats with a final, rather as harness races in Britain today, and at this small village event there were two heats and a final where J Knowles' Brown Duchess beat T Wharton's Countess by two lengths. Countess was almost certainly a local mare, because of her owner's name. Les Thackeray of High Scales, Scout Green, said that when he was a boy, Ravenstonedale was still a place where the men were keen on trotting horses, and he mentioned the Whartons of Sunbiggin and the Hullys of Bousfield who were rival supporters of the sport. He says that the trotting was 'rather a different thing,' from keeping work horses and Fell ponies but even so, there were some remarkably fast trotting Fells.

Now, whether a pony really could catch a steam train over the last mile of a six mile journey is anybody's guess, but in a tall tale told by Les's father, the railway is near the end of a notorious four and a quarter mile climb up Shap Bank. The worst part of the gradient is 1 in 75, one of the steepest in the country which usually needed an extra 'banking engine' coupled on at Tebay. Modernised 'steam special' passenger trains make around 50 mph up here, but they are often beating the times made in the 1940s. If a heavy train was unlucky enough to be tramping up Shap behind a single engine… and there were enough passengers and produce being loaded to make it wait at the station… who knows, the pony might well have made it.

When my Dad worked at Selsmire, they had a Fell pony and it was a real go-getter sort of a thing. They would put it in trap and they used to go to Shap station, with butter and eggs for Penrith. He reckoned one day they were going over railway bridge at Toll Bar, when train went under; and they took gear off t'pony at the Greyhound, and stabled it, and he catched t'train! (Les Thackeray)

In the early years of the 20th century, Orton 'Pot Fair' was held in June, and trotting races were part of the fun. Here is the school headmaster John Falshaw, in 1983, interviewing Horace Wilson, retired woodworker of Orton:

> HW: There was wrestling - Cumberland and Westmorland style wrestling - running and jumping. There was some goodish athletes who used to come from about Tebay and Ravenstonedale. And there was quite a few used to come from Kendal…
> JF: And was there any betting on them?
> HW: Oh yes, the bookies were always there.

JF: So this was like the traditional Lakeland sports.

HW: Yes… and then there was the trotting round the village. The Whartons [from Sunbiggin] had trotters. They used to go twice round the village - they reckoned it was about a mile.

JF: These trotters; when they were trotting round the village, did the riders go on the backs or were they in sulkies?

HW: No. They just rode them as jockies.

JF: Yes, and they actually trotted? They didn't gallop?

HW: No, they were purely and simply trotters. Hully's from Bousfield, they would have a few trotters, and the Hullys and the Whartons were great rivals. But there were others who used to come from a way off.

JF: What time of year did this take place?

HW: June, in summer… Wrestling, jumping and trotting, all spread out. And children's races, the children were very involved. (*Memories of Orton,* 1998)

The Dargue family's early ponies were notable trotters and so were the Linnel ponies. From the FPS Archive, from Mr Charlton's scrapbook, comes this newspaper clipping from the 1930s (just prior to the export of a batch of Fell stallions to Spain): it gives details about the Welsh cob, Trotting Comet, kept at Hully's farm, Bousfield, near Orton:

In 1856 there appeared in the Shap district of Westmorland in the hands of some betting men a big dark brown trotting cob, named Comet. Nobody could tell now exactly where Comet came from. [author's note: Mr Charlton states in his later book, *A Lifetime with Ponies* that the 'wonderful Welsh cob stallion' came from Tom Jones Evans, Craven Arms, Shropshire] Linnel Comet, as were other Comets, was a descendant of the original Comet, and it was the sire of both Alston Comet and Blackthorn… At Brough Hill fair this year he (Mr Charlton) had had a talk with Tommy Birkbeck, of Brough, a well-known pony judge, who remembered Comet very well. For one winter Comet was stabled with the father of the late Mr Thomas Bell, Moor House, Orton. The late Mr Bell himself told the lecturer (Mr Charlton) that he got a sovereign from the owners to give Comet a bit of extra corn. Comet remained in Westmorland, and was the sire of Daddy's Lad. Tommy Birkbeck told the lecturer that Daddy's Lad was the only pony he knew that was faster than the original Comet, and Comet trotted ten miles on a hard road, well mounted, in 33 minutes. (Courtesy of the FPS Archive)

Paul Metcalfe's great-grandfather was the man to whom Comet was entrusted. He lived at New House, Orton (known locally as The Kennels because the Lunesdale hounds were kept there in the 20th century). When Paul was a boy there was a photograph of Comet in the house at

Bousfield, hanging on the wall in the stairwell. Comet was a rough looking, heavily built, common headed cob whose appearance gave little hint of the speed he possessed. That speed ensured a ready sale and fame for his offspring, but it had its disadvantages too: Paul's father was once driving 'a Comet horse' that bolted with him. 'Those Comet horses could be a bit like that.' It ran down the hill into Orton smack into the back of a wagon that was standing outside the shop, and killed itself. Paul Metcalfe tells that a horse, which dropped dead as it crossed the finishing line in one of the trotting races, was buried in the garden of Ellerhowe. Another racing distance at Orton was from the gates of Petty Hall to Street Farm and back, to make a mile. At one time Street Farm also had its own racecourse in the fields to the east of the farmstead.

Much of the toughness and speed that was required in the old Fells still remains in the Fell breed. Barbara Bell took part in endurance rides in the early days of the sport and also did Fell Pony Society pleasure rides with Waverhead ponies.

...long distance rides; Golden Horse Shoe rides. That Golden Horse Shoe went up by here and came back by Dash and over Skiddaw; we would come back probably down Swineside and Mungrisdale - there was a lot of road work. You just hadn't to loss any time, it was quite a fast ride. And we did a lot of those Pleasure Rides with the Fell Pony Society, every year a different area. Used to enjoy those rides - they went through some lovely countryside. I always never missed a one. (Barbara Bell)

The FPS News of 1968 carried the following report:

> Those wishing to qualify the 40 miles rode another ten miles back to Threlkeld. On both these rides there was a good turn-out of Fell ponies who acquitted themselves well. One of the Fell ponies, Sleddale Angus, belonging to Mr Robinson of Troutbeck, qualified on time and distance, but as the minimum height is 14.2 h.h., Fell ponies are debarred from the G. H. S. Rides.

Countering this exclusion, Peter Robinson used to suggest there should be a competitive ride that made the ponies

Guards Joseph at Sizergh Show, ridden by Sue Wardle.

and horses carry a stone of weight for every hand of height!

More recently, Sue Wardle's Guards Joseph has performed magnificently across country and so have Joan Hopkinson's Hesket Raffles, Alison Knight's Lownthwaite Romany and Fiona Carradus's Uldale Black Raven. They don't have the long legs of their Arab cousins but they do have a turbo trot that, once fuelled by competition, leaves the Orientals wondering what it was that went by in that flurry of hairy legs.

Mining

PONIES have been long associated with the exploitation of Cumbria's mineral wealth. There were mines burrowing underground following veins of ore, and 'drift' mines working into the sides of the hills, but open to the sky. The Dargue family bring out stories from over a century ago; the mining paths around Dufton have steps cut in them for the pack ponies to ease their passage over the steep ground:

Pauline: Dad used to say they used the ponies to bring things down from the mines. There's a mining trod up there on the fell, with steps. He kept saying, 'we'll have to go and see where it is,' but I don't think you can see where it is now. It's got proper steps. He used to say we should show people where it was, because after his day nobody would know where it was.

Derrick Byas: they've put slates in, to make a lip [demonstrates with hand - one flat and one vertical, the vertical standing proud of the flat surface to give a secure foot place for the pony]. Then they didn't go over t'edge. What did they call coal mine over t'Back? It was a drift mine and it was on Back Fell. There were some lead mines on Back Fell as well. You've got Smelt Hill, coming down to Flakebridge towards Appleby. They used to pack the ore down to Smelt Hill and smelt it there. It was probably using 'white coal' there, using wood out of Flakebridge woods. I imagine that's how it would be. London Lead Mining Company had it all mined; it was a national resource. These houses were built by the Lead Mining Company; they used to mine Silverband up the top there. They used to mine it before the War as part of the War effort, to get lead - I suppose for bullets - and goodness knows what else - paint, water pipes -

Mrs Dargue: And now they've discovered it's bad for you. My Grandfather, he used to say they tied the tails - from one pony to the next one - from the mines. (Dargue Family)

Mining looms large in the stories that are told. People sometimes think that 'mining' only means pit ponies pulling coal tubs, but there are many minerals to be got: a local one is gypsum, used in making plaster and plasterboard:

A lot of the people who lived in Milburn would work in the mines, at British Gypsum or Silverband. And a lot of them got a big garden because they kept one of the mine ponies. (Christine Morton)

In Northumberland the ponies were used to carry lead ore, mined in the heights of the Pennines, down to

Newcastle. I mentioned that I had heard the ponies on the mining trods were muzzled to prevent them eating lead-laden grass and so being poisoned, but Derrick Byas explained how he had found out that this might not be the case. When his wife Gwendy brought ducks to Silverband, and they died, the Merrythought Veterinary Investigation Centre (VIC) told him the cause was poisoning by lead ore in the garden soil. The VIC advised him not to eat roots or tuberous vegetables grown there as they would contain lead from the soil. However, the VIC also said that the reason sheep on the fell did not suffer from lead poisoning was because grass does not take up lead. So if the pack men put muzzles on the ponies only to prevent poisoning, they were probably wasting their time! Rather, muzzles may have been used to encourage the ponies to keep going at a regular walk and not just amble along as they would when grazing.

Sarah Charlton: This is a 'lead road' through here; all the names like Jingling Gate and Clickham Inn are all related to these pack ponies and lead trails. There's all sorts of BOATS [Byways Open to All Traffic] as well, but the pony trails were pack trails and they weren't wide enough for carts; and there's a lot round here.

Bob: They didn't use carts for that sort of job.

Sarah: There's a very old fording point. As you go up it the bank goes right above your head because it's been worn down with traffic.

Bob: [Lead] would all go to the staithes [loading docks] at Newcastle. And they would come back with coal. (Bob and Sarah Charlton)

The Newcastle coal would most likely be 'sea coal' washed onto the shoreline from undersea beds by the action of the waves. The antiquary, Leland, visiting the north in 1769, wrote: 'The vaynes of the se-coles be sometyme upon clives [cliffs] of the se, as round about Coket Island.' Coal was dug from these seams in opencast mines wherever they outcropped inland, but the term 'sea coal' was still applied to it. Daniel Defoe in his *Tour through the Whole Island of Great Britain* also uses the term to mean coal brought 'by sea' to London: 'The City of London, and Parts adjacent, as also all the South of England, are supplied with Coals, called therefore Sea-coal, from Newcastle upon Tyne, and from the coast of Durham and Northumberland.' Where there were mines worked inland in Tyne & Wear and in County Durham, either opencast or underground, we find stories of Fells working for the coal pits. Most of them went eastwards to work in the pit yards or on the dairy farms. Only a very few of the smaller sorts went underground, to the coal face.

Some went into the mines. Frank Ward, [of Ward Bros., Wolsingham] he would buy some off Dad, and they would go into the coal mines in Durham. (Frank Wales)

I know the pit ponies the less they were the better they liked them. If you'd a one that was anywhere near fourteen hands that went for pulling milk drays, any of the big ponies. They had their own dairy herds you see and used to milk and that was how they distributed it out in Ashington and such places.   (Chris Thompson)

Joe and Chris Thompson's father made a nice profit on sales of four-year-old geldings; when a buyer from County Durham was due to come over looking for pit ponies, he got the boys to buy up any that were available, and cornered the market before the pit buyer arrived.

I can remember father buying three- and four-year-old geldings to go to the collieries - and milk ponies - Ashington Colliery in County Durham. They probably didn't all go to Ashington, but that was the main one. A man called Robert Sloan used to come and buy them, round about on the hill farms, round Bampton and Helton. Sometimes he sent as far as twenty each year. Father said that was another bullock cheque coming in! (Chris Thompson)

And then they were brought down in the autumn and the ones we didn't want, went up to Kelso sales, or to the pits. A lot of those colts went to Ashington and places. They didn't work underground because they were too big, but they worked on the top, on the farms. (Mrs Ailie Newall)

They very rarely went to the coal face; they were too big; but they pulled a lot of machinery about on the top, you know: when the coal tubs came up they would probably move them around the yard. Where they actually did an awful lot for the coal industry was on the farm ground they owned, because inevitably wherever there was a pit there was also ground on top and they farmed it. And they nearly always seemed to be milk farms. And all the milk was delivered in horse-drawn milk floats. I think my grandfather once went into Ashington and there were 18 of his ponies lined up in milk floats getting ready to take the milk round the village. (Bob Charlton)

Joe Thompson, I was talking to him at Rosley one night, he said a feller used to come and they sold a lot to go down pits. It was when he was a lad. He said they'd never see daylight again he didn't think. He said this feller - his father used to ga to him and they used to take him down t'mines to see them; he said they were tret like kings. Oh yes. They were looked after well. (Ivan Alexander talking with Henry Harrison)

'Tret like kings' contrasted starkly with a question I was recently asked by an editor: how true was it that Shetland ponies were deliberately blinded and their eyes sewn shut in order to work in mines? This horrific question arose because the editor had been researching the background history to Shetlands in America. Henry and Ivan made it clear that the Fell ponies were well-treated, so I discussed this question with them. They received it with polite scepticism, 'Beware: you hear people talking about these horses down mines - You can't say it didn't happen, but - I think if someone abused one, I think he was abused.' Certainly I found very little evidence of cruelty in British pits: there was Ralph Hodgson's much-quoted short poem *The Bells of Heaven* which describes 'wretched blind pit ponies'; some fictional stories that, from internal evidence, were clearly not written by horsemen; and third hand accounts that asserted, for instance, that the animals lived down the mines 'from the day they were born,' all of which have to be dismissed as ignorant nonsense.

First-hand accounts posted on the internet do explain that pit ponies' eyesight could become very sensitive to light from being constantly in the dark conditions of the mines, so that at first they found it hard to see in normal daylight when they came above ground for their annual 'holiday'. They were also unused to 'real weather', to changes of temperature, or to digesting fresh grass. These were real, but temporary difficulties. Other than that, the ponies appeared very well cared for. (Godwin, 2004; Shaw 2004.) Dalemain Fell Pony Museum contains a pit bogey (truck) and several pit bridles which have metal guards to protect the ponies' eyes.

Ethel Fisher of Seaton, on the Workington side of Cumbria, lived on a farm above a colliery which used pit ponies to haul coal from the working face to the shaft. In *We Ploughed by Moonlight* (2001) she explains that the farm had the contract to supply feed for the pit ponies. Benny Moore was one of the men who looked after them. She says they had to work hard in 'appalling conditions' but they were 'very well cared for and got every attention. According to Benny they were his 'family' and he saw to their every need.' The ponies had straw bedding, and were fed crushed oats and chopped hay and 'the odd sack of carrots.'

Roy Charlton in *A Lifetime with Ponies* devotes a whole chapter to pit ponies and underground conditions in the early 1950s, which he had observed at first hand in mines both large and small. Ashington Colliery, he says, employed 1,400 ponies. He describes the dedication of the picked men who were the horse-keepers: the electrically-lit and spotlessly clean stables, the good food, the fine physical condition of the working stock and the care taken to keep them that way. All hair was clipped off, including manes and tails. The ponies would wash themselves off in a big warm plunge bath after their day ended, then go to their own stalls to be fed and watered and groomed. Mr Charlton compares the pit life very favourably to a 'free' life on the high fells; in the pit the ponies had an unvarying local temperature, with no rain, wind or snow, no extremes of hot or cold weather, and no biting insects. Pit ponies were brought above ground for gala days each summer and proudly shown by their handlers in condition classes. Other English colliers' accounts (Godwin; Shaw) describe the camaraderie of their work, as well as its danger; and they tell of good quality ponies whose work normally lay underground, being taken to compete at agricultural shows in the summer. One has to conclude that if there ever was any maltreatment of pit ponies, it certainly was not Fells in Britain who suffered it.

Farming

THERE were uses for Fells on the farm. The uses, though, varied according to local conditions and personal preferences. Bessie Cox of Orton recalls that during the Second

World War her family's farm used 'two Cydesdale horses and a Galloway.' Chris Thompson's grandfather 'would keep one or two for trap ponies and that; to Penrith and anywhere he went. They would use them for shepherding, probably working the hayfields and suchlike.' Mrs Newall also said, 'We just had two working Clydesdales, we didn't have a tractor, and the ponies did the things like helping in the hay and that; single ponies. Which they did quietly and sensibly. We sold quite a few to farmers locally for looking their stock on; and also we sold them to people in the Borders who wanted them just to ride, and enjoy, or wanted them for their children.'

Old Billy Wilson used to use two Fell ponies [at Bracken Hill, Greenholme] - he used to mow with them. You always knew where Billy was mowing because he had a petrol engine on the mower. The ponies pulled the mower and the knife ran off the engine. Billy had these two la'al Fell ponies, Diamond and Dapper they called them, and they were just like pulling the machine out of gear. You could always know when Billy was cutting because of this pop-pop-pop-pop of the engine going. (Ivan Alexander)

Although Ted Benson did not work his own ponies at Adamthwaite because they were too small and the land was too steep, he recalls that Fells used to work on the farms around Caldbeck. Margaret Wilson, of Townend, Caldbeck, told me that the mares worked on the farm while they were in foal; they were used for all the farm activities. The foals would be shut in whilst the mares were working. One of the side effects of working the mares separately from the foals must have been to make weaning more gradual and less stressful, since by autumn, the foals would have learnt that Mum always came back, no matter how dreadful it seemed the first time they were shut in without her. Mrs Bell also told of Caldbeck farmers using their Fell ponies, though the Waverhead ponies did not do farm work.

Billy Winder, he had Fells and he did quite a bit of work with them; he was on the bottom of yon fell, the high fell. Tommy Pearson at Faulds, they used to cut all their grass with them. (Mrs Frances Bell)

Frank Wales said that his family did not use them much for farming. On their steeply rolling fields they needed the greater strength of the Clydesdales, but one year the big work horses got grass sickness and died, so the Fells had to be pressed into service.

I've cut grass with Fell ponies; cause our Clydesdales died with grass sickness. Would be during the War, 1941. The eleven acre field, we cut it into four plats, because the ponies went quick - and stopped - then quick and stopped; if they'd a long way to go, they couldn't, they used to stop and run back and it used to spoil them. We used to use two in a single horse mower. We were cutting a four foot swathe; our machine was an Albion. (Frank Wales)

First recollection of them was when we were leading brackens with sled, and hay. When we would ga to school, if you could sit on a horse, you would take sled back up on

163

to the hayfield, that's my early recollection. I went to school from Midwathstead in them days and ponies were up at High Steads, up Bretherdale. We used to take milk every morning down to Greenholme School, with pony and trap, and if we were good lads we got a ride, if we were bad lads we'd to walk and lasses got a ride! There were seven of us used to walk out of Bretherdale. If we'd to walk, we walked over North Side, and if we got a ride in the cart we come down to Bretherdale Hall and picked a can of milk up. One day we'd just come through gate at Bretherdale Hall and a wheel dropped off cart - we'd a runaway. Girls was in trap and me and Malc and Edward and Ernie was walking behind. Anyway, pony just went, maybe a hundred yards and Uncle Ben held it and we just picked milk cans up -and we were all right. We'd to walk on to school.

When we lived at Potts Valley we fetched milk with a Fell pony. We've been on outlandish farms, and just had Fell ponies to do t' work, you know; we did everything. When we lived at Potts Valley, we'd mow t' grass with two Fell ponies; and field was that steep, you could only mow down-hill - pull t' machine to t' top empty, then when you turned round you cut one way down t' hill and if such a thing as a mouse nest got on finger bar on top of it, well you just went to t' bottom and took mouse nest off at bottom and had another go; it was literally straight down like, and same with hay - you turned it with hand - and used to sweep it with ponies and just pull it downhill with t' sweep. I've done everything with them, I've hoss raked, and I've cut

grass, led muck, and literally everything with a Fell pony.

Uncle Kit had a new sledge, well I would think Tom Stivvison made it, at Orton, and this bloody sledge, it had wheels on t' back - runners on front and wheels on. Anyway, we were pulling coming down off Bretherdale Bank with a load of brackens on. I think it was Malc and me, we didn't realise you'd to ga that way then that way [dog leg]. We were gaan straight down as a nearer cut home, and sledge hit a bump! well sledge run into back of t' hoss and knocked hoss off its feet, pushing it downhill, hoss was sitting on its bum on brackens like! New sledge you see, it went itself, it didn't need any pulling! But the sledging job, it was mar-vellous - it was where you got your experience for riding and that. Soon's you could walk, up onto hoss's back - hoss used to walk in t' middle. Up Bretherdale there was a lot of laal narrow lanes and that where you'd to ga and it never touched wall, hoss knew where it was gaan. (Bill Potter)

I remember the Dobie family at Abbey St Bathans near Duns in Berwickshire who asked me to make a sketch of them for the FPS Newsletter, showing them with their homebred Fells droving cattle from one pasture to another in the 1980s. Bob Charlton recalls doing the same in earli-er years:

When I would be about ten or twelve, my father used to take grass parks over at Blanchland which is ten, twelve miles away. And we would drive, from here, Galloway cat-tle which are the wildest brutes on earth, four or five of us riding ponies and we drove them from here to these grazing *grounds at Blanchland for the summer, and back. We took them straight up the lanes to as far as you can see and then out onto the open grouse moors and down the other side. With one in front and a couple on each side and one behind - 20, 30, 40 Galloway cattle. And that was about the last time I remember actually driving cattle on the loose; you know today you wouldn't dare. (Bob Charlton)*

Heltondale Ruby III and Heltondale Polly Perkins VIII were featured in the 1999 FPS Newsletter; both were being used for shepherding cattle and sheep in North Yorkshire. Frank Wales tells of a horse he had for shepherding:

[When I was shepherding on the fell], sheep that had twins had to come down [they needed better grazing than they could get on the fell]. I had a horse, and I could tap its knees, and it kneeled down. I had a plough cord on it, while I catched a sheep, and I catched its lambs. I had a rabbiting coat, with pockets; I put its lambs in t'rabbiting coat, and t'hoss kneeled down, and I got on, and I pulled t'sheep up and I carried it on t'horse back and brought it down with twins.

A lot of farmers in the village used Fells for shepherding, just round about the fields. Specially some of the elderly men who didn't walk so good. (Frank Wales)

I remember that John Gate, formerly of Mosedale and now retired at Tebay, had an unusual pair of stirrup irons made to suit his preference for going to 'look the stock' in clogs or big boots that would not fit into a normal stirrup. The irons were made from quarter inch by one inch steel bar, with an eye at the top for the leather. The steel was bent out at a right angle, with a six inch 'tread' and a small lip at the outside, rather like Peacock safety irons but without the rubber bands. John swore you'd never get dragged with open irons like those. You couldn't run the irons up the leathers for unsaddling, because they would stick out like horns, so you had to cross the irons and leathers over the saddle.

Ponies would be used for haytiming; I think they would go shepherding. I mind them riding horses like. And then, in winter they'd maybe take hay out on them, bags of hay. (Henry Harrison)

Shooting-ponies

THE Charlton family recalled the ponies being used for various sporting purposes. The sporting gentlemen would go shooting 'on the hill,' and the ponies would carry the shot game back in panniers; or the gentlemen would stalk the deer and the keeper would rope the shot stag over a 'deer saddle' specially constructed, with rings to take the ropes, and a breast-band and crupper and breeching so it would not slide forward or backward. Although a deer saddle is not a comfortable thing to sit on, I am told that riding the empty saddle on the way up the hill is still preferable to walking up with a hangover!

Bob: A great number went to Scotland for the stalk, for the deer.

Sarah: Grandfather-in-law used to produce ponies to go and be riding ponies for the hill - bringing the grouse or the

165

deer off the fells. All sorts of jobs like that. He used to pro-duce ponies for old gentleman riders of 'Some Stature.' There's a lady just over the hill who's only just given up using the ponies for bringing the grouse off the fell - Daphne Scott-Harden. (Bob and Sarah Charlton)

Breeding police horses

NATIVE toughness was put to good use by E P Taylor when he imported Fells and other British horses to Canada in 1966. Unfortunately, the progeny were mainly crossbred and even purebreds were not registered with the Fell Pony Society but only with Canadian authorities.

Frank: The first Fell pony mares that Mr Taylor got, he used to put a Thoroughbred stallion on them, and if he got a filly foal, he kept that till it bred, and he put that to the biggest, to a horse maybe 17.2; and a lot of mounted police horses in Canada are bred off that. He bought the Fells to put substance into the horses for Mounties; because they're hard of their legs, you see. (Wales Family)

Carriage and other harness work

Sarah: There used to be an old lady used to live in my moth-er's house; she died about two years ago; Ella Turnbull. And she was just about a hundred. She could remember going to mart every Tuesday, that was one of the treats out; pony and trap, taking the eggs and pigs to market, using a Fell pony. (Bob and Sarah Charlton)

When I was a boy, most of the farmers had Fell ponies. Dad sold them and they used to go into the fruit carts, and 'rag-and-bone' carts, to Lancaster, and to Blackpool. Some went up into Scotland for carrying deer, deer stalking. Our local butcher bought one for his butcher cart. Last one we sold to Lancaster, he was a rag-and-bone man. It was a long time since. (Frank Wales)

Rag-and-bone carts used to be a common sight. BBC TV viewers will remember the famous comedy series *Steptoe and Son* whose main characters collected anything and everything that people wanted rid of from their houses, and sold it on. The modern equivalent is the 'house clearance' man. The last rag-and-bone cart I saw was in Chester in the 1970s and I remember thinking that the grey pony looked remarkably like an unregistered Fell I used to ride.

Mr Gedling, the grocer from Caldbeck, he used to come here every week; he always drove a Fell pony, to Wigton, on a Tuesday and bring calf meal back. He did it when we came here, when my Dad came here in '32, and he did it for a good few years. How long he'd done it I can't tell you now. He'd a shop in Caldbeck below the school; he stopped when he got older, delivering, but he'll have carried on a long time with the shop. And our neighbour, she used to milk Galloway cows, and make butter, and she would carry twelve pounds of butter over that field, to meet Mr Gedling on Brocklebank, for a shilling a pound. Beautiful butter. He used to take eggs, as well, in his trap, when he came up here with our groceries once a week. That's what he did, with a little, black Fell pony.

Then there was John James, and he was a sharp one. If one of us kids touched his trap he would turn round with his whip - 'You buggers, get off it!' and rattle our fingers. But his pony had a bit of summat else in it - it was still like a Fell but it had summat else in it. (Mrs Frances Bell)

Modern Carriage Driving

THERE are profits to be had in breaking and selling colts. Bob Clegg from Lindale, who once worked as a horseman on the farm at the Newton Rigg Farm School near Penrith, used to buy batches of young stallions in the 1980s and 90s which he would break and then sell as quiet to ride and drive. This was his hobby in retirement!

Bob Clegg would come and buy perhaps four at a time; he used to give me say two grand for four. And he used to take them uncut. He would say, 'Next time you're having a roundup give us a shout.' They would just be tied up; and he would come, and he would buy four, more or less wild and still stallions. He broke 'em in, he would cut 'em. One batch, I think he sold one over to Ireland for two grand, so that was like his main money back; and then I think he sold one into Scotland for about one and a half grand, so that was like getting his expenses; so t'other two were just profit for him. Then he'd come up and buy another four. (David Trotter)

I remember in June 1987, when the dealers were coming up from London for the Appleby Horse Fair, that the North West Driving Club held a carriage drive at Tebay. Afterwards, when we had unyoked in the Old School Yard, we ate sandwiches and let the ponies graze on their halters. The drivers were admiring ponies that had gone well, and trying to tease people into selling them. 'Tony Port', one of the London dealers, had been trying for a couple of days to sell back a black gelding, Minder of Tebay, to David Trotter. David half wanted him, because he had a customer, but Tony's price of £600 was too high. However, Tony reckoned it was worth having another go and we stood around to watch the fun.

'All right, this is a one-off special for you, Trots. Now listen carefully. Give me two hundred quid and I'll sell him to you.'

David brought out the fat, chained wallet known as 'the Royal Bank of Tebay.' 'That'll do me, lad. About time too.'

Tony grinned and pocketed the notes, and said, 'You weren't listening like I told you. That's my two hundred quid. Now I'm going to sell him to you. And the price is six hundred!'

I think there's quite a big strong market there for quiet driving ponies and ponies that's done a bit. When Mark Jopling bought Rosanna, she was a mare five year old and she was full of fire - I said, 'if you are going to start and break that, it's going to be some work for you!' He's done very well I think to break them as he has done. Because he can go anywhere with them. He's even yoked up and taken

Santa Claus around Stokesley; now, night time and crowds and that, they've got to be good, haven't they! (Chris Thompson)

I like driving, but it's not much fun on your own, is it? I suppose being a one man band you never get into it. And you see Murthwaite's a bit of a one-eyed hole, you've a lane that's a mile long, and very rough and very steep in one place; and then, you've two directions you can go, and you've got to come back the way you've gone. It's ideal at Sleagill where I live, you can get round. For a week or two one summer I took a pony back there and had it at my neighbour's farm; I broke one or two in to drive, and I once did get one crossways on the main road; and it got stuck and I nearly had to lift the horse round...(Thomas Capstick)

It certainly did a lot of good for the public profile of the ponies when HRH Prince Philip took to driving Fells instead of big Cleveland Bay/Oldenburg type horses. He is still joyously competing in national Horse Driving Trials with a team of four.

I was judging an obstacle at Lowther Driving Trials and the Prince came along with his car and he was walking the course... I suppose he saw me looking at him and he turned and walked straight towards me. He said, 'Good afternoon. I think you would like to speak to me, wouldn't you?' I said, 'Yes I would, Sir.' We had a little chat, and he said, 'what particularly?' so I said, 'Well I think you have one of our ponies at Balmoral. And then you've had her down at home

to drive. You remember Linnel Rose?' He said, 'Yes, exactly. When the others walked, she trotted, and when the others trotted she cantered. She was a pain! I couldn't keep her back with the others. So I'm afraid we had to put her in foal and stop driving her.' (Bob Charlton)

The end result of driving schooling could be quite impressive. Harness work was a starting point for other ponies that went on into quite different disciplines:

Philip Cornthwaite, up Keswick way, was wanting one to chain harrow bracken; he couldn't do it with a tractor; and one he could shepherd on. So he shepherded on him, and he got all his brackens chain harrowed with him; and then the pony come back down to me. He went down to Sheelagh [Myers] at Flookburgh, and he was very good at dressage, under saddle. And Sheelagh'd shown a lot, so she entered him, showing him in these dressage classes; and he was unbeatable. (David Trotter)

Dressage

MORE recently Townend Patrick has performed well for Vicki Brown, who says, 'Over a period of only two summer seasons Paddy went from 0 points to 110 points. In those days you were awarded 7 points for a win, 6 for second and so on. The first 50 points were novice level, the next 50 elementary level, and the remaining 10 points he won at medium level. He was then and still is now the only Fell pony to compete sucessfully in affiliated dressage at medium level. Once into medium, his half-pass and collected work earned him very good marks but the extended work let him down. He had reached his limit, but what an achievement for a Fell pony that some die-hards say should not even be allowed to canter!!' He had a block about counter-canter, because once having learnt to canter on the correct leg, he found it unbelievable that anyone could ask him to canter on 'the wrong one'! At the age of 22 he is still doing a bit of

Townend Patrick ridden by Vicki Brown, performing in a dressage competition at Malvern NPS Show, 1988, photograph courtesy of 'Eventer' (Peter Doresa).

jumping and dressage at Northallerton Equestrian Centre.

In 1999 Lownthwaite Star Boy qualified for both the summer and winter UK Riders Dressage Finals and won a class at the latter. In 2004 two Fells, Linnel Cragsman and Greenholme Kelly, and two Highland ponies, won the Riding Clubs' Quadrille at the Horse of the Year Show.

Riding and Driving for the Disabled

FELL ponies are widely used by RDA centres helping both adults and children with disabilities. Their determination to take care of themselves translates itself into a wonderful talent for taking take care of others. Linnel Mozart 'in his latter years was a staunch member of the Slaley RDA.' Waverhead Andrew currently works for Westmorland RDA and won the exercise cart class at Westmorland County Show in 2002.

Swindale Rose, foaled 1980, was rescued from a 'meat wagon' by Sarge Noble when she was three. She went to Brough to be broken in by Bob Atkinson, and returned to Sarge for sale in September 1983. I bought her from him as 'quiet as a sheep, I would say.'

After a five year spell with me in leisure driving, a tiny bit of ridden and in-hand showing, some driven eventing and private driving, she was bought jointly by Hazel Hindmarch and Brenda Harrison, and qualified to do RDA. (Brenda is probably better known now under her married name of Hodgson; with her pair of Welsh ponies she took a Gold Medal in the World Disabled Driving Championships at Hopetoun in 2004.) Rosie is a bold and unflappable pony, who has taken most things in her stride, including people on crutches, people in wheelchairs, and the wheelchair ramp falling off her carriage. Her attitude is one of 'Come on, you silly human, sort it out! Do I have to do everything for you?'

She paraded with different disabled drivers at Lowther Show in 2002, '03 and '04. Although now aged 24, she is still ready to flirt with any good looking male Fell who comes within range!

Hunting and jumping
IDEALLY all stock should go on to have a use, preferably riding or driving, if they don't breed. Mrs Bell says of the family's early ponies, 'Ours didn't do anything, they didn't even pull a cart.' But as Barbara and Nancy grew up they used to break ponies and use them, while Bob Charlton's Linnel Mozart 'had 250 days hunting under his belt' and Glenis Cockbain hunted on Townend Maydew. 'Townend Flash went hunting too - people used to look down their noses at the 'little hairy pony', but he could go - he could keep up as well as anything else.' Christine Howe wrote in the 1980 FPS Newsletter that, 'For a special treat I took Glenda to a meet of the Quorn Hounds. On arrival faces turned towards us in some astonishment. The children were thrilled - 'Oh look mummy is it a Shetland!' Glenda became the centre of attention until we were silenced by the Field Master who addressed all the children on ponies about

Mountain Roamer in cart gears at show, photograph courtesy of Ted Benson.

what farmers did to small people who rode over corn - I was definitely included as I was at the right level. We were off and Glenda effortlessly trotted with the large hunters much to their owners' surprise.' In large areas of the Fell's home country horses take no part in hunting; the Bewcastle, Blencathra, Lunesdale or Ullswater hunters follow the respective packs on foot or in a Land Rover, so hunting is probably not the Cumbrian Fell breeder's biggest market. The ban on hunting in 2005 is likely to affect the southern English studs more than the northern ones.

We used to hunt; Mayflower hunted a lot. We used to have a lot more ponies than we have now, but we used to break them in more or less for ourselves, we didn't do anything else. That's when we had more - there was always just Nancy and I used to work with them. (Barbara Bell)

Crosses using Fell stock inherit their cleverness and hardiness. I know of two cross-breds by a Hackney stallion who are in the front rank in Horse Driving Trials. A Hanoverian x Fell from West Cumbria went on to be a top grade junior show jumper a few years ago and commanded a five-figure price. Bob Charlton has several very nice, light bay, small hunters of 15.2 hands, which are got by his Fell Linnel Reynard out of a thoroughbred mare.

They've got to have a job, haven't they? Pleasure; driving; RDA; showing; endurance; dressage; well, that they can do. And I always say, inch for inch, Fell ponies going Open here at our Performance Trial are jumping bigger than the great big 17 hand thoroughbreds who do our British Eventing. (Sarah Charlton)

Sold to the Gipsies

PEOPLE liked a good pony whether it was registered or not, you know? Somebody, a gippo'd buy it and it would go somewhere, it would ride and drive. I don't know what gippos did with them – but they'd be well put through their paces! (Henry Harrison)

Oddly, it was not always necessary for a pony to be any use to make a sale to 'the gipsies': some good looking ponies have ended up being pasture ornaments and never doing a stroke of work:

Some of our ponies, the gipsies used to buy the pony – just to look at. Some of these wealthy scrap merchants used to buy them. They just kept them in a field in front o't house for ornaments, if t'was a good 'un. It's always been the case. Just to look at. For relaxation he brings them in and puts them out every day. (Frank Wales)

That's Mountain Roamer; out of that mare Stouphill Pride, got by Heltondale Prince. He was reserve champion at the stallion show as a yearling. I sold him and he went to Selby, Yorkshire; he wasn't a Fell pony man really; a sort of a gipsy type, but he was a very good horseman and he liked his ponies. It was a toy really. (Ted Benson)

Children's ponies

You can sell four or five big ones where you only have one market for a little one. And that's for a kiddies' pony and it's got to be absolutely bombproof. (Chris Thompson)

My daughter did ride at the National Pony Society show at Malvern one year when she was just nine, and was third in her class with honour, who was not just so broad as some of the others. But they're not really suitable for very small children, because they are very strong. They don't put it on, they just are strong, strongly built and broad. We used to have races bareback on them and have fun with them – it was such a pleasure. We used to go for miles on them, and the children used to ride them. Then they wanted ponies for the Pony Club; but they still would have a ride on a Fell. (Mrs Ailie Newall)

I used to ride a Fell pony to school. I used to put it in a barn here in the village [during the school day]. I used to gymkhana quite a lot as a boy; a friend of Dad's had a wagon and I went with him. I used to go to Alston, and Black Dyke Band used to play for Musical Stalls. A lot of people used to buy them for their children to ride. Dad can ride it, Mam can ride it, and children – and they look all right. (Frank Wales)

Forestry Work

AN occasional job that ponies do is 'snigging' wood out of difficult ground, where machinery would do too much damage. Bill Potter told of a hard winter when he and his brother yoked a pony up 'and we were pulling tree branches for a bonfire, with this Fell pony.' The FPS uses promotional photos of Walter Lloyd working his ponies in a similar way.

Derrick Byas trained Townend Huey to this work in 2003 and I have used Swindale Rose to float out big pine logs from our riverside wood to a point at which the tractor could take over. Although Fells are not heavy enough to pull the weight that, for example, a Clydesdale x Dales would handle, they can make a useful contribution with lighter loads in tight places.

Lowmoat Sambo working in the wood, photograph courtesy of FPS Archive.

Conservation grazing

CONSERVATION scientist David Murray has been exploring the grazing habits of Fells with a view to recommending projects for which they might be suited. It is his opinion that Fells are needed on their native hills and that subsidies should support those of the breeders in this book who still maintain their semi-feral herds, because a breeder, inevitably, must be strongly influenced by financial considerations in what he breeds and how he presents it.

Fell ponies and their owners in fancy dress for Kendal Charter Pageant, 1975. Left to right: Heltondale William Rufus (Peggy Crossland), G Ibbetson, Greenfield Ruby (Beth Connell), Waverhead Robin (Jeff Potter), Bill Potter, Castlerigg Prince (Thomas Capstick), Lunesdale Peggy (Ernie Potter), Mrs M Ibbetson, photograph courtesy of FPS Archves.

There's not that many people who want them for snigging wood out. Or cutting grass. Now all this conservation grazing with Exmoors; a friend of ours, who is part of the Moorland Mousie Trust, buys a lot of these Exmoor colts who otherwise just disappear – they bought 20 off Exmoor this year, which probably would have all gone to meat. The point in favour of the Exmoors is that they have smaller littler feet, and not so much body mass, so they don't necessarily 'plunge'; but if you have a large enough area, Fells won't either. (Sarah Charlton)

Training, working and having fun

ONE of the great assets to any breed is a large number of single-pony or single-horse owners who simply take their animals to have fun in public. Fell ponies are used for re-enactments and demonstrations of Roman cavalry work, medieval tournaments, Victorian crop harvesting. Fells compete in hunter trials and performance trials of all kinds, acquitting themselves well with competent riders and giving confidence to the less experienced.

Stock who are not fully occupied with breeding can be useful pets or performers, and in an active home a gelding or a geld mare can be as great an ambassador for the breed as a breeding mare or stallion. A British native pony should be an easy care ride-and-drive, economical, powerful and useful.

And finally: you can't put a Fell to the wrong job

THE best thing about them I think is that they're very versatile in various conditions; and don't want a lot of looking after. If you've a thin skinned pony well you've got to rug it up and keep it in haven't you – whereas these things will stand any storm! If you're trekking them and that, you have to give them some feed, but they don't take a lot. If you take the weight that they're carrying and put the same weight onto another pony the same height – which would go the further!! (Chris Thompson)

Townend Septimus at Sizergh Show, 2004.

LIVING ON THE FELL - WINTER AND SUMMER

When you ask the families who have bred Fells longest, 'Where did your ponies come from?' they just say that the ponies were always there, as they have always been, out on the fell. Some can pinpoint dates in the nineteenth century when ponies came into the family, but the stock were out on the fell. They were Fell-Galloways, so that was where they ought to be.

Stock numbers on the fell have fluctuated over the centuries, and so have the proportions of different livestock making up those numbers. Medieval monastic land ownership by abbeys and priories, such as Cockersand, Conishead, Furness, Shap, and Watton, meant that many of the commons were given over primarily to sheep. The Tebay fells, curiously, were better known for cattle (Lambert, 1996). When the monasteries were removed from land ownership in the sixteenth century by Henry VIII, their estates were given to favoured courtiers. The Lordship of Tebay, for instance, went to Sir Thomas Wharton; from his family it passed to the Lowthers of Meaburn Hall in 1728.

The tradition of using the common land for ponies as well as sheep and cattle is a long one, going back to at least 1794 and probably very much earlier. In that year Anthony Pringle reported to the Board of Agriculture, later the Royal Agricultural Society, on the state of agriculture in Westmorland and other Lakeland counties. He reported that 'The (Westmorland) Commons are numerous, extensive and valuable...' and added that they were mainly stocked with Scotch sheep, black cattle and geese. He observed, frustratingly briefly, that 'a few ponies of the Scotch breed are reared upon the commons, but the practice not being general, need not be dilated upon.' He also dismissed the work horses of Westmorland, 'As there is but a small portion of the county under crop, the horses are not numerous, nor has any considerable attempt been made to improve the breed of these useful animals. They are small, not exceeding fourteen hands and a half in height, are said to be hardy, but they are neither strong nor handsome; sixteen or seventeen pounds are reckoned a good price for a horse at five years old. They are often turned out upon the commons in the intervals of labour, which, as the farmer very probably has neither turnips nor fallow, are very frequent in the summer months.' Notice that he distinguished the work horses and the ponies by using different names. The word 'Scotch' is tantalising because although it may mean the 'Galloway' type (a wide term including ponies that were later called Highland, Fell or Dales) Pringle did not feel a need to explain it.

Life on the fell is the central influence that made the Fell pony what it is today, and that keeps it true to its type. The annual cycle of life on the fell is relatively simple. The mares spend mid to late summer on the tops, grazing and looking after the foals. Ponies are not involved in the long summer days of work, when grass is mown on the in-bye land, and turned, and led home as hay or silage. They are only disturbed by the men gathering the sheep for clipping, or separating-out lambs at weaning. The ponies will not be gathered to take off the colt foals and surplus filly foals until the shortening days of October or in some cases, not until Christmas or the New Year. After that, they spend the rest of the hard weather out on the fell again, continuing with their pregnancy but without the strain of feeding a foal. When they foal in May or June they are brought down to the allotment or fields and stay there for a couple of months to be served again. The notable points in this cycle, however, always have to be fitted in with the requirements of the farm.

On the fell, the mare normally knows her own area and tends to stay on it. She relies on her extended family to keep her safe, as they in their turn rely on her. She teaches her foal, and her previous foals if they are still with her, to exhibit correct behaviour with other ponies and to be knowledgeable about the ground on which they live: where to shelter when the wind comes from any direction, where the streams and sweetest grasses are, and how to avoid bogs. Henry Harrison observes, 'If some foals were never taken off, they would still hang together, yearling and foal, when they were born - they clang [stayed close] together.' Ivan Alexander agrees, 'Yes... there was a cluster of them at finish. Once you found one, you found they were all there together.'

The herd may travel several miles in a day, the direction and purpose dictated by the boss mare: across to one ghyll to drink; down into a sheltered hollow or over the tops onto a lee slope to escape an oncoming gale; sometimes right down to the fell wall when snow is on the way. They share the grazing with sheep, and occasionally cattle. The feeding preferences of the different species keep the sward even, and the extensive nature of the grazing, together with this mixed stocking, helps to keep the land clean of parasites.

Life out on the margin of the farm business has its own characteristics. On the whole it is peaceful. Walkers, on their way to who knows where, may attract the ponies' interest from time to time but if ponies are not fed on the common land they do not expect food and generally move steadily away about their own business instead of pestering people. An exception is on the Caldbeck Commons where Shetland ponies, including entires, have been turned out for so long and so petted by visitors that they are a definite hazard, shoving their heads into open windows of parked cars to demand food in a most ill-mannered fashion. On another area of seasonally occupied common land, Sunbiggin Tarn Pasture, serious damage was caused to a car a couple of years back, where a cattle grid securing the road onto the pasture was obstructed by a mixed group of horses and ponies. The lady driver stopped, but she was afraid to get out and chase them. Because it was a picnic place where they had been given titbits before, the horses thought the stopped car would have food and so they besieged it and began biting and kicking it and each other. They did a thousand pounds' worth of damage to its bodywork in the twenty minutes before someone local came along and chivvied them off. I heard this at first hand from the driver who, not surprisingly, was extremely upset and was seeking the horse owners to claim compensation. Both examples carry a strong argument for discouraging the hand-feeding of any ponies on a public common.

Shelter, and the going underfoot

THE prevailing winds in Britain are from the south west and carry a lot of rain. However, strong winds from the east in winter can bring a snowfall several feet deep. Always, the fell tops are exposed, with no trees and very low growing herbage.

On the Howgills: *Any of those ghylls – they're very deep – and because our winds are from the south west, if the ponies get down in the bottom, it's a different day from what it is up on the tops. But some of these ghylls that go back into Howgill, will be the least sheltered, because they face into the wind. (Thomas Capstick)*

On the western slopes of the Pennines: *Mrs Dargue: There isn't any trees though.*

Derrick Byas: No, it's open fell. You've got heather about six inches high, but it's not much use to ponies! It's surprising how much shelter there is in dips and hollows. If weather's coming bad, you'll oftimes find t'old mares and young 'uns going into the bottom of High Cup Nick. Can't say whether they still do or not because it's three or four year since I've been up there. When I used to walk up there with Jos – if weather was coming bad they used to come to Front Fell [on the west side of their range]; if it was snow, well usually you found them down the bottom of High Cup, come down with weather, and you couldn't get em back out again; they tended to head there in really bad weather – it must have been sheltered and a bit better place. (Dargue Family)

At Shap: *On Hassocks, there's them trees; last weekend, I'd visitors and we went up to Hassocks, and one of them saw how that pony stood in back o't bush, and I said, 'That's the shelter for winter. Wouldn't that be a beautiful picture? Standing out o't wind, back o't bush.' That's all we have for shelter in winter, and hill ends... that's why, if it's too bad, I don't give them anything. You're dragging them out of shelter; that's worst thing you can do. Wind'll take flesh off them faster than anything. (Barry Mallinson)*

The extensive range of most fells gives the ponies the chance to move before the wind and find shelter under a lee slope. Although Fells, with their average height of 13.2 hands, are sometimes cited as being short enough to shelter behind a stone wall, they mostly do this when confined in fields; on the fell, their preference seems to be a sheltered ghyll or a valley out of the wind, or a big clump of whin (gorse) bushes.

If you went out on a wet day and stood aback of a whin bush you didn't know if it was blowing, or raining or what – there is some where Tat [George Tatters] used to be and they were good shelter. You go up Tebay fell, up them valleys, and it was grand, they just were under t'hill... They were sheltered from wind from the west or from the east. They knew it was going to be bad before we knew. You know? It's like a rabbit; they say if they come out in t'afternoon it's going to be a bad night. (Ivan Alexander talking with Henry Harrison)

As a generalisation: ie, on most fells (not all)				
Approx dates	Mares	Stallions	Foals	Young stock
May to mid-August	In-bye for service	In-bye or stabled OR on parts of Heltondale fells, out on fell with mares	In-bye with parents	May have been gathered and sold, otherwise on fell most likely in small band, separate from main herd.
August to October	On fell with foals	In-bye or stabled	On fell with mares	On fell; most likely in small band
October to December/ January	On fell, with foals if foals not sold	In-bye or stabled	May have been gathered & sold at autumn sales; otherwise on fell	On fell, most likely in small band
December/ January to May	On fell without foals	In-bye or stabled	Weaned and brought indoors indoors with other foals	On fell, most likely in small band

Given sufficient area to roam, ponies can take advantage of changes in the soil; they can move up to a dry shoulder of land to graze in a wet summer, or to the edges of boggy ground for fresh grass when there is a dry time. Most of the fells are acid soil. Even where the underlying rock is limestone, the high rainfall counteracts its sweetening effect and even lime-hating plants such as heather can grow well on limestone fell.

On impermeable rocks like slate, granite or shale, the higher land wears a thin, fibrous peaty soil while the hollows can be boggy and treacherous, growing water-retentive sphagnum moss. What the ponies like is the high, grassy country, with fine, quick-draining ancient turf close to the rock; they avoid the heather moorland and the bogs.

The line along the top here, more or less the Pennine way, separates the wet Back Fell from this side. They don't go there, it's too wet. (Christine Morton)

You never see them grazing where heather's at, unless it's been burnt off and starting to come through maybe, a five or six year old patch, they might ga on it then, but they won't go on it, you can't chase them on it. (Bill Potter)

Below, the black pony asserts dominance over the bay, who accepts it and moves away.

Right, Tebay Jenny, a daughter of Victor, photograph courtesy of Thomas Capstick.

Below, the Lownthwaite herd on the fellside in the far distance.

Above, young handlers at Sizergh Show.

Opposite, top, Bill Potter's mares on the fell, early spring 2003.

Opposite, below, three in-foal Fell mares in April 2004, working their way across limestone land at Fell End, near Sedbergh.

Clockwise from top:
Ponies on the fell at Stoney Ghyll.
The ruin in the background lies on
the route of the Galloway Gate, an
ancient packway and drove road.

Ponies grooming.

Three generations of the Wales
family, and the Prince of Wales -
another horseman whose grandfa-
ther invested in Fell ponies - with
Lownthwaite Bramble, photograph
courtesy of Christine Morton.

Of course there was difference of times of year. In summer, obviously, if it come a really dry spell, well they would hang more to the wettish sort of land; because the dry parts of the fell, some of that Howgill fell, used to burn off, where it was near to rock. They would hang more to the wetter ground then, in the really dry spells. And obviously vice versa if it come very wet, well they would move onto the dryer stuff.

Tebay fell is suited with a dry summer because it's a wet sort of fell. Then you get further over into the Howgill fell, where it's more grassy, but it's nearer the rock, it doesn't stand a very dry spell so well as Tebay fell. (David Trotter)

There's some bracken on Howgill and on Cautley front and a little bit on our side on the front; you tend not to find them there, and you certainly tend not to find them on very very steep areas; it's as if they know their limitations. (Thomas Capstick)

There is one cycle of stock movements on and off the different areas of the fell which mirrors the availability of the grass due to seasonal or local weather conditions; and another which is dictated by the demands of the breeding season.

Hardiness and weather sense

OFTEN the ponies shelter in ghylls when the westerly gales bring rain, but the very worst cold and snow will come from the east. When bad weather threatens, most breeders say the ponies come down to the fell gate. They do this before the weather breaks.

Drybarrows (Askham Fell) - They were quite good weather merchants. They knew when it was going to change and they came to the lower ground. I won't say they come right home but you would see them heading down the fell and probably the next morning we'd three or four inches of snow.

I've seen in winter time they've come home with a big ball of snow on their tails, and there's sheep come following down afterwards, when there's been a lot of snow. You wouldn't have seen that if it hadn't been for the ponies; I don't think sheep would ever have come! I've seen it quite often. These last twelve or fifteen years we haven't had any winters, but before that, we had some winters... and I was there and saw what happened; a pony or two would come, and about half an hour to an hour after, a lot of sheep come and you could see them coming Indian file down the track the ponies had made.

But your older ponies quite often came and you'd probably got to go and look for the younger ones. Maybe if they'd missed the older ones coming away, they were to bring down. They can please themselves. They'll stand a snow storm and be hungry for two or three days; if there does come a thaw they can break away and find what they want. Rug them up and look after them like that? it's not my opinion of a Fell pony... I suppose it keeps them clean, but they'll stand any storm that comes along, without being covered up. (Chris Thompson)

183

If it was a real windy day, they were hard to find, they'd be down in a ghyll somewhere. And when you got to them, they were very sheltered, you could light a fag [cigarette] just about. They knew where to get in them gullies and when a wind come, they knew where to go to. (David Trotter)

David Trotter had a brown gelding which someone wanted to buy and he had noticed him grazing along Longdale Bottoms, so he made a note to go and catch him at the weekend, but when he went to look for him, he had gone. The Bottoms are on the north side of the Howgills and shortly afterwards there was snow out of the north. David did not see him there again until after the snow had melted. He'd gone over the tops to the south side into shelter before it started – four or five miles over land rising to 2,000 feet.

The ponies not only know where all the sheltered places are, and indeed they will travel extraordinary distances in one day to reach them when the weather is about to change, but their instincts remain very sharp. They predict the arrival of snow with uncanny accuracy and will always arrive at the fell gate near the farmstead 24 hours before a snowfall… 'The Fell ponies know when we shall have snow.' (Bert Morland, *A Lifetime in the Fells*)

At the other side of the Howgills, Ted Benson's Adamthwaite ponies would move down towards the farm. 'They would go away, but they'd a habit, if it was going to come stormy, they would land home. Right down into t'corner. They would do that all year round, even in summer; if it was just going to be maybe heavy rain or a low pressure coming in, they would land home till it settled again, then we would maybe never see them for weeks.'

Like the sheep on the hills, they come down into the lower field when it's going to be stormy. They're so wise, the Fell ponies. (Mrs Ailie Newall)

At Windy Hall, Lownthwaite, Christine Morton said there is a plantation of trees, and a big shed for winter shelter. In snow time the fell gate is opened, and the Lownthwaite ponies are given hay there, though not till the New Year. In frosty times, much of the surface water freezes; 'the ponies won't try to cross a stream if it's frozen. They know if they went through and broke a leg they'd be dead.' The spring at Windy Hall doesn't freeze, so the ponies can come in from the fell to drink, and they are also let in there to graze in March, 'the hungry month', when mares are heavy in foal but most of the natural grazing has been eaten already.

One time in their lives when young ponies are vulnerable on the fell is when they 'change their teeth'. When they are shedding their milk teeth and growing their adult incisors at around three years old, they find it hard to graze close-cropped turf, and occasional youngsters may get into a poor condition before the new teeth grow up enough to meet and grip the grass.

The winter of 1947

IN January 1947 an extraordinary change in weather conditions appears to have taken everyone by surprise. Reports tell that there had been an unusually mild spell which rapidly turned to a severe blizzard. Once the snow started it scarcely stopped for weeks, while constant below-freezing temperatures prevented it thawing. Hedges, fences and stone walls alike vanished and trees stood up to their waists in snow. Level stretches were six feet deep with drifts of twenty feet and more; there are tales of men, digging out ways for milk wagons to reach farms, hanging their jackets on the arms of telegraph poles while they worked, or cutting notches on the poles to record the depth of the snow. There were few mechanised snow-ploughs then, and even where farms had horse-drawn ones, the horses had a terribly hard time because they had to struggle through chest-high snow themselves to pull the plough. It was said that two million sheep died that winter and many farmers went bankrupt, though at least one of my neighbours received Ministry of Agriculture compensation payments of £3 a head. Another neighbour at Greenholme, Les Thackeray, remembers that the snow went on so long that his family ran out of basic foodstuffs and paraffin oil for the lamps and heaters – there was no mains electricity in Greenholme till the early 1960s and most households cooked on coke or coal-fired ranges.

We had no paraffin, and no bread or flour left at the farm. Barry Airey and I set off one night, walked under the railway 'creep' and made a beeline for Orton. It was bright moonlight and snow was that thick, we never saw a wall or hedge till we landed at the back of Grandma's on Front Street. Hully's were friends of ours and they opened up the shop for us, so we bought anything that was useful and carried it home in the moonlight. It went on for oh, six or eight weeks, and the sheep wouldn't see a green blade of grass in all that time. Ours were in-bye, but such as Shap Lodge, theirs were on the fell and they lost a lot. But I never heard tell of what happened to the Fell ponies. Maybe Jim Thompson was the only person who had any around here at that time. (Les Thackeray)

Mrs Sylvia McCosh wrote in a FPS newsletter that Mr Jim Thompson's 8319 Syble, a dark brown nine year old mare, was out on Roundthwaite fell with her foal 'during the terrible winter of 1947, and it was some time before her owner located the pair in an exhausted condition, but eventually they were brought safely home and recovered.' Miss Peggy Crossland bought Birkett Bank Polly that spring and wrote in the FPS Newsletter of 1980: 'It was now March and that ghastly '46/'47 winter was coming to an end. I rang Mr. Relph and asked if I could go to see him, and my mother, sister, and I duly went to Birkett Bank. There were still large drifts of snow about. They had been so deep the ponies had been able to walk over the walls. The losses among the sheep had been terrible.'

Pauline Robson says that her father, Jos Dargue, was living at Bow Hall in 1947. 'We can remember Dad saying that how the ponies survived, was by eating seaves. The sheep ate seaves too, but not to the same extent. On Bale Hill allotment, which was shared grazing, they nearly ate the seaves down to ground level; it took years for them to grow back.'

In south west England conditions were so bad that ponies were found frozen to death. 'They had an aircraft from Chivenor to get out to them, to take out some food for the ponies, when they got out to them they were all on their legs, they sort of fell into one another, he supposes they cuddled into one another for heat, and they were dead. Frozen to death. Yes, standing up.' (Cyril Wyburn, recorded in Somerset County archive).

> Birkdale [above Dufton] has the reputation of being the most isolated sheep farm in the kingdom; there is no road to it; the previous tenant used to travel on horseback when he went to do his shopping… Mr Airey… told us that out of a flock of 700 sheep he had only 110 survivors, after the blizzard, and only 30 lambs... Never have I seen so many dead sheep lying about in various stages of decomposition; everywhere there is the horrid, pungent smell. It may be asked: 'Why don't they bury them?' The answer is that the job is beyond the power of any one man. How could a farmer, with other jobs to do, set out over a wide area to collect and bury two or three hundred sheep? Nature in her own time will do the work of getting rid of them and soon all that will be left will be the bones. (Sir Clement Jones, 1948, *A Tour In Westmorland*)

Ivan Alexander reminded me about 2540 Heltondale Romer, bred by J W Rowlandson at Longbarrows, Bampton, in 1939. The stallion was dark brown, with a black mane and tail, and stood 13-2½ when he was measured on 25th August 1945. 'I can remember Sarge saying they'd named him Romer – and if you look at pedigrees he's been all over; everybody used him!' He survived on the fell that winter, despite fresh snowfall every day from January to March, an undeniable tribute to the vitality of the breed. 'He didn't come in until March. Sarge said he was just like a shot crow, he *just* sort of survived.'

The winter of 1963
IN the winter of 1962-1963 my family were living on 'mild' coastal Merseyside. School was shut, the sea was crusted with ice floes, and at Chester the River Dee froze solid from bank to bank; my mother has a photograph of me standing on the greenish ice, which was at least two feet thick. Television showed us that high villages were cut off, power lines were brought down and trains were cancelled.

Farmers could not reach some of their livestock, and once again many starved to death in the constant severe frost. Again, aircraft were brought in to carry food to outlying farms. I remember a Thelwell cartoon of the time showing a kitchen with a splintered ceiling, and a couple sheltering under a table surrounded by scattered bales of hay while through the window can be seen a distant helicopter. The caption read something like, 'Stay where you are – there's a ton of cattle cake still to to come.' My mother recalls that when the thaw eventually came, the grass was pale yellow and the soil stank from being covered so long.

Christine Morton says, 'My mother says it was very cold before Christmas, and it snowed on Christmas morning. The main challenge was the wind from the east, dry and cold. Roads were unblocked only to 'blow in' again overnight. The ponies came home across the snowdrifts, over the fences. Johnny Walker joined the mares the same way and they all went into the middle pasture and into the wood.'

David Trotter remembers the house water supplies freezing underground in 1963 because of the prolonged, intense cold, but says that there was not as much snow as in 1947, when he was at school. He compared the survival of his two herds in 1963: Tebay Campbellton Victor's herd, running on Fair Mile and Tebay Fell, came to the fell gate in Tebay and were fed with hay there during the hard weather. Heltondale Heather Lad's herd stayed over the north side of the Howgills, along Longdale Bottoms, and never came home or had any extra feed. They were all in better condition, when the thaw came, than Victor's herd which hung about the fell gate for hay.

Christine Morton says very little is recorded about ponies in the Lownthwaite farm diary for that time. The family's main concern was for the dairy herd and getting the milk collected. 'Presumably the ponies stayed at the fell and got fed with the sheep. Fell ponies did die. Old ponies and very

young ponies. Four died in Knock Ore Gill. It was the in-foal mares who survived.'

The odd thing about those two notably bad winters is that you cannot see their effect when you look at the Fell Pony Stud Book. There was no dip in the number of foals registered: 35 were born in 1946; 40 in 1947; and 44 in 1948. That upward trend was similar in 1962, 1963 and 1964. Bill Potter remembers stock losses in 1947, 'I think we lost eight ponies that hard winter out on t'Howgills, but we had two or three left up at Uldale.' And again at Greenholme, in 1972, 'We selt a lot and we lost a few. That winter come a right hard winter, and we lost a few. That learns you – when it hits your pocket, it learns you to cut back.' Obviously the Stud Book, recording only births and not deaths, cannot tell the whole story.

Foals went to sell in October on 'yellow forms', applications for registration, which were given to the auctioneer, who then passed them to the buyers. But a lot of foals on yellow forms never were registered. You can't measure the actual losses in those bad winters because the ones you lost on the fell would have been on yellow forms, and not yet registered anyway. (Christine Morton)

Herd behaviour

THE ponies live in small groups, with an old mare as the leader. If fillies are left on the fell they continue to run with their dams, but if they are returned to the fell in spring after being weaned indoors, they drift off in separate little junior bands, in the groups established during their winter confinement. Thomas Capstick says, 'although I let them all out together, they split up into the two groups. I've never seen them all together. They tend to stop on their own. The older ponies seem to rather pick on them.' It seems that a herd is a tight-knit entity, and leaving the established hierarchy means a pony cannot easily return to it. On most fells the adult mares come off the fell in summer after foaling, for service, so the yearlings and other young stock are on their own for a couple of months.

In-bye - *You always have a boss mare; and one who thinks she's boss. If you put the stallion with them he's always on the outside. He's the lowest of the low. And then you always have a boss mare, which is old Star Turn, and a mare who thinks she's boss, which is Nora Batty; she does all the ruling but if Star Turn comes, everything else just fades away. It seems to be that you always have two main mares. One lead mare that stays out of the group, on guard as you might say; your other lead mare seems to be with the herd. Out at fell there's fourteen in one group and in t'other group there's seven. If they're all together there'll be a bit of squaring up, but there'll still be two mares in charge. Any mare can square the stallion up. He is the lowest of the low. (Christine Morton)*

It all depends how many are in a pasture. There's always the pecking horse. Top of the line is always an oldish mare. Then down the line away from that. When they change,

you'll find, if you take a pecking mare away, she has a struggle to get back in, struggles to get back to the top. She has to be there a long time. I found that with my old brown mare, cause she was always the boss, on Hassocks. I put her back on this time when I found out she was geld, and she wasn't bottom of the line but she was two or three down. It's queer how it happens. You shouldn't interfere with Nature, in one sense; she wouldn't have gone out of the group and she'd have been the boss mare. (Barry Mallinson)

The stallion, either on the fell or in-bye, is on the outside of the group, and he keeps out other adult males. The herd's own colts over two years are not tolerated at all; he drives them off ruthlessly. Two adult stallions who meet in spring may have a serious battle resulting in injury or even death, unless the area, such as the Howgills or the Heltondale fells, is sufficiently extensive to allow them to roam without clashing.

On the fell - *In the breeding season the stallion won't have anything to do with the young ones, he chases them off. Sometimes they split up and you'll see four or five at one place and a similar number at another place; they don't all hang together all the time. The mares at present, there's about a six and a five at two different places, and there'll be one or two dotted about; quite often they go back to the ground that they're used to going to; they're rather like sheep, they heaf themselves. (Chris Thompson)*

Heather Lad used to run Longdale Bottoms; and on this

side [Tebay Fell], and onto Fair Mile, was Victor. But no, they didn't clash, they had their own little herds. You'll have your boss mare. Maybe the mares stuck to their own little areas and then the stallions stuck with them. The stallion ran out with them all year round – no we'd never any savaging or owt. He might sort of shift, say a yearling or two-year-old colt, that hadn't come in and was out there; he perhaps wouldn't wear him, he'd shift him out; and sometimes you would come across a little parcel of perhaps three or four yearling and two-year-old colts, that neither stallion would wear, hanging about for company. (David Trotter)

Oh they can be terrible, stallions, can't they; I've seen stallions up on the fell, if a youngster appears… There was a black and white stallion out for quite a few years. I once saw this youngster – it would be a two year old, only a little raggley thing – it came and tried to join this herd and he went to it and got hold of it by the back of the neck and downed it and just shook it like a dog would shake a rat. He gave it a good shaking and then he let it go, and it wasn't long afore it was out of there! It wasn't to tell twice! (Thomas Capstick)

Travelling on the fell

IT is surprising the distances that the ponies will travel in a day when they are roaming freely. Chris Thompson describes the unpredictability of keeping ponies on a large area and how a breeder has to be prepared to do a bit of hunting round to find the ponies when he wants them.

If they're out on the fell, I've lost them for eighteen months and presumed they were dead, and then they've turned up. This stallion that I have now, I lost him for eighteen months; and then I lost three 2 year old fillies, probably about twelve years since; and I think it was just that they'd been chased away with motorbikes, and didn't know where they were to come back home. I did actually find those three on High Street. And the stallion, he come down to Askham end. Well he'd more or less gone back to where he was brought up at you see, but he'd overshot and gone further. If it hadn't been for t'bit out of t'ear, well I might not have been able to find him then! It's surprising you know – like he was two and a half year old when I found him and he wasn't a year old when I sent him out; he'd grown and changed considerably. (Chris Thompson)

Derrick Byas: Bad to say what they do in a day – they tend to sort of amble about and rest, stick their heads down and graze, and as they graze they're wandering along – they're not just stood in one spot. It doesn't take them long to get from one side of Front fell to t'other side; putting it down to distance I wouldn't like to say – it'd be between five and ten mile a day depending on the time of year and what it was like and whether they were disturbed or not. There's so many variables. Year on year fells vary. They're not always the same. Spring of the year if it was really good… If they got onto a good patch, you might find them there next day. If weather was right bad they might stop on Front of fell for a day or two, a week or two. But then guaranteed next time you wanted them, they could be somewhere down Street and you'd gone right the way past High Cup and goodness knows how much further after that, so they'd maybe travelled that in twelve hours since you've last seen them. You think 'I'll go out and get them hosses tomorrow morning –' and time you'd gone, you'd got a fair old walk! (Dargue Family)

Some of Thomas Capstick's ponies prefer Tebay Fell, a range six or seven miles from the main farm below Harter Fell. A few of Henry Harrison's mares would typically graze five or six miles from home, in Mardale. Such preferences for distant areas of a large fell can be inconvenient for the owner, because he cannot know with any certainty where the ponies may have wandered to, except in extreme weather when he probably would not want to gather them anyway. Ted Benson considered that the ponies move round the Howgills in a regular cycle, and Ivan Alexander agreed.

You could gather, fetch them in to t'fields; gather yan area that you thought they were in: Bowderdale, Longdale; go back three days later, and like sheep, they'd come in and you could get t'rest. It's your movement again – what you found in Langdale today, if you went in four or five days' time, they would be different horses; cause they'd moved out and t'others had moved round. If you saw a cluster of horses in a valley they wadn't stop there – they would move

out and another lot would move in. There was always some in but they were different ponies! (Ivan Alexander talking with Henry Harrison)

They travel about, and there's a lot of people think, because you have, you know, twenty ponies on a fell, that they stick in a herd, but they don't. I suppose because you winter your yearlings inside, they go out and they tend to stick in a little group. Otherwise they would stay with their mothers.

The ponies that stray onto Tebay Fell, they're always the same ones, that'll come back; and they'll be back within a day or two. And even if you let one out, it'll find its way back. You'd have thought it'd stop with the first group it came across, but it didn't. (Thomas Capstick)

When Barry Mallinson bought his first mare from Sarge Noble, she was for sale because her little herd ran in Martindale and Fusedale, territory that was, and is, difficult to reach from Bampton. It is only five miles away, but separated from the farm by high steep country, so it was a day's work for Sarge and Thomas Noble to go and fetch the ponies, who as a result were not handled very often and were difficult when they were caught.

I just wanted 'a good Fell'; Heltondale Fusedale Daisy, it was. He was wanting rid of them, they were that far away over to Martindale, and I ended up buying it. Job was, moving it! Never been touched; she'd be eight year old I think when I bought her. My brother and some others decided they would halter her; she left her imprint with her back feet on one or two of them! But they did it, they haltered her, and I could catch her, and I used to lead her down to Geordie Cowin's to his Twislehope stallion at Rose Cottage. (Barry Mallinson)

Gathering

WITH the advent of quad bikes it is less trouble to gather than it used to be when all the work was done on foot.

Henry: They used to just go to yon side of Swindale; some of them used to go as far as Mardale — but I sold them!

Ivan: We'd no motorbikes!

Henry: Took you a long time!

Ivan: Trouble is they're like a sheep, once they've gone over there and they've had a foal over there, that goes back – so you're making work for yourself. (Henry Harrison and Ivan Alexander)

Mostly the breeders today gather using quad bikes, but in earlier days someone would give them a lift in a car or Land Rover to the far end of the fell, and from there they would walk back to the farm, pushing the ponies ahead of them in the same way that they would gather sheep. A few people would ride ponies for gathering, but on the whole they were not accustomed to riding for long periods and said it was easier to employ 'Shanks' pony.' It is a straightforward job to gather a fell such as Birkbeck, where there is only the one herd; but around Wet Sleddale, other farms' ponies would run with the group for a while then break back, taking away with them the ponies that were wanted.

David Trotter used to ride little Tebay Campbellton Victor up the fell to fetch in mares. 'I always used to go shepherding on Victor! Even though he was so small, he used to carry me up hill and down dale, right over into Longdale Bottoms, and yeah, he never broke stride. And actually he was good to take out, because if you were looking for mares or summat, he would know where they were you see, so you more or less just let him have his own way and he would take you to them.' When I mentioned this to Henry Harrison he agreed that it made sense because 'when they're mating the stallion will round them up.' It was natural for Victor to get the mares going in the right direction.

We brought a big bunch in off the fell; of course some of them were colts. We'd perhaps bring them from over that Ravenstonedale side. We were riding; we'd saddle two or three up, and away out on Sunday afternoon and have a look round them. Lynn was – how old was she when she broke her teeth helping us? She was still at Tebay school. (David Trotter)

Unfortunately, the extensive nature of the fell can make it hard to gather cleanly and sometimes a breeder will miss a mare and foal. Sometimes, ponies come home after being missed for over a year; and sometimes they never come home and you don't know if they have died or been stolen, unless someone finds a body when gathering sheep. In the 1990s David Trotter's daughter Lynn almost certainly had a good driving Fell stolen with a Hackney cross foal at foot, because they never found the mare or the foal.

These motorbikes, the quads, have revolutionised the job; because now you get right side of the ponies and they'll come home, absolutely no problem at all. You would walk up before. I think I've only once ever brought them in on horseback. It would probably nearly kill me... when you're not used to riding, and then you go and do a job like that for two or three days, you feel like you've been run over by them, not ridden them! But aye these quads, they're marvellous, you can go up and find the ponies. But then again sometimes you don't find them! Even so it still takes you two days. I mean I helped Bill [Potter] and Colin [Roberts] to gather, this spring. I did 30 mile; we all did 30 mile and we all went different ways... (Thomas Capstick)

Henry: We used to gather on foot. Shanks' mare – Shanks' pony... Used to go over in Land-Rover right to t'other side, then we set off back.

Ivan: ...Rather like beaters – Used to take us to t'far end and let us go!

Henry: Nip on bike now and it's nowt of a job.

Ivan: Only trouble we used to have... Bill Benson, he used to have an odd 'un or two didn't he – and when you fetched them out of Swindale around that top by Tailbert —

Henry: — nearly get 'em halfway and those two'd scuttle out for Shap Abbey, to go home.

Ivan: Once you got 'em down below t'cement road they used to follow away round, but these two used to take 'em you see. (Henry Harrison and Ivan Alexander)

Until very recently the European Union and DEFRA have, effectively, encouraged farmers to overstock the fell with sheep for the sake of the subsidy on each ewe, whether she produced a lamb or not. The resultant overgrazing on some areas has now forced a change of policy towards 'conservation.' The devastation of the sheep flock by compulsory culling during the foot and mouth outbreak of 2001 revealed very clearly how strong was the influence of the sheep: the following year saw a huge change on empty fells, with normally short-cropped grass flowering several feet high and nettles and thistles appearing from nowhere. Breeders not only commented on the difference that the lower sheep numbers had made to the ponies, but said that until the 1950s nobody fed hay to animals on the fell. There were lower numbers out there, which could survive on the grazing that was available. Increasing numbers forced supplementary feeding, but there was no such thing as a 'feeding right' – only a grazing right.

I've a feeling since foot and mouth there haven't been as many sheep on the fell and the mares have sucked the foals better. Mine seem to have grown better these last two or three years (whether it is that I've been taking them off – but then, they were taken off before that!) And handled inside, they're getting a better start I think now. It stands to reason if there's more for the mothers to graze at, you know, they're getting plenty of grass and that; I'll not say there used to be twice as many sheep but there used to be a heck of a lot more sheep. (Chris Thompson)

If you put any feed out on that fell, nobody officially can stop anybody else's stock from eating it. Cause there is a thing where you can't dog anybody else's stock from the fell. I once looked through that 'fifty years back' column in some of the old newspapers, and there were people fined at Ravenstonedale for dogging other people's stock away. (Barry Mallinson)

The general feeling given by all the breeders in conversation is that so long as the numbers of any one species are not excessive, mixed grazing with cattle, sheep and ponies works best.

THE LOW-MAINTENANCE PONY

This chapter is not really intended as a compendium of 'Fell Ailments' but a brief note of a few things that occasionally trouble the Fell pony keeper, and some remedies that Fell pony breeders have suggested for them. Adult Fells are 'constitutionally as hard as iron.' Their inheritance from centuries of ponies who have lived all their lives on the fell makes them hardy and self reliant. You might compare them to tough, compact alpine plants, well adapted to flourish in harsh conditions. However, unlike alpines, Fells don't usually rot away and die of the transfer to an easier life in the lowlands!

Paul May MRCVS, of the Paragon Veterinary Centre just outside Penrith, gave this opinion of their constitution:

You don't see an awful lot wrong with them. Of the horses we see, Fells are no more than ten per cent, because they don't tend to ail a lot. When they do ail something, if they've got a bit of a bump, then because they're not doing high level competition, owners will just give them time off. The ones that are constantly coming to our door are the Thoroughbreds and Warmbloods that are always doing something to themselves; you've no sooner turned them round than they're back again. You just have to look at the horses in our stables here; it's all joint problems from what we do to them or we expect them to do.

It isn't fair to generalise completely. For the likes of

cuts, they're very variable; some of them do react. Some of them react to mud and get mud fever, but others never get it. In general you'd say they are a good, robust, reliable pet. (Paul May MRCVS)

Lush grazing

ONE of the biggest worries for a Fell owner on lowland ground is the knowledge that the ponies are bred to live on the fell where the grasses, perennial rather than annual, are thin and tough. Fells are adapted to digest less sugar and protein, and more fibre, than is usually found in lowland pasture. Ponies can eat happily for sixteen hours a day, and on the fell they use that time to travel large distances, grazing as they go: five miles a day is a conservative estimate, while I was given many instances of longer journeys. Over the year, the energy used balances their grass intake. In a more lush environment they are less likely to walk off that intake; not only is it stronger stuff but they have to walk fewer miles to get it. The result of eating to excess, as any weight watcher knows, is accumulating fat! Fat ponies in ridden work must suffer extra strain on their legs and joints, while both Barbara Bell and Carole Morland observe that fat mares tend to be harder to get in foal.

One of the fears, for an owner of a fat pony, is that it will become laminitic. Laminitis is 'an inflammation of the sensitive laminae of the foot. In Great Britain it occurs most commonly in overweight ponies... Usually only the forefeet are involved... The normal blood flow to the foot is disturbed so that some areas, notably the sensitive laminae, receive an inadequate blood supply... without which the cells become damaged and ultimately die... inflammation (laminitis) and chemical mediators (eg, prostaglandins)... cause pain. The inflammation causes swelling, which within the close confines of the rigid hoof wall, contributes to pain. The cause – over consumption of lush grass...' (Hayes, ed. Rossdale, 1987)

While Fells are not immune to laminitis (any search on the internet will turn up a story or two) they do seem less susceptible to it than some of the smaller native breeds and they can get over it.

Miss E. Firmin from Essex writes to tell us about her eighteen year old gelding, Wolds Heron, who was diagnosed as having chronic laminitis in September 1980. He was so bad no-one expected him to ever be sound again but thanks to a very good vet and farrier working together he gradually recovered. (FPS Newsletter, Autumn 1989)

Hoof care

ONE of the major attributes of a Fell is the 'hard blue horn' of its feet, and perhaps for this reason very little was said by the breeders about the care of hooves. Ponies on the fell walk over varying terrain and don't stand about in mud, and so they can wear down their hooves more or less naturally. The excessive 'turkish slipper' growth seen in neglected field-kept animals is far less often seen in ponies who are free to move long distances over extensive but sheep-nibbled grass on the fell, with no lush feed.

A tendency of Fells however – along with other native ponies – is for the hind feet to grow rather too long at the toe, which can cause stresses throughout the hind legs and quarters, and can totally alter the appearance of the hind-leg conformation.   Bert Morland demonstrated this at the Jubilee year gathering at Lownthwaite. He slipped a small block of wood under the heel of a pony's foot to show the improvement that a slightly steeper hoof angle made in the rest of the leg joints.

As the holder of a Farrier's license for many years, I would not advocate trimming your own ponies' feet without advice and supervision from someone familiar with these necessary angles. I frequently come across ponies in the show ring, when judging, that are obviously suffering from back discomfort which can easily be understood when I get close and see the angles that their hind feet are trimmed to! Trimming your ponies' feet to an incorrect angle can also result in the pony becoming sickle hocked and by putting stress on certain ligaments, can result in lameness, which would be a high price to pay in comparison to paying a farrier to do the job correctly! (Bert Morland, email on Fell Pony discussion group, 2004)

It has long been traditional for many, many generations of 'Northern Fell Men' to show off their ponies' action by shoeing their young stock for important shows such as the

Stallion Show. Many, including myself, go to the trouble of having special small shoes made which are removed soon after the show, so that growth of the foot is not inhibited. Lunesdale Henry was shod as a yearling for the Stallion Show. He is now 26 years old, has never taken a lame step in his life, and could still give start to many ponies half his age!! Likewise his son, Mountain Mist. They have both got superb round open feet and good sound limbs which early shoeing for the Stallion Show has done nothing to diminish. I have followed this policy for well over 40 years and none of my ponies have suffered any lameness or detriment. The last time that this subject was discussed by the Fell Pony Council, the late Jim Bell, of the Waverhead Stud said that in his opinion more young ponies were ruined by NOT being shod than were ruined by being shod. I agree with this sentiment. (Bert Morland, email on Fell Pony discussion group, 2004)

Catching semi-wild ponies and trimming their feet is difficult, but not impossible; in fact one of Bill Potter's ponies was once shod by Bert Morland before it was halter-broken!

Dentistry
Frank: If one had a tooth rather longer, it couldn't eat could it? Christine has a tool, and you put it in the mouth and it has a handle each side [to hold the mouth open], and the blacksmith used to come and file that tooth that was long. Twas a very very difficult job, because the horse shook its head around, and it was a terrible hard job to do it, a terrible

delicate job to file a tooth.

Christine: Now this is something we never do. We never have their teeth done.

Frank: We only got it done if it was one doing badly and we didn't know why it was doing badly, but you see because one tooth was longer, the others wouldn't shut when it was pulling the grass.

Christine: Is it just a modern fad? Or do these horses that are kept inside, on artificial food, need it? (Wales family)

As usual the answer is, some need treatment, some don't. Of my own two ponies, one has teeth that wear evenly and can be left for years without rasping. The other when bought was apparently in bouncing health, in fact looked a prime candidate for laminitis; but when I had her teeth checked routinely by Paul Chambers, he said, 'You wouldn't believe that a pony that looks like this – pig-fat – could have such big ulcerated holes in her cheeks!' She gave no trouble though and in fact was treated standing in the middle of an open field.

One of the distinctly good points of Fells is that their incisor bite is usually correct. Some judges check this in the show ring; I do myself, having learnt as a trainee from Mrs Newall and from Bert Morland. Overbites or underbites in my observation are uncommon. One would expect this to be the case, since a pony with an uneven bite cannot gather food efficiently and will do poorly on the fell.

Hair and leg care

ANOTHER good point in the breed is that Fells have very well-made legs and unlike some British ponies, dishing, plaiting or interference in their action is uncommon. Movement is generally very straight and lameness is not a common problem – they are 'hard of their legs.'

They don't have all the joint problems. Because a lot of them are used for driving, working on hard surfaces, ringbone is an issue, as are chips in the knees, and problems, such as spavin, in the hocks, but whereas you see Warmbloods who will get these at five, six or seven, Fells are getting them at twelve, thirteen, fourteen, well into their teens. And instead of seeing the acute inflammatory problems, the early joint diseases, this is something much more of mature age, a form of arthritis, wear and tear. (Paul May, MRCVS)

Fell pony feather is most at risk from muddy ground, which is seldom met with on the fell because of the extensive nature of the grazing. Some fells and some farms have soil that is likely to wear hair off the lower legs; some less so.

The fell's the place that you get the hair, definitely; if you get the one in the field, and that, it doesn't seem as if it hairs up the same as the ones that are out on the rough fell ground. Out on the fell they never find that poached ground you see; I think that's one thing that does happen. And it doesn't matter what you put on it, you can't always preserve that hair. (Chris Thompson)

Some local applications were suggested that might help the feather not to break; these ranged from pig-oil-and-sulphur to pink paraffin mixed in rapeseed (canola) oil. These also were recommended for the treatment of heel mites:

There is nothing that destroys untreated feather as quickly as mud. Our Fell ponies which are wintering high on the Cumbrian fells in their native habitat, are exposed to extreme weather, but not extreme mud! There are bogs, but they usually avoid them, and much of the high ground despite heavy rain fall stays dry. Many many times I am asked at shows in the summer why our Fell ponies have so much feather and the answer is, in addition to careful breeding, that their feather is not covered in mud all winter. For those of you who are not in a position to run their ponies on high (mud free) ground, you will retain your ponies' feather much better if you wash it once a week and apply liberally to the feather a mixture of pink paraffin and rapeseed oil (mix in a bottle one inch of paraffin to five or six inches of rapeseed oil) - the paraffin kills mites which cause 'grease' and the rape seed oil nourishes the feather and applies a certain amount of water proofer and thus helps to stop the mud destroying it. (Carole Morland)

Mud fever is another common problem with ponies who are forced to stand in muddy fields, particularly on heavy clay land. The skin behind the heels, which creases with every step, becomes 'chapped': sometimes just itchy, and sometimes cracked and painful. It's mostly the hind feet that are affected. Ponies with heel mites do a lot of stamping, and sometimes creep backwards onto projecting rocks or hedge-stumps to scratch their itchy heels. Veterinary recommendations include stabling the pony or otherwise to provide dry conditions underfoot, treat with ivermectin, and to clip off the feather to allow the skin to dry – at which the showing Fell-owner will cringe, because of the time it takes for feather to re-grow! Frank Wales remembers having to put 'chapping ointment' on the Clydesdales' legs when they suffered from this problem and were heard stamping in the stable. Chapping ointment is zinc-and-castor-oil cream. Carole Morland's recipe for preserving feather and killing mites is also useful in waterproofing the skin. I keep my used kitchen cooking oil and use an old paint-brush, and judging by their wiggly top lips, the ponies seem to enjoy the sensation of having the oil vigorously brushed into the creases of their heels.

Sweet-itch

THIS is an allergic, itching reaction to the saliva injected in the bites of blood-sucking female culicoides midges (no-see-ums). Like humans, some ponies react and some don't. The ones who do, scratch themselves on any available object, damaging stables and fixtures and fences as well as themselves. In Cumbria the midges bite between April and September, ie 'when the grass is sweet,' hence the name. In lowland situations I have seen sweet-itch sufferers (of other breeds) pair up and scratch each other endlessly, removing mane and tail hair, and often breaking the skin. Sweet itch appears to be hereditary: Mrs Newall remarked that one Fell pony she had, which suffered it, produced two foals with the same problem, but her other mares who were free of it did not. There are many suggestions that are said to help with mild forms of this allergic reaction. They range from applying proprietary oils or ointments, through feeding high quantities of garlic, to mist-spraying with human urine which deters the flies, but the only solution really is to prevent the midges biting the pony, by stabling at dawn and dusk, or by covering the pony outdoors with a light, very fine-mesh whole-body blanket.

...my Fell gelding developed sweet-itch for the first time last autumn and rubbed most of his mane out and the top of his tail was red raw. I tried every wonder potion on the market... finally came to my senses this spring when once again all the potions failed. Within days of the Boett blanket going on, Blackberry stopped rolling and went back to his calm usual self. His mane has nearly grown back to its former length and once again he looks a splendid jet black shiny fellow when we ride out. (Jenny Keen on Boett blanket web site, November 2002) This pony can be seen in the foaling photograph of Heltondale Lucky in Chapter 8.

Even this may not be a complete answer. I have known of ponies becoming so frantic with the pain of the bites that the kindest course was to put them down. Fortunately the number of Fells suffering from this allergy is small. It does not often appear in ponies living on the fell, and one can only speculate as to the reasons. Certainly the air moves more there, which would be enough to defeat the weak-winged midges, and there is very little stagnant water in which they can breed, so perhaps the ponies are living above the midges' range.

Grass sickness

I can't mind them ailing a lot bar they got grass sickness. Maybe about 1950 we had three [Clydesdales] died about hay time. And then one year we had how many Fells died with it – three or four? I took one to Edinburgh, to the Royal Dick Vet College. They don't know, they still don't know, what it is. (Frank Wales)

Fiona Chalmers wrote in the 1980 FPS newsletter that Fells in her area (Morayshire, Scotland) had had grass sickness. The illness is still being researched and has not yet been solved.

We live in an area where every year one hears of cases in the locality, and this year we ourselves had two cases. Our daughter's horse and my three Fell ponies were grazing the same ground and two of the Fell ponies got it. A five year old mare died after ten days and my nine year old gelding is now convalescent.

The mare didn't show any acute symptoms and simply gave up. She would eat nothing in the way of branmash, only occasionally nibbling at some grass, and drank nothing, eventually becoming so weak she was put down.

Some old treatments

IN earlier times it was common to dock ponies' tails. The practice was outlawed in Britain in 1948 but there were many reasons for it, not just fashion, though that came into it. Harnessed horses could sometimes trap the reins with their tails and so take control from their driver. A long tail was a nuisance when working with implements, as the hairs got caught in the equipment. Long tails became muddy and could dirty the goods or food being carried on a cart, mares urinated down their tails which could over time make the leather of their harness breeching rot and break, and overall they just involved more time and care.

I've seen us dock them… you put a bit of string onto t'tail, and you put tail over t'wall; on t'wall there was a block of wood – you put a bit of string on and held t'tail, and come down w't axe and cut it off quick. (Frank Wales)

Frank Wales: And when we fed them up to sell, you know, sometimes we took blood from them. We bled them.

Christine: A bleeding-knife looks like a modern day glass cutter. It's not a knife as such. It folds up like a penknife, but it hasn't got a blade like a penknife; it has like a roller on the end.

Frank: That was terrible sharp; and that was in like a knife casing.

Christine: They bled for everything; it was a cure-all.

Frank: If they got laminitis, then you were too late for doing it. But this is more Clydesdale horses that they bled. I've seen them take maybe a calf bucket – would it hold a gallon and a half? - they would take that much blood off a Clydesdale. And then when it settled there was that much fat on the top. Twas to stop them getting a thick leg.

The Fells used to get colic sometimes, and you know, roll. Sometimes if they got colic – you know a boiler, a set-pot? – well we used to light that, and tip hot water on their tummy, if they got colic. I've seen me trying to give one turpentine – well two prisoners of war and me. We used to put it backwards in the stall and put a halter on; then take two forks and hold its head up with t'halter; and then somebody else tipped it in. It used to sit down and all sorts. Last one I doctored, I never got any in; it never swallowed any; but it sweat that much, it mended it. You hadn't to let them lie down. You walked about with them.

They got colic if they were sweating. If it was sweating you only had to allow it to have three swallows of cold water and no more. If you brought it in and it was sweating and it was thirsty, it could swallow three times. Then you'd wait till it cooled down before it had any more. If it got more than three mouthfuls it used to 'syme'. That meant that the fat settled. The fat in its body, it cooled off too quick and the fat went hard, and they were jiggered for a long time; you couldn't work them for months.

If it got a cough you used to lap the bit in a bandage, put 'electuary' on it and lap the bit with it.

Christine: It had a strong smell, a bit like chewing a Fisherman's Friend. (Wales family)

Worming

PONIES on extensive grazing such as the fell are less likely to pick up parasites than those confined to pastures with other worm-infested animals. They are not forced to graze round recent droppings and pick up more worm eggs. Horse-specific parasites can be eaten with impunity by other species such as cattle or sheep, and vice versa, so where extensive grazing is shared with them, this effectively removes parasites from the pasture.

Henry: I don't worm them, no. I never have. Just the odd one or two if they're inside a bit.

Ivan: But then again, why were they wormed just cause they were in, rather than they weren't wormed when they were on t'fell? Because they'd more room on t'fell?

Henry: When ponies are spread out, the chance of another coming onto there is minimal.

Ivan: Mixed farming works better than one… they won't eat after themselves, will they? But put some cows in, they'll eat it off and vice versa. (Henry Harrison and Ivan Alexander)

Derrick Byas: Christmas, if and there's time, we sometimes just try and we'll worm them. Whether they need it or not! Well there was always a debate with Jos whether, actually, mares needed worming or not. We could never really get a strong decision as to Yes they needed or No they didn't. But if there happened to be a time when they were somewhere handy we could get em in, they got a dose for

the hell of it! And that's all the handling they got. We used the pen – as you go up to the allotment to fell gate there's a pen by the stone wall. It was a bit of a rodeo really. It's been like a big pen with a smaller pen in it but the walls are breaking down from where we've tried to get one or two in a corner. They sometimes got the full dose and sometimes didn't! Whatever – we did our best. We weren't really scientific – we set it to where it looked about right. But it's a bit sin' we've been up at Christmas to worm them. Obviously if we missed it didn't make a lot of difference, because they don't look any worse when they don't get any, when they're extensively grazed, and not having a lot of ponies on the fell either... (Dargue family)

David Trotter gathers wild garlic leaves to worm his ponies. He cuts the leaves up and adds them to a handful of feed along with vegetable trimmings and fruit leftovers from his grocery round. The garlic is very pungent when it flowers in May – you would not pick a bouquet and share a car with it – but the ponies seem to eat it readily. Both the wild and the cultivated varieties are well known as a gipsy remedy for all kinds of horse ailments including coughs and bacterial infections. However, feeding garlic does depend on someone being able to catch or stable a pony, and it being willing to eat from a bucket. In some cases this is difficult!

If we can handle t'mares at all we worm them. But we've started now with this pour on – you don't need to touch its mouth at all; it just goes on its skin, on its fur. You can do the wildest of ponies now and it does everything, worms, any sort of parasites on it or owt, it is 100% better, you're not apt to get knocked down. The safest way is to crowd them into a dark hull and use the quietest mare as a shield. Half the time they can't see you coming, and anyway they haven't got room to kick. (Bill Potter)

Fell Pony Syndrome

FELLS, as we have seen throughout this book, are tough. They seldom ail much; they do not give in, but survive 'the thousand natural shocks that flesh is heir to.' However, there is one problem which has become visible in the last twelve years and which has on occasion made the national press. This is a condition most usually called Fell Pony Syndrome: 'a congenital fatal immunodeficiency that commonly leads to anaemia and lymphopenia' (Thomas et al., 17 May 2003). It is a bone marrow defect, and foals die from random opportunistic infections. 'This immunodeficiency is unlike any other seen in the horse or indeed any other species, including man.' (Carter, cited in FPS *Jubilee Celebration Book*, 2002). It was first drawn to the attention of the veterinary profession by Paul May:

The first time I was aware of it was in 1993 - as long ago as that. Probably three years before that, we'd been seeing individual foals, and trying to make a judgement as to what was going on. The thing with the syndrome is that, if you've seen them as an individual, there's nothing; there's frustration there because you haven't cured it, but there's nothing that rings any great alarm bells, if they die quickly. But if

they drag on and on and on and you see the anaemia and you see how pale they become then you realise that this is something new. It took two cases – it was the third case when I realised that what we were seeing was something that didn't fit into any of the normal foal diseases.

If you look at what happens to them, they get recurrent diseases, recurrent infections; well, you can get that in certain individuals anyway, maybe ones that didn't get the full dose of colostrum, they are always weak. But by the time you've come to the third one, bearing in mind that we've said they are robust and hardy anyway, that really did ring alarm bells. You can allow the odd one, say, 'Okay that was a weak foal, and couldn't throw off infections,' but by the time you've got to the third one something starts to worry you. And then if you make it survive long enough that you start to see the anaemia as well, then that's when alarm bells ring. Then history takes over…

In the early days it was all very gloomy - because we didn't know what was causing it, we didn't know how to go forward with it. That's the trouble when you've got a completely novel disease, you can't predict anything. (Paul May, MRCVS)

We have seen throughout the book that it is usual for breeders to leave their mares to foal outdoors, and often on the fell. They bring them home just for service and turn them out again once they are served. Because of that, and the fact that ponies are normally run as part of a farm which also suffers losses around lambing and calving, occasional foal deaths are accepted, resignedly, as a natural occurrence. Chris Thompson's comments are typical of the fell breeder's observation. Although his remarks about mares losing foals after service fit right into the pattern of the syndrome, individual farmers are not ideally placed to compare clinical case notes.

I'll have lost an occasional foal, as I have had mares which I thought have been in foal, and they've come in without a one; and I've had mares come in foaled, to the stallion, and gone back and lost an odd one; but not of any consequence, just the odd one you don't worry about. (Chris Thompson)

Unexplained losses in the first few months of life could just as easily fit with an accident as into the syndrome pattern, so identifying a single common cause is difficult, and the syndrome might therefore not have come to public notice but for the work of Paul May.

Certainly in the early stages, they all seemed to scour. They all seemed to scour about the time of the foal heat. Most foals scour at that age anyway. Speaking to breeders before that time – they'd come in and say, 'Oh, I've got a foal's scoured, I need some scour medicine' or whatever; and you'd do that and you'd never hear any more. Some of those won't have survived. Some of them will have done. Natural losses are accepted – 'Well, we didn't win with this one. I've got another twenty – let's move on to them.' And it isn't until you bunch everybody's results together and realise there is something going on – unless lots of neighbours got together and

said, 'What have you lost this year?' – unless that happened, you'd know very little. (Paul May, MRCVS)

Horses are not in any case prolific animals. Mares may miss a year of production for several reasons. Examination of published Fell Pony Society foaling records in the early 20th century indicates that still births, 'slipped foals', and neo-natal deaths were fairly common. Live foaling percentages for a stallion could be as low as 29%. In 1916 for example, the FPS records show that 313 mares were served of whom 175 had live foals, making the average foaling percentage 55.9%. In 1918, only 43% of served mares had living offspring; the rest lost or simply did not produce a foal. Neonatal losses are known risks in farming, and it is pointless to whinge about them. Taking figures such as these into account, it is hardly surprising that modern losses, some of which may have been from the syndrome, were not always recognised as such by breeders. Confusingly, the symptoms of the syndrome can vary year on year and foals die from a variety of infections.

They present differently every year. What you tend to get is, you get one year when they all do one thing. One year they're all scoured, or they'll all cough; but they all do different things in different years. Two years ago we had a whole lot with arthritis, swollen joints. You can get them as early as five days. The whole thing about it is there are no rules in it. Okay, there are the average cases; you can say, yes, the average doesn't present till a month, and dies four weeks later, or whatever, but the youngest we've had was five days of age and died overnight. We've had one that didn't show until it was twelve weeks of age. Normally you can say by the time you've got through eight weeks you're safe, yet suddenly at twelve weeks it started up. So there is an enormous range there. But what happens if a foal gets a [routine] illness during that time? The only test that there is, is a bone marrow biopsy. At the moment the opinion is that, 'there's no way of finding out, so you just have to bumble through and if you've got one you've got one and it will die.' But at least if you've got an ill foal we can tell you if it is a syndrome foal or not. (Paul May, MRCVS)

Other potential tests, such as for significantly reduced levels of certain immunoglobulins, have been suggested by recent work done at Liverpool University. Breeders and vets have formulated a range of theories as to the syndrome's origin and how long it has been in existence. The working assumption is that it is genetic, but whether it is recessive or involves more than one factor, is not yet certain (June 2005). There are potential sources in genetic 'bottlenecks' (low numbers in the breeding population, or extremely widespread use of just a few stallions) one of which occurred in the years around the Second World War, and another in the 1950s. Under the Enclosure scheme, single stallions were able to be extremely influential and several were used for three successive years. However, there were FPS comments as early as 1914 about the stock being potentially inbred, due to the sire lines then nearly all coming from Blooming Heather 325, and in 1916 some stallions were so heavily used that the Board of Agriculture was moved to propose that no Fell should stand as a Premium stallion in a district for more than four years in succession. So it is difficult to say which animal might have been the source of the faulty gene, or genes.

What the researchers were trying to do was just to work back by mathematical prediction; they reckon it's some time, some people even say between the two wars, in the late 30s or early 40s. The whole breed at that stage was very poorly represented – what we are assuming is that this is a genetic mutation – it would allow that genetic mutation to become easily distributed through the breed. A lot of people said, 'Well, why has it suddenly appeared?' But you don't see it in any sort of numbers until it is pretty much right through the breed. (Paul May, MRCVS)

Dr Gareth Thomas estimates that 33-50%, and perhaps more, of Fell ponies are carriers for the condition (FPS *Jubilee Celebration Book*, 2002). A recessive genetic mutation can manifest itself whenever two animals carrying the mutated gene or genes are mated, and clearly the likelihood is increased, when the mutation is widespread, of any mating being such a carrier-to-carrier mating. The foal then has a 1:4 chance of not inheriting the gene. It will never produce a foal that will die of the disease though it might produce carriers if mated to a carrier. It has a 1:2 chance of inheriting the gene from one parent, and thus being a carrier as they are; although, barring 'normal' risks and accidents, it will not die in foalhood. It also has a 1:4 chance of inheriting the gene twice, once from each parent, and then it will display symptoms of the syndrome and die. Even from a carrier-to-carrier mating there are three chances in four that the foal will grow normally and survive. It is estimated that fewer than one in ten of Fell pony foals each year actually succumb to the disease.

For a while we thought the numbers (of syndrome foals) were reducing; but I think a lot of it just depends on how many are being reported. And it got so much bad press that you can't really blame people for not reporting them, because it was attracting all this ridiculous coverage: 'Fell Pony Plague!' At one point somebody was publishing information saying there was a secondary syndrome that they might get in adulthood. It was a total fabrication – wherever they got that from I don't know, but scaremongering like that can destroy a breed. A lot of people were saying that the breed will die out because of the scaremongering, not because of the disease.

There is all the pressure of trying to get a test out so that if anyone's worried they can get a test on the foal at an early stage. Once you've got a test, that's fine – but what are you going to test? Are you going to test the parents? Are you going to test the stallions? Are you going to test the foals when they're born? The foals when they're born, that's not controversial at all, that's fine; that just allows people to know whether they're clear, or whether they've got a carrier. Testing stallions is politically very difficult, because what are you going to do with the results? You could say,

well, nobody needs to know if it's a negative; but if everybody goes around publicising that their stallion is clear, then for anyone who remains silent the assumption will be made that theirs is a carrier.

You look back over ten or fifteen years of it and ask, 'What has it actually done to the breed? Has it severely weakened it?' I don't think it has had a major effect on it. It's caused a lot of attention to be brought to focus on the breed; but there's still plenty of Fell ponies going to shows. They're definitely not dying out. (Paul May, MRCVS)

Fell ponies nowadays probably do as well as they ever did in terms of percentage foaling rates. FPS certainly register a larger number of foals annually than was recorded 90 years ago. To put it into perspective, the 1916 stallion progeny records showed 175 foals born (not all of whom would go on to be registered); the 2002 stud book registers a global foal crop of 274 colts, geldings and fillies while the 2003 stud book registers well over 300. While this still puts the Fell within the 'endangered' category of the Rare Breeds Survival Trust (fewer than 500 breeding mares), the increasing numbers registered have to be regarded as a positive fact.

'There isn't any survived [the Syndrome] yet. My last one was to be put down; I kept it alive, it wasn't getting any better and it wasn't getting any worse, so Paul said he would start taking samples, and we just put it down. Cause we knew it wasn't going to get any better; it was just hanging on so you might as well put it down at word Go.' (Only one breeder discussed the syndrome, so I chose to leave the identity anonymous here.)

Various teams have done work on it over the past twelve years. 'Fell Pony 2000' raised funds for work at Liverpool University and at the Animal Health Trust at Newmarket. The Rare Breeds Survival Trust offered its expertise in proposing breeding strategies for use once there was a test for the disease. In 2004 an American multi-disciplinary research team has become involved, and because their findings may then be used to inform research into certain forms of congenital bone marrow failure in children, this work is likely to receive good funding and thus be carried through to a successful conclusion.

Foal syndrome is a subject that always provokes the expression of strong opinions. For Fell pony breeders the most important aspect of the research is the test that can subsequently be constructed, which will enable them to identify which of their ponies are clear non-carriers and which carry the syndrome gene

Facts about the Fell pony foal syndrome

* A fatal disease only known to affect Fell pony foals.
* The onset of the disease has not been seen beyond fourteen weeks of age.
* It is totally unlike any disease reported in any mammal.
* It is not known when the syndrome came into the breed.
* It is unpredictable in character which is why it is hard to diagnose as a purely genetic problem.
* A presumptive diagnosis is made from a combination of clinical examination by a vet and laboratory testing. Confirmation at this stage relies on post mortem determination. (Author's note: there are now tests that may be used ante mortem.)
* It cannot be confirmed as fact that it is wholly genetic but evidence so far suggests it is caused by copies of a faulty gene inherited from each parent (carriers) ie both sexes are equally important in propagating the disease.
* It affects the bone marrow resulting in reduction in red blood cell production and some white blood cells.
* In 1998 87 foals were volunteered for testing from all over the UK. Eight went on to develop the syndrome. This suggests an incidence rate of less than 10% per annum of Fell foals are affected.
* The level of incidence is unlikely to increase. The mathematical maximum is 11% of Fell foals per annum assuming breeding pairs are randomly selected.
* The disease is not likely to grow. Based on data, it is calculated that the numbers of carriers are near maximum. Therefore, the prevalence of the disease should not get any worse.
* Carriers are themselves perfectly healthy and normal ponies. It is calculated over 50% of ponies are carriers.
* Research is being conducted to develop a test for carriers and an early indicator of the disease in foals.
* It will not lead to extinction of the Fell pony. (*Fell Pony Society Newsletter*, Spring 2002)

or genes. When they have that knowledge, it will be time to choose a policy for eradicating the problem.

What it's going to need is some very very clear thinking and bold and brave enterprise, people going out there who will say, 'Look, you will destroy the breed if you just say, 'We are only breeding from A1 clear stallions!'' because those stallions may not be good breed type anyway. You look, for example, at the scrapie testing in sheep, and they are saying that a lot of the good sheep are the ones that are poorer in genetic resistance to scrapie. There is no reason why good breed characteristics should be linked with the syndrome, no reason whatsoever, but it does seem to be linked to a strong breed type of some kind. There is a possibility there that, as in scrapie, there is a genetic susceptibility but they've still got to meet the agent; and susceptible ones are more likely to succumb than non-susceptible ones. It's possible that that's involved in it. Who knows? There are so many questions. (Paul May MRCVS)

Saffron Townsend of the Rare Breeds Survival Trust points out (cited in FPS *Jubilee Celebration Book*, 2002) that in small breeding populations such as the Fell, genetic diversity can be lost much more quickly than in large ones, when genetic 'erosion' can lead to a poorer quality of animals and a higher incidence of genetic disease. Because of this, if syndrome carrier animals were simply dropped from the breeding programme, this would drastically reduce the genetic diversity and might, ironically, prove to be a very much worse choice than continuing to breed from them. It is very likely, for instance, that excellent and popular stallions, and prizewinning mares who rear excellent foals, will prove to be carriers. Do we have to stop using them because of a theoretical one in four chance (in practice, a one in ten chance) of a diseased foal? This is something that all breeders are undoubtedly thinking about, because it is they who will have to make those decisions.

While we have to acknowledge that this lethal syndrome can affect the breeding of Fells, it must not be forgotten that all Fells belong to individual breeders. They may receive advice from the society, veterinarians and the RBST; policies may be suggested, and perhaps financial incentives could even be given to support difficult breeding decisions. But, whatever the advice may be – whether it is to remove carriers entirely from the breeding programme; to minimise inbreeding; to prevent carrier-to-carrier matings; or to just trust to luck – it is what each breeder chooses to do about the syndrome, that will have far more effect than the syndrome itself on the long-term health of the breed.

Showing and Judging - and a few less obvious influences

Showing is just one of many influences on domestic breeds of animals. In some countries in the European Union, a Breed Show has the aim of examining livestock and pronouncing a definitive Yea or Nay on whether they are of sufficient quality to become breeding stock. In such an instance it would be unlikely for a gelding to be made a Supreme Champion. In Britain, however, a 'breed show' is a show for animals of the named breed, more of a testing ground where breeders seek opinions on their own animals, see which studs are producing good stock, and keep in touch with what's going on. It is also a showcase where prospective buyers can study what is available and identify farms that produce what they like. Few of the breeders have time to turn out all their own stock as a finished product, but some have formed useful long-term relationships with 'producers' (in the British sense), who are good at educating and polishing a pony's manners and performance, then showing and selling the results and thus keeping the stud name in the public eye. Showing requires dedication not only to the ponies' training and transport, but to the maintenance of a sound cash flow to support all that. Families who farm for a living seldom have time or money for the polishing of all their ponies.

A big show for any breeder is a long day out under considerable pressure. Like a family wedding there is often a long journey before and after, much cash and energy expended, lots of preparation and high expectations; but the smallest, local, shows still have very much the same holiday atmosphere as they must have had a century ago.

The tales of quality show ponies from all the studs are endless, and to tell them all would make another whole book. If I tried to chronicle everyone's successes in this one chapter, inevitably I would have to leave out great chunks of the families' achievements. Instead, I'll try to put the showing of Fell ponies into some kind of context.

Historical Cumbrian shows: Victorian times

ORTON Show was founded in 1860, when it held two classes for ponies. At its Spring Fair on 3 May 1862, Orton village offered a prize of £1.10s for the best Agricultural stallion and £1 for the best pony stallion. Eight miles away, not to be outdone, Shap organised its first show in 1861. It held three classes for ponies under 13 hands, and seventeen were forward. Shap Show grew and thrived and was later described in the local press as 'one of the best agricultural shows in the district.' It was held 'opposite Brook Field - just over t' la-al Force Bridge there. That's Shap Show field.' (Henry Harrison)

In 1880 at Shap the height limit for ponies had changed to 13-2 hands, for whom there were classes for 'Mare and Foal', '2 year old' and '1 year old'. Entries for these classes were ridden or led from Shap, Greenholme, Orton, Helton, Whale, Crosby Ravensworth and Thrimby; the furthest distance travelled was about nine miles. There was a fashion at the time for the owner of a local stallion to sponsor a foal class, for example: 'Mare with Foal at foot and stinted to Jack's Delight,' a well known fast-trotting stallion bred by the Relph family from Southernby (this is not the Jack's Delight 1214, foaled 1921, who was owned by a later Relph family living at Birkett Bank, Threlkeld). Interestingly, there was a class for 'Highland pony colt or filly, saddled and mounted'; but no Fell pony classes as such.

Whereas today agricultural shows are held from mid June through till late September and are fitted in with the cutting of grass for silage, in Victorian days they seem to have mainly been held late in the year, allowing time for the hay crop to be taken. However, in the third week of July 1880 the Royal Agricultural Society held a show at Carlisle, at which there were classes for 'Agricultural' horses; Clydesdales; Suffolks; Hunters; Coaching horses and Hackneys; Ponies 13-14 hands; 12-13 hands; and under 12 hands. Horses came to this show from all over England. (Ten years later in 1890 the local Penrith newspaper reported that the show had been held in Plymouth and made £5,931 - just over £1,500 less successful than the Carlisle show).

A much more local affair, Temple Sowerby show was held in the third week of August in 1880. It had classes for agricultural horses, including pairs of them; 'Ponies not over $13\frac{1}{2}$ hands'; 'Cobs over $13\frac{1}{2}$ hands and under $14\frac{1}{2}$ hands'; 'Hackneys over $14\frac{1}{2}$ hands'; hunters; 'hurdle leapers' ('three times round the ring and over three hurdles') and cobs or hackneys in harness. The art of pure show-off driving was also alive and well in Cumbria, because there were five entries in the Tandem Harness class, a difficult discipline that still attracts many fine Northern drivers today.

Pony and cob sections were sometimes divided at 13 hands, sometimes at 13.2, and sometimes at 14 hands. No doubt this was set according to the organisers' local knowledge of a 'split' that would produce a fair number of competitors for each class. There was no definition of what type was required; the division between pony and cob seems to have been simply one of height.

In 1893 the Shap Show classes were still described as for 'ponies under 13-2 hands.' Not until 1894 do we have our first glimpse of recorded, dated, 'Fell history' when Hesket New Market held show classes specifically for Fells. In 1895 the local newspaper also reported 'Pure Bred Fell Pony' classes at Shap. M H Atkinson of Orton Hall offered prizes for foals by his stallion Just in Time (two prize winners recorded) and A Bainbridge of Shap offered prizes for foals by his pony Young Sir George (three prize winners recorded).

At Brough, 20 miles east and at the foot of the Pennines, in 1895 there were pony classes for: brood mare and foal; yearling; two year old; Dale pony; best rider; leaper; and lady's hack ('lady equestrians in the ring'). Here we have a mention of another breed, the Dale (not, at that time, Dales-with-an-S); but no classes for Fell ponies, nor even 'Brough Hill ponies.' An individual class was 'James Hunter's Special Prize for a colt or filly by Young Comet'; there were two entries, from Brough and Brough Sowerby.

Historical Cumbrian Shows: 20th Century

Frances: That's Jenny, the pony that was bought for six guineas - she had been to Ireby in 1920 to the show.

Barbara: Usually they'd ride them there.

Frances: That's what Jimmy did. (Mrs Frances Bell and Barbara Bell)

The local agricultural show was strong and healthy at the turn of the century. Margaret Wilson's photograph of Ireby Show is worth studying. There are plenty of men watching the show classes for Fell ponies and Clydesdale horses. There is not a woman in sight at the ringside; they were probably elsewhere making and serving lunches and teas, or criticising each other's sewing, baking and preserves in the 'industrial' tent. (I have

On the back is written: 'an old photo which was in three pieces which came from Grace Teasdale at Longlands. Ireby Show. Eddie's father in dark cap (Townend). Also Johnnie Little's father (Guards). And Rob Bellas' father (Moor).' Photograph courtesy of Margaret Wilson.

209

often wondered why such classes are not called 'domestic'). There is a man with binoculars watching a race - perhaps a foot race or more likely a hound trail - beside the band at the bottom of the photograph. In the background you can see the line of boards on which the 'bookies' chalked the odds at which one might bet upon the outcome of various races. Notice how little feather or spat there is on the Fell ponies' feet. They look, too, as though they have been brought in from the field that morning and groomed for the show, in sharp contrast to the highly produced show animals of today.

For some exhibitors an important consideration was the length of the rope they used to lead the pony. Mrs Newall says that some of the pony men would use it as a lunge line to get a good trot out of their animal without having to run too much. On the East Fellside of the Pennines, farmers would show their ponies even more simply, by running them loose into a ring of onlookers who closed in around them.

In those days at the shows, I've seen people come in with young ponies on the end of a very long rope and the pony would charge one side of the judge - you had to be nimble on your feet if you were the judge! (Mrs Ailie Newall)

Mrs Dargue: I remember Dad used to say that they showed them loose, didn't they, on the village green at Dufton.

Pauline Robson: When Dufton show was held on the green, people used to bring their ponies down, drive them down, and everybody used to stand round to make a ring.

Mare and foal classes are relatively tame these days, because mother and child are shown together, and suckling mares are not allowed to be shown in any other classes. Foals are no longer shown solo as they once were. In the FPS Newsletter of 1980 there is a tale from the 1960s about Jim Bell's Jenny o' the Hill who was, 'tied up to a thorn dyke at Hesket Newmarket Show while her foal was in the ring. It was quite usual to do this and naturally the mares became fretful. Jenny was tied firmly to the dyke with a strong rope halter, but where there's a will there's a way and, after a tussle unnoticed by anyone, she galloped into the ring with the thorn dyke on the other end of the rope, and there was no stopping her until she had found her foal.' Gilly Trotter - not wishing to follow the same path as the thorn bush - let go an agitated foal she had been given to hold at Blackpool Show, and it dashed into the ring seeking its foster-mother. The Bell family later avoided these trials by taking just the foals and leaving their dams at home, but this would only be possible when the foals were well grown, willing to eat and drink out of a bucket, and able to stand a long day without nursing.

Frances: Everybody takes the mare in the ring with them now, it seems to be the pattern.

Barbara: But we used to show them as foals on their own. Bim Tyson used to have the wagon at Caldbeck and we used to take them to shows, just taking them themselves without the mothers. It'll be this last 20 years it has changed. It isn't that many years since they stopped mares sucking foals being ridden; just since Breed Show [1970s]. (Mrs Frances Bell and Barbara Bell)

Gilly: We had one that mare foaled and it died, didn't it? That was Beauty. We were on our way to t'Dales stallion show and foal went to Brays over at Kettlewell to a mare that they had - they'd lost the foal. They mothered it on and took it. Then they were showing, weren't they, at Blackpool, and I was supposed to be holding this foal while they went in the ring, because they didn't want foal. Well, it set off and it danced and thingied, so I let it go, you know me, I'm not a lover of 'em. Foal obviously going to be a grey goes up to this black mare and starts suckling... so we had to sort of explain. (David and Gilly Trotter)

I have not dwelt on show results in this book because it is unfair to single out a few, when so many Fell studs produce excellent stock which may go on to win in other hands than their own. And many, many good ponies are never shown, but they are still good ponies! Showing is influential but its effects can be unpredictable and it is well to

Pictured above: Penrith Show, 1963, left to right, Barbara Bell, Jim Bell and Bim Tyson who is holding Waverhead Blossom (1st prize). W Molly was 2nd and W Jester 3rd. Bim Tyson used to drive the wagon for the Bells when they went to shows. His father was the first man to drive a cattle wagon in to Wigton auction. Photograph courtesy of the Bell family.

remember that it is just one of many ways to measure the worth of stock. It may give a stud either a good or bad reputation, yet achievements or failures in the ring can depend on so much that is circumstantial. Was the judge, for instance, competent in judging that breed? A frequent accusation is that he owed someone a favour or had a bias of some kind, and as such idiosyncrasies are entirely personal they are hard to prove or disprove. Then, how far can the owner afford to travel and how much time can he spend showing? How many quality animals of that breed were in the class? Were some local rules in force that altered the way results turned out? Is a first prize at Little Puddleworth (East) really of equal value with a win at the Royal Agricultural? A potential sire or dam can't be judged on the quantity of first ribbons it has won. Two of the most informative classes at the Fell Pony Society Breed Show are those for three ponies by the same sire, or out of the same dam, where one can judge the ability of a pony to pass on good quality to its offspring.

Cumbrian Shows: fun with Fells

THERE was a period when the FPS showed great enthusiasm for displays of the Fell's versatility, and they took part in pageants and period re-enactments of all sorts.

Molly Laing was a great one for dressing up. This photo is at Lowther - we had to sort of charge around; this one is Early Britons. This photo is the ride at Linnels... we had a great time. I made a map up to hang at the meetings, of where we actually went. It was a glorious day and the trees were so lovely... This photo was at another thing that Molly

Waverhead Magic and Leithenwater Caraway carrying a litter at Carlisle Jubilee Pageant, photograph courtesy of FPS archive/Bell family.

did - we were Border Reivers. That was a four year old, newly broken, never been to a show - well she had been to a show in hand - and that's me as a Border Reiver. It was all such fun... The whole society was on the go and full of enthusiasm; we had such laughs! (Mrs Ailie Newall)

Frances: Jimmy used to say: 'Well, Mrs Newall goes all the way down south, to a lot of shows, and to stop overnight and all that, many a time, when a lot of them doesn't know the road over Shap.' ...That's a picture of the pageant at Carlisle. [Waverhead] Magic and [Leithenwater] Caraway. That 'litter' was made with wood pegs. The ponies just had to have very little harness on. Miss Crossland was very keen; she used to come over here and go with us every night and it went on for a week; there were a lot of Fell ponies used. And I think show days was better than what they are now. Do you not think? Really? There was more fun in it.

Barbara: 'Twas more fun - it was more like one big happy family, years and years ago, really. (Mrs Frances Bell and Barbara Bell)

Everybody was much more pleasant in those days. And at the shows, at the big shows, all the different breeds, they used to mix; and you used know, oh that person has Connemaras, and if you got as far as the overall championship, you knew all the people. (Mrs Ailie Newall)

Presentation

WHILE the straight-from-the-field tradition was fine for the pony that only went to one local show a year, to show at the county and national shows really demanded a higher standard of turnout. The Charltons and Mrs Newall explained the requirements of production for the show ring. It isn't so much the polish on the top that is important, as the work put in behind the scenes. Careful selection and patient training, regular schooling kept short and including much variety, are keys to producing a pony for the ring. Then there is 'strapping' - strong massage on the large muscles of the pony's body on the neck and quarters with a leather pad or a 'wisp' made of twisted hay. Add to this good feeding and plenty of exercise, and you would end up with something worth watching.

Sarah: You've got to have a good pony; you've got to produce it right; and you've got to present it right. It's no good going into the ring and showing a pony that won't trot up, won't canter, or what have you. So you've got to get it right. You've got to start off with the basic goods.

Bob: We use 'show sheen', but that's about it. In the old days they used to use paraffin. It was good and it kept the flies off. Baby oil though - when you've done THAT [smoothing action by an inspecting judge] on the tail - YACH! (Bob and Sarah Charlton)

They were always groomed properly, and rugged-up; I have exercised over-fat ponies in a jute rug, to sweat the fat off them, because that's the only way to get the fat off the Fell pony. Now, you see, they just wash their ponies the night before; a lot of show horses are like that. But it's the strapping brings the muscle up.

I used to do a lot of schooling - not a lot of time, but just before you went out on a ride; take them into the field for quarter of an hour; and they did lots of circle working, both legs, and turning in a circle both ways, and standing still, you know; and going round walking, then breaking into a trot, halting, reining back, breaking into a trot, halting and walking, breaking into a canter; cantering in a straight line, on each leg. I had a lot of teaching; I went to a very good place when I was at boarding school, which taught me all these things, and how to change your weight, and which leg to use, and how to not pull on their mouths, and I was given all that knowledge; and it worked. You'd to work harder with a Fell of course, but they became just as good as anything else. That girl, Metcalfe's sister in law who was doing that passaging at the clinic a few weeks ago - I could do all that on Jim at the trot, and leading with one leg to the other; I could stand him still and passage standing still. They're very intelligent, Fells, if you just give them the time. The riding ones were given at least an hour out on the roads, where they would get a bit of cantering, and perhaps somewhere there was a log lying, jump them over it; you know, we'd give them an interesting ride, and see things. And they were always glad to come in, in the spring, and get toshed up; and they were always glad when the show season's over

- 'Oh it's time for me to go out and be free! And grow my woolly coat for the winter!' (Mrs Ailie Newall)

Preparation of course did not stop a cheeky Fell from upsetting the organised routine. I can remember chuckling at the baffled look on Bob Charlton's face when he realised he had lost Linnel Romany Boy at the Stallion Show one year. The 'naughty boy' was quite determined not to be caught again but the combined guile of the spectators outwitted him.

Sarah: We couldn't keep a head collar on Romany Boy.

Bob: The Stallion Show once or twice was on a disused Army camp at Lowther on the Askham side - did you come to that? Anyway I was showing him that day, I don't know why, and round we went, and as I came out, suddenly I thought Hell, I've just got a rope and no horse. We had sewn the headpiece of the halter in to his head with black cotton, totally fixed it, and he still got out and snapped it. And of course he galloped off in amongst the bodies and under the trees and so on; it was quite funny, 'cos he was a nice horse, but he was a naughty boy, and I remember there were about fifteen or twenty of the farmers, they saw it all happen and they just went down and they did a circle and they all walked in until he got to the trailer. Then he was a bit awkward, but they brayed him and he went into the trailer loose. (Bob and Sarah Charlton)

That Stallion Show at Lowther was in a nicer location than the old 'Foundry Field' in Penrith. Mrs Newall remembers attending it with Roundthwaite Lucky Jim. He was a gentleman and never allowed to become otherwise.

This is Lucky Jim at the Stallion Show, at the back of the slaughterhouse in Penrith - d'you remember that? No? it was terrible - That's him at 24 at the Stallion Show. He won the riding class. I'd take him to the Stallion Show, in the little trailer; tie him up outside it, and he behaved perfectly, never did a thing. That's Peter Dean hunting him! He was tall - legs down here - I used to lend Jim to Peter for the winter and he did the Pony Club things, and hunted and that. I said, 'Now you're not to teach him to jump! Because I'm not having him jumping out of fields and crashing down walls!' (Mrs Ailie Newall)

Roundthwaite Lucky Jim aged four, when he was Fell champion at the Royal Show, 1956.

Lucky Jim's breeder was Jim Thompson of Roundthwaite. Bert Morland, who was his neighbour, used to give him a hand, and so became involved in showing, 'through Jim Thompson, who lived next door. He had one or two he used to show; a two year old and a yearling; I used to help him to show them for a few years.' Without help, for the 'one-man-band', it could often be difficult to get to shows at all.

I didn't see much of what was being shown years ago. It's only since I started farming on my own, since 1990, that I've been my own boss, that I've been able to go. The stallion show, I've always tried to go to that, but I've always had to be back to milk. You've to be there for milking morning and night; you have. So when I started having to stay back perhaps for the championship, with old Prince, I sometimes got a mate to go and milk for us. (Thomas Capstick)

Roundthwaite Lucky Jim had only been broken to harness a fortnight and he won down at the Ponies of Britain Show at the Great Yorkshire Show. We had to be in fancy dress for some reason - and the judge got in, driving, and she said, 'Do you do a lot of driving with him?' and I had to say airily, 'Oh - yes - quite a bit!' (Mrs Ailie Newall)

Judging
THE judges were very thorough in those days. You want to measure the bone, see if their teeth are OK; you just say 'nice pony' [gesturing as though rubbing a knuckle over the pony's muzzle and lips] and you can feel it. (Mrs Ailie Newall)

If you go into a show ring, doesn't matter if you're just spectating, horses, cattle or what, you think to yourself, well, if somebody asked me to take home what I liked, it wouldn't always be what judge liked! Or anybody else. (Ivan Alexander)

If we're going to encourage people to breed the best, the judging's got to be the best, because people are going to go away from a show thinking, 'Well, that's what we've got to breed.' (Bert Morland)

You should look through the 'production' to see which is the better pony. (Bob Charlton)

In the Fell's home country, showing is entertaining because there are so many immensely competent and opinionated spectators around the ring who freely pass judgement on the quality of the judging as well as the worth of the stock! However, where that factor is not present, judges need to know the breed standard very thoroughly, and they need to be strong enough to make decisions in the ring that reflect whether the exhibits are representative of that standard. It's hard for breeders to uphold a standard if the judging fraternity doesn't know the standard well enough to reward it when it sees it.

There can be fashions in judging breed classes. One does not have to look back very far in more rapidly-breeding animals such as dogs or cats to realise how thoroughly a breed can be changed yet still ostensibly have the same standard. In the late 1970s, my Siamese cats' idea of a rollicking good afternoon's fun was to go out hunting and bring back anything from a live rabbit out of the wood to a five-pound roasted chicken, whole, sneaked out of the back door from a kitchen in the next street. However, when I last went looking to purchase a kitten in 2000, instead of the six or seven in a litter from which I was used to choose, there would only be two or three. They all appeared to be dainty, delicate-boned fireside creatures unable to survive without vaccination against several deadly diseases. Fell generations are rather longer than cat generations but Heaven help the ponies' physical and mental health if 'fancy' or 'production' breeders discover them and promote their own vision of 'perfection' as the breed standard. It has happened to other breeds.

Anne Sutcliffe pointed out in her 1981 book, *Breeding and Training a Horse or Pony*, (p23-24) that the Arab 'is a very beautiful animal, and because of this many breeders have kept Arabs for show purposes alone.' Arabian mares were bred regardless of conformational defects or flighty temper, which did not matter in the stud paddocks, but of course when a gelding from the third or fourth generation was bought to be trained for riding, accidents happened. There were sound, sensible strains of Arabs who performed well in endurance work, working hunter classes and even competitive driving, but the bad press of the untested 'show' stock gave Arabs generally a doubtful reputation. It wasn't the judges but the irresponsible breeders who were at fault. We are fortunate that the Fell breed at home is guarded by outspoken characters such as we have met in this book.

Showing and judging overseas

MANY British Mountain and Moorland breeds are known across Europe, America, and Australasia, and the Fell too is spreading. Shows have been held in recent years for Fell as well as other M&M breeds, and appear to be on the increase. Some invite judges from Britain, and others do not, and as the years go by and numbers of shows increase, British judges are inevitably going to be less frequently invited than more local ones. That is understandable on the grounds of cost and accessibility, but there may be a tendency for show results to favour the types that the local area finds appealing. There are already little nuclei of people outside Cumberland and Westmorland who appear to think they are 'improving' the breed by making the range of Fell types converge into one: in some places, modelled on another fashionable breed; in others as a sport pony or a draught animal; a totally black pony without white markings; a long necked, high headed or flashy actioned pony, or one that is consistently up to height; it does not matter *how* they redefine the breed. Such leanings towards 'improvement' may be acceptable in one breeder's choices for his own stock, but they narrow the genetic base of the breed if they are imposed on everyone. Fells were not purpose-bred and of one exclusive type. They were 'just always there' in the background, versatile and useful, so their variations within the breed standard should be kept because they are healthy.

Height in particular is a thorny question. If ponies born overseas grow taller than the breed standard allows, is that because of feeding, management practices, or the original export of taller stock who are genetically more likely to breed tall offspring? What can be done about it? Rescind their registration? One hopes the poor ponies would not then be born to a starvation regime just to keep them from going over height. It could be argued that people are taller and heavier than they used to be in Victorian times, and need bigger ponies - such arguments can put serious pressure on breed standards - but I don't think any of the breeders would take a 14.2 hand pony seriously as a Fell.

Less obvious influences

SHOW judging is very easy to criticise, and most spectators do so! Magazines and newspapers, breed newsletters and photographs remorselessly chronicle its effects. However, there are also supporters and promoters who have influence within a breed behind the scenes. Such people are energetic and resourceful and often the salt of the earth; where would our breed societies be without them? It's the volunteer committees and sub committees who run the shows, print the newsletters, tend the archives, man exhibition stalls and sell everything from teas to T-shirts. Visitors to country shows will often know them better than they know the people in the ring, and certainly better than they know the judges. Most supporters in the Fell's home area really know their stuff and they willingly share their knowledge, because so many are also breeders themselves.

Breed societies occasionally decide to enforce restrictive

rules across the board. Simple examples of this are FPS decisions at various times to debar piebalds, skewbalds and chestnuts, and only to register foals out of registered stock. In recent years however they have cautiously amended the breed standard so that it 'discourages' excessive white markings but still allows registration of ponies that have more than the earlier permitted 'small white star' or 'little white on the hind feet.' There are very good reasons behind this. The Fell is still too short of available breeding stock to take otherwise good ponies out of the gene pool without good reason, and registrations of white marked ponies have not increased significantly over the years. Breeders may well choose not to register or breed from mismarked ponies but that is still their own decision, not an edict from the society. It is more important to value the animal that is true to its type in its home area; that can live as the breed does under normal circumstances; and that, most importantly, is healthy, built right to work well, be safe and versatile and stay sound. Only after that do we need to worry about other cosmetic criteria such as quantity of hair, colour or white markings.

Supposed origins and 'history'

ANOTHER thing that is worrying is that the energetic breed supporter outside the home area sometimes gets a wrong handle on something relatively simple and then vigorously publicises it. For instance, a common and fairly recent promotional line links the Fell and Friesian breeds by their modern appearance alone - ie, black colour and length of hair. This supposed Romano-British 'history' is an attractive myth which I am going to tackle here, because it does crop up frequently in conversations with non-Cumbrians about Fells, and it upset breeders when they first heard the term 'mini-Friesian' as a new 'spin' on the breed.

Clive Richardson, whose well-known and definitive book *The Fell Pony* (1990) is a much-quoted source for this topic, has pointed out in more recent discussions that the modern Friesian is nothing like it was even three centuries ago, let alone two millennia. While Frisia did contribute auxiliaries to the Roman Army in the North, the men who manned Hadrian's Wall came (in alphabetical order) from countries now known as Algeria, Belgium, Bulgaria, South West and Eastern France, North Germany and the Rhineland, Greece, Holland, Hungary, Iran, Iraq, Italy, Morocco, Romania, North and North West Spain, Switzerland, European Turkey, Syria, Tunisia and Wales (see www.hadrians-wall.org, 2004). Cavalry are indeed likely to have brought some of their own war horses with them, because not to do so would be like taking a tank regiment overseas without any tanks, and this may possibly have been a source of foreign equine blood to cross with the local British pony; but that could have happened *anywhere* in Britain where the Roman Army penetrated. Until the conservators of the Vindolanda tablets decipher a Roman military stud list, we can only deduce the types of horses in the Fell's homeland from the bones recorded in archaeological digs. We know nothing specific about whether there were any long-sustained crosses, the numbers that were bred, how many crossbred horses might have been kept as breeding or working stock, or how many offspring survived to produce further generations. It is equally possible that there were dark coated ponies all over Britain and Western Europe from which several modern breeds descend and that the Roman Army had little or nothing to do with any of them.

Admittedly, physical similarity between a few modern specimens may make the phrase 'like a small Friesian' into a useful introduction for people who have not seen the Fell breed at home, but why place undue emphasis on supposed events that are so far back in the past as to be nearly irrelevant? The difficulty with the Fell enthusiasts who advertise the breed with the nice 'nugget of Roman history' is not that they are changing history, but that by making a fuss about the Friesian they may turn the Fell pony in the 21st century into something it probably never was, just by talking about it too often and too loudly and changing people's expectations of the breed.

This is not strictly a chapter about history, so with apologies I am going to jump over the intervening centuries to more recent times. If there is any Friesian influence on the Fell, here is a much less romantic story! In the 17th century, Dutch drainage experts came into Norfolk to drain the Fen country, bringing with them trotting horses that contributed to the Old English Black, later the Shire. There

used to be chestnut and roan coat colours in the Friesians, which rigorous 20th century selection has bred out, but which at the time might have passed into the Norfolk trotting cobs. Such 'roadster' blood might have contributed any of those former Friesian colours to the Fell, which were certainly in the breed in the early days. Of course it must equally have carried something of the 'trotting cart horse', from which the Norfolk cobs originally sprang... but we hear nothing about that! A cynic would say that this is because the Norfolk Cob and the Shales breed are almost unheard of nowadays and thus no use for promotional purposes. If this Norfolk cob input has been smoothed over by the passage of time, so must any Friesian influence have been. It does the Fell no favours to market it commercially as a small version of an entirely different breed.

Other 'alien blood' in the foundation stock
FELL pony breeders of the late 19th century were not originally breeding 'a Fell pony' or even a pony for sport or work, but 'a useful sort.' Some fancied crosses with the Highland, Welsh cob, Dale or Hackney as well as Norfolk Roadster 'types', as recorded in the early parts of the Fell Stud Book: Norfolk Swell, a 14.2 or 14.3 black Norfolk Cob; Yorkshire Fashion, a 15 hand 'pure Dales cob', but also said in some registrations to be by Norfolk Cob; Daybreak, by Norfolk Cob. C W ('Kit') Wilson bred fast, strong-actioned ponies from Fell (and Welsh) mares by his famous stallion, Sir George, who traced to Flying Childers

and Darley's Arabian, through horses that we would now classify as Arabians, Thoroughbreds and Hackneys.

In the early years of the society there were indeed registrations which recorded blood from outside Cumberland and Westmorland. There were local strains such as the Dargues' grey trotting ponies, some of which had been bred to the grey half bred Arab stallion, Telegraph, whom we have met already in *The Next Generation*. Frank Garnett, the Secretary for the Northern Committee of the National Pony Society, wrote in 1914 that the Highland 'Galloway' Pony and the Fell Pony were of the same foundation breed, whose stallions had been used interchangeably 'time out of mind,' and that such crosses were to be recommended for bringing in fresh blood. Given this statement, and the clear records of Dales stallions in the breed, it is curious that so few Highlands (Glengarie, perhaps Highland Laddie and Mountain Hero 2nd) are noted in the early compilations of the NPS Fell section.

Broken-coloured ponies included The Mikado 200, a 20-mile-an-hour trotter who was skewbald ('black-brown with tan and white hind heels') and, like Sir George, was said to trace back to Flying Childers; Park End Fanny 4503, a black and white mare by Park End King; Sporting Times 916, a black and white stallion out of Park End Fanny by Valence Heather; and his son Sporting Times II 1328 out of a mare by Daybreak. Daybreak was by Young Comet, who was out of a mare by Comet II (from the Bousfield stud at Orton) and therefore carried the Welsh Trotting Comet blood line.

The point here is that the earliest registrations were just local ponies within the 'Fell' area defined by the Polo and Riding Pony Society. The aim was to identify tough, hardy foundation stock, to be top-crossed with the Throughbred or Arab to get fast, sound weight-carrying riding and polo ponies. The Board of Agriculture and Fisheries appointed a committee to consider the Mountain and Moorland breeds in 1912.

Observing that the M&M breeds were of common origin with the same characteristics modified by the environment, it was the opinion of the committee that these characteristics should be recorded with all the available history of each breed. Believing that all native ponies were descended from the ancient British pony, they attributed the various types firstly to their surroundings; secondly to their treatment by man; thirdly to selection for the work they had to do; and lastly, to the attempt made at different times to improve the herds by the introduction of crosses of more or less alien blood (Fitzgerald, 2000, *The Dales Pony*)

'Dales' vs. 'Fells'

THE Fell Pony Committee in 1916 must have been aware of the ease with which a foundation breed could be altered and perhaps lost completely with the introduction of such 'alien' blood, and at their spring meeting in 1916 they agreed to discourage the cross with the high-actioned Wilson type stallions, which 'had too much Hackney character for local needs.' Mares also had to be of approved Fell Pony type if their owners wished to breed them to a Premium Fell Pony stallion. By the 1920s, the only 'alien' stallions that the Fell Pony Society permitted to be used on Fell mares, were from the Dales breed.

A few random examples of Dales stallions in the Fell Stud Book are Dalesman, 14 hh (572 in Dales Stud Book); Teasdale Comet (904 Dales) who was a 14.2 grey; Brown Jock, 14.3 (973 Dales); possibly Yorkshire Champion, brown, 14 hh, though the breed is not stated. The progeny of Dales stallions, it must be remembered, were allowed to be registered. But gradually, fewer Dales were seen in the Fell registrations.

It's type as much as anything; today I think there's quite a bit of difference between the Fell pony and the Dales pony; more than there used to be, definitely. (Chris Thompson)

None of the breeders talked of using Dales stallions in recent years, but it was common enough to use one in the first half of the 20th century. Fell stallions were sent over the Pennines to be used on Dales mares, while Dales or dual registered stallions were certainly used on Fells, before their use was prohibited by the FPS. Some people, such as the Charltons, the Hullys, Walter Tuer and Joe Baxter, kept stallions of several types at the same time. In 1952 for instance, Joe Baxter owned a 'vanner', a big black cob cross type

with a white star and white hind feet; Brown Berry (a Dales); and Master John, a Dales who was also registered as Fell 2883. He was the final stallion to travel to Fell mares, and his last foals were produced in the early 1960s.

Hutchesons at Wythwaite, they had more like half Dales. It was quite common, to get a bigger pony to work with, for the smaller farmers, because they didn't have the Clydesdales. They'd maybe have just the one Clydesdale, because the Clydesdale was a big stint. So you got a horse that was more capable of doing agricultural work on a small farm. We never used a Dales stallion; but my Dad'll have sold two or three stallions to go onto Dales mares. (Frank Wales)

...that Black Jock II, he was a Dales; I don't think he's been up here [Shap] but when you look in t'Black book he's there; he's come out of t'Dales side. But it was allowed, wasn't it? (Ivan Alexander, talking with Henry Harrison)

They weren't a very unique set-out; they varied quite a bit. Fell ponies did, then. They were nothing like as unique as they are nowadays; strong Dalesy types, a bit more than a pony. Well they used to work, you know, on farms, up Uldale. (Ted Benson)

It is sometimes forgotten these days that one of the areas of Fell pony breeding was centred on Middleton-in-Teesdale, on the east side of the Pennines, an area now more associated with the Dales breed. The exchange of stallions over the great watershed was common enough from the outset, although the formation of the Dales Pony Society at the end of 1916, and the resolution of the Fell Pony Committee in the same year to become a Fell Pony Society, indicated a strong feeling that there were in fact two types of pony in the Pennine area, the smaller, western, Fell, and the larger, eastern, Dale. The 1920s saw a general resurgence of interest in native breeds, such as the foundation of the Exmoor Pony Society in 1921 and the Highland Pony Society in 1923. In 1922, the FPS re-formed itself on more liberal lines to attract more members to support the Fell breed. But for another thirty years the ponies of the Pennines were considered similar enough for ponies to be registered within either the Dales or Fell stud books, the choice of which register the foals should go in depending on the registration of the dam and following the convention of tracing the female line.

'Although there was general agreement that cross-bred Dales and Fells should be registered in the dam's Stud Book, the progeny of the Dales mares Robinson's Gipsy and Linnel Dale, Dell, Dinkie, Coquette, Lady (by Sir Horace) and Linnel Belle II (out of Stanhope Beauty) had all been absorbed into Fell stock. Of the 30 Fell colts entered in Volume 25 all but one had Dales Grand-sires or dams or both. All the 101 Fell mares of known breeding had Dales forebears in at least one line.' (*Iona Fitzgerald*, 2000)

Naturally Fitzgerald's argument works both ways! Fell stallions were still permitted to serve Dales mares in the late 1970s, but not vice versa. In 1948 the Fell Pony Society had ruled that the progeny of Dales or other stallions out of Fell mares 'may not be registered until it is two years old except by discretion of the inspectors.' These steps were taken towards separating the two types of ponies, but the occasional exchange still took place, which was no doubt healthy because it brought fresh blood into both gene pools, which for most of the time were developing separately on either side of the Pennines.

A hundred years ago we're not necessarily talking 'the breed' but a type that was HERE - which is why we have problems pulling the Dales and the Fell apart when you go back that far. (Sarah Charlton)

In 1958 the resolution was passed by the FPS that 'no colt or stallion may be registered on inspection only, but that both sire and dam must be entered in the Fell section of the NPS Stud Book.'

An even less obvious influence: Official vs. 'real' pedigrees

PEOPLE sometimes ask how accurate pedigrees are. It is hard to answer this question. In the beginning breed societies were gentlemanly and trusted owners and breeders. Records depended on people filling in and returning service slips and registration forms. Breeders were very likely to want this information recorded correctly, though many were slow at actually submitting details to their society. In Vol VI of the FPS newsletter (1983) the Editor pleaded for pony registrations to be 'meticulously recorded in every detail.' But tracking ponies through sales, private or public, depended on the readiness of buyers and sellers to inform the breed society of a change of ownership. It is obvious that not everyone would have found it vital to do so, but one cannot begin to estimate how many that might have been.

There wasn't that many about - not registered. I remember Jos Dargue telling us - and they've had Fells as long as he could remember - that you can only go a limited way back because as he said, a certain amount weren't registered. Up these fell areas, they were Fell ponies and a Fell type stallion used, but they weren't registered. Farms'd have a 'black Fell' - no pedigree - a work hoss, and they thought, 'Oh well, we'll join t'society and we'll have a foal out of it,' and that's where you set off at. But they were proper Fells. They weren't inspected at first, were they, that came a long time after. (Ivan Alexander talking with Henry Harrison)

Lots of the earliest ponies registered were indeed simply named ponies of Fell type out of a 'Fell pony' mare. Many did give the female line for three or four generations previously, but occasionally neither parent's name was given.

Until the advent of blood typing, DNA testing, microchipping and age limits on registration, there may have been many reasons why the recorded details might differ from the real pedigree of a pony. For instance, breeding

on the fell itself might require 'guesswork' in identifying the stallion in a pedigree. His identity will only have been a certainty on the commons where only one herd ran, or where no entires were permitted at all, so that all services had to be on enclosed in-bye land and under a degree of supervision, if not actually performed in-hand. But on the Howgills, certainly until the 1980s, several different herds would run with their own stallions, and on the Heltondale Fells it is still possible to run stallions out during June, July and August. Only 'heaf' instincts would keep those bands of ponies apart. Clipping time for sheep is also June, July and August, so if the local farmers disturbed and mixed-up the herds when they were gathering sheep, who could swear that foals born eleven months later were from one stallion or another? Sarge Noble recalled a nine-mile trek by a stallion to serve a mare. There was a possibility that odd colts could escape the autumn gathering, remain on the fell entire until they were mature and so sire foals. Owners would make an informed guess about which fell-going stallions were responsible for which foals, but there was no cast-iron certainty.

Until very recently, too, the droves of foals that went to the autumn sales were sometimes registered and sometimes not. Dealers would buy a bunch of ponies - in the case of Fells, so many black or brown animals who were often undistinguished and wild - and collect them by the wagonload at the end of the day. The poor and raggedy colts, the types so often bought by the meat man, would seldom be registered, but there was potential there too for confusion. Breeders knew all their own of course, and ponies were identified for sale purposes in the same way as cattle, by a round or oval paper number stuck to their rumps with a thick dab of brown glue combined with their 'yellow form' by which registration could be applied for. But even if the numbers were recorded, eventually they were removed or wore off and you just had a bunch of rather similar ponies in the field. With the best will in the world, there might have been uncertainties later about which papers went with which ponies and whether or not they had in fact been registered. The same kind of uncertainties arose through sales at Appleby Fair.

Them gippo lads, they didn't care anything for t'papers. They'd come on to me or Sarge - 'What've you got on to sell?' - and take whatever we'd got, and take 'em to sell on Fair Hill there. I'd sometimes give 'em papers but you'd know they weren't going to be passed on, cause they were like that, papers meant nothing to 'em, they were just a nuisance. They just wanted the pony. Then months, even years later, someone down south would ring up and say they'd bought a pony, and they'd been told it might be our breeding and were there any papers! If they sent us a snapshot, maybe we'd recognise the pony and be able to tell them what it was out of. But sometimes we couldn't. (David Trotter).

Then again, people lost their own ponies' certificates; sometimes families even lost interest in breeding Fells. For example, Norman Handley's family at Haygarth had been breeding ponies for years, yet Mrs McCosh observed in a FPS newsletter that by 1946, due to the difficulties of wartime the ponies had become very crossbred; and in the 1960s good quality ponies from their herd either had not been registered, or their certificates could not be found.

For 30 years, good Fell type mares and geldings could be accepted into the stud book by inspection. This is not the case now. Sometimes a breeder will have sold the pony without registering it because he felt it was not worth the expense; either it did not show the quality he wanted to represent his name, or it had a bad fault that he did not want to pass on within the breed. Much as the society might like to help enthusiastic new owners, it would be impossible for them to identify such ponies.

While we have all heard of crafty 'horse-trading' such as most people blame for 'wrong' pedigrees, the tales I have heard at first-hand over the years came mostly from the mid 1960s and the dealers involved are long dead. They did have the qualities that 'horse trading' has come to typify, attempting to pass off an aged, grey-faced mare as a three-year-old, or a gelding as a filly; but they dealt in other breeds as well as Fells, so any irregularities they may have caused are not confined to our breed! If a dealer sold a pony whose buyer chose to leave the certificate behind for any reason, there was little to stop him applying that to another pony of Fell type. One, at least, used to collect spare certificates from the gipsies moving south after Appleby Fair!

A little preliminary conversation with buyers would give enough information about their expectations to ensure a pony could be 'fitted up' with a certificate that suited. For sales to other dealers, no doubt it was done more off hand-edly, 'What breed is it? What breed d'you want it to be? Well, ratch in the kitchen drawer there, you'll find a certificate that'll fit it.' Later such a mare would not be inspected for type in order to breed, because the owner would already have the necessary papers. There was nothing to stop a colt with 'creatively applied' papers being sold entire. If it was good-looking and a typical Fell, had good feet and legs, a neat head, moved well and straight and didn't have too much white, it might be licensed as a stallion. It might even have gone on to be an influential sire, and who is to say the breed was any the worse for that? Such ponies were just as likely to be 'proper Fells' as were the first recorded generations of Fell pony stock, or even the 'inspected' ponies; they just might not be the same 'proper Fells' as the names written on the paperwork!

I am going a long way round here to explain that if you take an interest in pedigrees you may gain useful insights into the general history of the breed, but the further back you go into the mists of time, and the more stallion lines and changes of ownership you encounter, the more inaccuracies can accumulate in the data, and the bigger pinch of salt you need to take before you believe absolutely in the distant pedigree of any particular animal.

On the other hand, the lines that have descended through mares in the hands of one family over generations, have an almost religious quality of accuracy. 'I've heard it said that if you haven't got a mare line, you haven't got a line,' said Derrick Byas. Barren mares and mares close to delivery may try to steal foals occasionally, but the ones they rear and bring home off the fell are almost certainly their own!

All breed societies will have learnt hard lessons over the years from having had to solve arguments over mixed-up paperwork, so I am sure this is not a situation exclusively found within the Fell ponies, nor is it particularly serious there. The adoption of blood typing, microchipping and DNA sampling should make it easier these days to guarantee pedigrees. But the Fell breeders themselves say that they pay far more attention to the qualities of the ponies, the faults which will need improvement in the next generation, and the progeny that ponies have already thrown. Barry Mallinson said, 'Papers, the breeding, is nothing. What's a paper if the horse is nothing? Everybody doesn't breed good 'uns. You buy the horse, you don't buy the papers.' It does not matter whether Neddy is descended from Pegasus himself; it does matter that Neddy must suit the job you want him for.

Breeders check they aren't putting closely-related animals together, and they might take into account the quality of the mare's mother or the characteristics of a prepotent sire, but they form their opinions from a vast net of knowledge of their own and others' ponies, which seldom needs confirmation from the stud book. They are inheritors of an old and stubborn local preference - in some cases, from long before 'official' records of any kind - for keeping Fell ponies for their own qualities; and it is their well-informed judgement that is the real influence on the breed. They do their best for the future, balancing knowledge and experience with hope for a bit of luck.

IDEAL PONIES

Breeders told me that they choose by eye, not from a paper; no matter how illustrious the pedigree, if the pony doesn't have quality or pass on quality, it is not breeding stock. Conversely, if a pony has good type and quality they said that its registration details matter very little. So at the end of each interview I asked breeders to pick out ponies, past or present, who showed the quality that they were looking for. Their pleasure and pride in good ponies, whether they had bred them or not, were very clear to see.

In the early days, I always thought there was two or three mares by old Heltondale Prince that Ted Benson had – that moved quite exceptional; Miss Crossland had one by him; then Brays had one by him. And Roundthwaite Lucky Jim – Jim Thompson's. They were all of a type and they were quite exceptional for the day, for the time. They varied a lot, but they can vary a lot today too. Best looking pony… you'd have to choose those that had won the stallion show a few times; Heltondale Black Prince III – because he won four times… Me and Bill Potter, we had to form a syndicate to buy Heltondale Black Prince III when we wanted him. It was just because of the quality of his stock that we wanted to buy him… And I suppose in the present day – Look at Me (p 66) — and Misty (p 84 and p 229)! I suppose she's maybe the present-day pony 'flying the flag.'

Another stallion that I think has been a tremendous improver of the breed over recent years has been Tebay

Campbellton Victor [6641]. And to look at him you would never have thought – he was 12.2, and built like a brick... he was a good looker in his own way. When he went to the summer breed show as a yearling he was in a class of his own, as far as feather was concerned, and bone. Although I never owned him, I have quite a lot of ponies got by him. These Victor mares seemed to click with Black Prince, although they were two completely different types of stallion. One of the best getters was Victor. (Thomas Capstick)

I tried to buy Tebay Campbellton Victor from Mr Trotter. I saw him at one of the shows and he wouldn't sell him! (Mrs Ailie Newall)

The morning he was born, down at Lune's Bridge, he'd silky feather right from the back of the knee to the floor. An Irish lad came over with Joe Carr, for Appleby Fair Hill; well sometimes they stayed with us. Jimmy said, 'What've you got on?' I said, 'I've just had the best foal born! what I've been trying to breed since I started, and it was born this morning.' And it was him that said, 'Will you do me a favour David?' 'Well,' I said, 'I will if I can.' He said, 'The best pony to come out of Ireland was called Campbellton Victor. Will ye call it after him?' So that's how he got his name.

The legs, and the little sweet head, and the little ears, and the mane down to his knees, that was all there. I said, 'if I can get mares and stock of that quality, I can sell 'em without papers.' And for so many years I didn't paper anything. It was when our Lynn come back from college and we were getting Victor's stock then; she says, 'What's this stock?' If it hadn't been for our Lynn, that would have been t'end of it. I would say he was the best pony I've had. Where he was good, was that he transmitted it. (David Trotter)

Best old time pony? I think without doubt Linnel Flighty; I don't think there was anything that could beat Linnel Flighty. She's gone, a long long time ago. She not only won lots of prizes, she was very rarely less than first. She hunted, she jumped, she was fun, she pulled, she was naughty, she bred some good foals, and yet anybody could ride her, as long as they could ride. I think she was probably – in my

Sarge Noble and Victor, photograph courtesy of FPS Archives and Mrs Greta Noble.

lifetime – the best. There may have been one or two others – Sandpiper [who was exported to Australia] was probably as good. And there was a pony called Sapphire when I was young. Grandfather had favourite lines; because he probably would have three, four or five of the same line. And he bred so many. Of our type I think those ones are ahead of what I call 'the Sleddale Ruth type pony.' I think Sleddale Ruth's very good – I think she won for Sylvia, the Mare Breed Championship or something? But I much preferred this type, of Sandpiper, Flighty type ponies. Again, because of the riding. So the one I'd have picked first, is Linnel Flighty. (Bob Charlton)

Sleddale Rose X, Breed Champion, 1979,
photograph courtesy of FPS Archives.

Linnel ponies had a very good name at the time, so we were showing against them all the time. Linnel Flighty was a nice pony. That was the one that I used to like. She was quite a sparky pony. (Mrs Ailie Newall)

Best old time pony? That one that's on calendar there that has a dog sitting on it – it's by Peepings Swell (p 148). It would be one of the most famous ponies, it would win at London quite a lot. In 1940s Dad got £40 for it. And Lowthwaite Star Trek (p 26), it won a lot. (Frank Wales)

Mrs Frances Bell: That's Bank House Polly (p 55). That's the stamp of them that they were.

I think I would prefer not to name ponies belonging to

*Heltondale Misty IV, photograph
courtesy of Laura Hart.*

other people, but obviously there have been many whom I
have admired. My own favourites have been Townend
Flash II [5278] (p 99); Birkett Bank Polly II; T Heather
(opposite); T Holly; T Candy; T Shula; T Dinkie; T Prince
[5118]; T Polly III (Polly III was the pony Eddie always
called his best)… and many more! (Margaret Wilson)

I've always liked the Sleddale ponies. But always a bit
long, is Sleddales, long the back. When I set off showing I
started with [16315] Sleddale Rosette VIII. She wasn't the
thickest horse, but the bone was nice bone, and I like the
action on them horses. I think that's why I've liked the
brown mare [Moorhouse Rosie]. Everybody had them;
Shap Abbey had them. They were Sleddale ponies.
Everybody seemed to want them; they used to shepherd on
them and that. (Barry Mallinson)

Going back years and years ago, my father brought a
stallion from Drybarrows where I am now, and that was
Rowland Boy [3032]. I think that was probably one of the
best that I ever knew. He was a brown pony was that one,
with four black legs and points; well he won at the stallion
show that year [premium for the Arnside Enclosure, 1946];
it was one of old Mr Rowlandson's breeding who farmed up
at High Drybarrows and he had as good a type of pony as a
lot of people. I think the best one probably that I had myself
was Drybarrows White Heather; that was a black Fell pony
of the original type. She was mother of Handy Lad. In my
own opinion, Thomas Capstick's mares are probably as good

a type of mare as anybody has. (Chris Thompson)

Tommy Capstick — he'll have as good a herd as anybody… (Ivan Alexander)

Best old hoss would be the one I got on its back as a two year old, Mountain Ranger, at Hully's. Best modern hoss: maybe Thomas Capstick's Heltondale Misty IV; as good as any I think. It's part Greenholme is that. Bert Morland's Lunesdale Rebecca; it's a good mare. (Bill Potter)

First one I had was Heltondale Princess. I think she was just about best mare I ever had. She was brown. I don't think she was as good as that mare of Bert's now, that mare he shows. There wouldn't be a lot of difference, but I think taking them all round Rebecca would be a better pony than Princess. (Ted Benson)

Bert's own comment on Rebecca is interesting. He does

Bert Morland with Lunesdale Rebecca, photograph courtesy of Fane Murray.

not run through her show achievements but remembers Sarge Noble saying he had never seen a pony that good in his lifetime. 'I thought that was the best compliment she could have had.' Sarge offered him a large sum of money for the mare. He turned it down.

I know the Bible says 'thou shalt not covet,' but I have to admit that I coveted that mare [Heltondale Princess]. I begged Ted to sell her to me on many occasions but he always refused. She epitomized all the good points as laid down by the Fell Pony Society and which Ted had always preached to me. She had good feet, joints and feather, marvellous flat bone and hocks, a beautiful head with small pointed ears and large nostrils, a well laid shoulder, good neck and short back. (Bert Morland, *A Lifetime in the Fells*.)

THE FUTURE

If we are going to look to the future we need to see what the present contains, and know what brought the Fell pony breed to where it is today. If I have done my job right, in 'reaching back' this book has provided that necessary view of the breed in its homeland. What assets does the Fell pony have that might be marketable, that need to be kept and built upon to go forward and assure its future?

As we have seen in the preceding chapters, a Fell is only considered a Fell if it is of typical appearance: a hill pony, adaptable, hardy, thrifty, and a good mother. And like all good M&M types, these ponies should have the less visible qualities of a friendly, willing nature, allied to the vigour, self reliance and brains which are vital to living on the fell.

Sarah: Father in law and Grandfather in law were interested in breeding the riding type. Then realising that the Cumbrian heavier type was what people were looking for, they had to try and get something in between, which is more marketable, more what people require or expect.

Bob: I think quite a lot of breeders have gone that middle way. (Bob and Sarah Charlton)

Even in so strongly typed a breed as the Fell, there is an acceptable and essential range of variation. Hearing the breeders talk about the uses of the ponies, it becomes clear that the breed was never really sharply defined by any one purpose. Some were fast trotting ponies under saddle or harness; just as often, ponies were expected to work sensibly in the fields or the pits with potentially dangerous machinery; and some of them never did any work at all but lived on the fell and maintained the foundation stock. They were just 'always there' – somewhere among the ponies that were available, there would be one for the job you needed to do.

The first definition of the Fell took place in the late 19th century with its recognition as a localised foundation stock for the production of high quality riding ponies. The Fell Pony Society grew from the need to ensure the original pony did not disappear in the urge to cross-breed. Re-definition was needed fifty years later when petrol-driven transport took the place of the trap (a process interrupted by the Second World War) and the Fell re-discovered itself as a versatile all purpose 'family' pony. Another fifty years on, pony and horse ownership now has a quite extraordinary pyramid of businesses balanced above it in the form of feed, equipment, accommodation and transport, passports, veterinary attention, competitions and the sponsorship associated with the competitions, publishing and advertising. For a long time the Fell pony had little to do with this pyramid because the major players on the 'luxury' stage were the ultimate athletes – racehorses, show jumpers, hunters in the Shires, eventers and dressage horses. But a maid-of-all-work such as the Fell will tackle many sporting pursuits and do them well.

Many riders will never go to a high level in any sport;

they want a pony to be an easy-to-keep friend with a nice nature, whom people enjoy having around. A Fell won't ever be expected to win a steeplechase or a point-to-point but she can still jump; and she can do very well indeed in long distance riding and various forms of competitive driving, Le Trec and dressage, not to mention the fun to be had showing and simply hacking out. So with no alteration needed, she is the ideal pony, with abilities well suited to many different kinds of rider, or a rider with many interests, and especially to the person to whom a competent, 'confidential' mount is more valuable than a highly strung performance animal. RBST have recently (Spring 2005) admitted doubts about the future of some horse breeds and forecast a slump in sales as a result of the ban on hunting, which at the time of writing has only just become law. I believe the pure pony itself is versatile enough to survive that possible slump because neither the Fell nor its crosses are limited to that single niche.

Breeders match ponies not papers
SHOW quality goes beyond utility, into excellence. Although each breeder keeps in his mind's eye the breed type that he likes, not everything he produces will be show-quality as well as workmanlike and typical. The show ring requires visible excellence of breed type, good conformation, and registration papers.

Pedigrees are now capable of proof by blood typing, DNA sampling, microchip identity markers and most recently the equine passport system with its requirements of registration, diagrams and detailed descriptions. The breeders are almost all judges as well as exhibitors, and so they regularly give their opinion on the type and quality of Fell ponies in the public eye - and type and quality are what 'pedigree' is really about. They said in Chapter 7 that when breeding they matched the ponies themselves, taking into account the quality of any progeny each had produced. They know the background of their own herds and the type they want to produce. They know how well certain lines and individuals 'nick' with each other, so they take little notice of 'papers'. On the other hand, they also say that they have difficulty in finding registered stallions of good quality that are not closely related to their mares. It requires a great deal of knowledge and experience to chart a safe and effective course between the wish to breed pure, and the need to maintain the health and vigour and quality of the herd. But as numbers increase, yet the popular bloodlines become ever more widespread, breeders increasingly require an ability to find and match unrelated stock and to judge the value of a given mating. A new technology that may therefore become important to them is the use of a computer database to calculate degrees of kinship between ponies; and they may need to develop knowledge and skill in the use of that information.

A closed breed with a small number of breeding animals can too easily fall victim to genetic problems, so when a test comes for the syndrome, breeders will also need to decide whether they should stick with a 'non-carrier' or risk a 'carrier-to-carrier' mating and here again, database technology may offer a tool that they can use. Over and over as I have written this book I keep seeing that there are two related but distinct gene pools either side of the Pennine divide. The Fell and Dale breeds each, periodically, drew on the other to maintain type and health. Perhaps a time will come when another 'inspection' scheme could be used to bring in fresh blood yet retain the right type. Above all breeders need to be given the latitude to make their own choices. What they certainly do not need are yet more forms, rules and costs. They have enough of those imposed by EU regulations on agriculture and the government's implementation of them.

Artificial Insemination (AI) is a regularly-used tool in the horse world; it is particularly necessary where breed populations are thinly distributed across a continent. It is also often used when it is not necessary at all.

Here's a question for you. What have commercial turkeys to do with ponies? Well, white broad-breasted turkeys are so heavily built now through constant selection for size and breast muscle that the jocks can't breed the hens naturally any more. They are not capable of living and surviving independently because they can only be reproduced by artificial insemination. Some pony societies, Fell Pony Society included, have developed strict rules for registration of foals from AI, partly to guarantee that animals coming into the Stud Book are genuinely bred the way that their registrations say they are, partly to make AI something that

is only used where there is no alternative. The FPS doesn't allow embryo transfer at all, and in this I think they are wise, because while it might indeed produce more ponies in places where purebred mares are few, it does not do anything at all to widen the gene pool. Although it might take a while to turn the Fell pony into a 'turkey', artificial insemination and embryo transfer are both potential dead ends simply because they sidestep the natural processes that keep Fells what they are, long-lived, hardy, healthy and born to survive.

While breeders take care of their stock and know them all and their lineage, they do require them to be capable of living naturally and hardily without the need for constant human interference. Normal matings and normal births are essential risks to test the toughness of a breed, and if one interferes too much, a weakness may be kept which would eventually compromise usefulness or even survival. Many of the breeders expressed their opinion that there had been changes to the Fell breed. The changes are external but, away from the high fell environment, might such changes be going hand in hand with less obvious ones within? Human preferences without a practical purpose – fashions – can narrow a breed's uses and move it away from its Mountain and Moorland qualities. Living in a stable, it can be looked after so well that any lack of hardiness and toughness will never be tested. But on the fell those invisible qualities are proved by 'benign neglect.' This is how the breeders keep the Fell pony true to its type; by testing on the fell, and removing the non-viable stock. The soft ones find more generous homes, leaving the hardy ones as the core of the breed. Breeders often sell poor ponies without registering them; they don't keep or breed from ponies with bad faults, and if the difficulties are temperamental, sometimes they even go to the length of putting them down. Responsible breeding is about producing good ponies, not just mating any pair with a registration certificate apiece.

Breeding ponies is fraught with risk and for most breeders it brings only a modest profit. The profits from sheep, for the sake of comparison, come mainly from quantity: even on a small farm, hundreds of sheep are lambed each year. But even the biggest volume breeders don't register more than a score of foals each year. For small breeders the loss of even one youngster can turn the pony balance-sheet red, and selling a poor colt without registering him will be a cost-cutting exercise as well as a decision on behalf of the breed. It's just as well that breeding good ponies brings immense satisfaction, and that satisfaction has evidently been enough for the long-term Cumbrian and Northumbrian breeders – because I would guess that most of the time they have lost money rather than made it.

If you'd seen Jos when Jos was on with ponies and you got talking to him about buying summat, he was always worried he might maybe charge you over much. He would feel awful bad — so he never would make money out of hosses because he'd look at it and think 'it's maybe worth that – I might give such and such for it – I would be happy

to give that,' and then he would usually be pretty well down in the market, not top of the market. And I would say to be perfectly honest he sold a lot of ponies for damn little money when he should have had more. (Derrick Byas – Dargue family)

National and international legislation are taking a tighter grip on horse and pony ownership. If it is going to be more complicated to own and breed and sell, and there is going to be more expense involved, then the breed's breadth of scope must be kept, its variations must be kept, to give the widest range of options possible for actual use.

I'd like to illustrate the dangers of mere 'preservation.' In the late 1950s, Sir David Attenborough travelled to New Guinea to film the famous birds of paradise. In *The Quest for the Paradise Birds* he wrote about having seen a group of native men making stone axes: was he looking back into the Stone Age? If so, he defined it as being in its last stages, because the men were using steel tools to finish their work. The axes that were being made had lost any work function. They were more flamboyant than any of the older stone tools, the blades too widely flared, their edges impractically fine. They were used only for display or perhaps included in a bride-price. Their purpose and inner integrity had

Looking forward! Emma Woolley and the homebred colt Littletree Bodini.

been eroded. Yes, they were still stone axes, but they would have shattered if used for work.

What are our Fell ponies capable of now? Can they still do what they did fifty years ago? Established breeders know the Fell breed's qualities thoroughly and are critical. If they were not, they would not know or admit what needed improvement in their stock. They are honest about the animals from which they hope to produce the next generation; recognising what could be improved and more importantly, what should be left exactly as it is. If they get it right, Fells will still be able to do as well, fifty years on.

Similarly, future owners need to be allowed to learn about Fells from honest promotional material. For instance, the mental energy of a Mountain and Moorland pony can be considerable. He needs to be used – a 'sensible pony' is still a *pony*. This needs saying because I have been surprised at how many enquirers seem to think that a Fell is 'My Little Pony', a groomable long-haired toy or a docile 'teddy bear.' Any pony has to be accepted as an active responsibility, whose energy will demand an equal output from his owner(s) – the cost of his upkeep should be discounted against his healthy character-building qualities!

The enthusiasts who become promoters of the breed, and to be fair I see more problems in overseas countries than in Britain, sometimes omit to point out such things in their desire to stir an equal enthusiasm in others. But it isn't fair to spin romantic stories to people who are too innocent to know fantasy from reality. As I have tried to do in this book, you must tell the reality as well. Northern breeders, at any rate, don't pander to this fairytale outlook. They tell potential buyers about the real qualities of a pony they are selling. Having bitter experience of the hassle of after-sale problems, they will not sell to people whom they consider are unsuitable, and sometimes they will not sell a pony that they know is not of good enough quality to fit the customer's requirements, even when the customer is willing to buy it.

Organisations affecting the Fell breed and its future

IT seems to me that the first, unifying and supporting resource for any British Mountain and Moorland breed has GOT to be its own breed society; particularly where ponies are being bred at a great distance away from their home ground, perhaps overseas. Mere ownership does not convey knowledge, not without experience. Supporters as well as new breeders need to have a good grounding in the nature, the purposes, the whole ethos of the breed. To maintain a rare breed in good health, show successes are not enough. Mare ownership and foal production are not enough. Even access to fell land, on its own, may not be enough. Enthusiasts need wise leadership and guidance and the Fell Pony Society needs to be strong, forward-thinking and flexible. Where else can you tap into such a wealth of sound collective knowledge? FPS Council members, who are mostly experienced breeders, take advice from specialists such as vets and even international lawyers, when such

The foals and the people are the future. Foal at Linnel Wood, photograph courtesy of Laura Hart.

professional areas become important to the breed. One never knows when bureaucrats in London or Brussels may make decisions that impact legally or financially on the Fells, or when a country's legislation may run counter to breed practices in Britain. The horse breeding organisations of different countries can make life very difficult for a pony breeder by insisting on exhaustive performance testing or exorbitant fees to comply with home regulations, and a new breeder will undoubtedly be given conflicting information about what he has to do with his chosen breed. He has got to know whose judgement he can trust, and that means a tough-minded and fair breed society must make it plain that it can not only guide him but fight powerfully on his animals' behalf.

Fell ponies have 'endangered' status with the Rare

Alison Morton on Lownthwaite Bramble after their win at Penrith Show, photograph courtesy of Christine Morton.

Breeds Survival Trust and are classed as 'rare' by the American Livestock Breeds Conservancy. Splits between, say, groups of breeders or between one group and their mother society, are regrettably common in breeds with such status, perhaps because the minority aspect attracts non-conformist characters. The splits are often unintentional, perhaps even accidental, but whether they are due to geographical distance, personal preferences or financial interests, they are detrimental to the future health of a breed. Breeding stock can be 'lost' from the global population just as easily through administrative arguments or neglect as through lack of a commercial market.

Connecting the newcomer to the established breeders can be a useful two-way exchange of ideas. Although there will be some uncomfortable encounters, on occasion his questions illuminate concepts or foreshadow problems that a breed society has not even considered. The wider the audience that begins to appreciate Fell ponies, the more of these problems the society will encounter; with every experience, council will find better ways to work to reach diplomatic solutions to them.

One has to be realistic about it: the core of long-term Fell pony breeders is small, and getting smaller, compared to the newcomers. There are many more people breeding Fells away from the fells than there are on them. The established breeders know that they must share their knowledge, as they do with their children and grandchildren who will form the core of the breed in the future. That sharing of information

237

is one of the cornerstones on which this book is based, and I believe it is also a reason why people were so helpful with its compilation. I hope that in return there will always be new people coming into the breed who are willing to learn from the original breeders. Fresh minds, combining local knowledge with their own, may well find new avenues that the versatile and robust Fell pony might explore, and thus assure its future. It will take some good marketing, and perhaps tough argument, but there is no real reason why the breeders at home who are getting the rough end of the deal in the agricultural sector should not benefit directly from a healthy market for their ponies.

The people I have interviewed for this book are the foundations of the Fell breed. Whether winning at shows, enjoying the making of good riding ponies, using them as workers, or taking an annual crop of foals to market (and they look forward to making money from their stock just as much as anyone else) their commitment has been passionate and lifelong. Although it's a sideline to their main farming activities, producing good ponies is a way of life.

Comparatively few people have the benefit of living and working with the Fell pony herds of Cumberland, Westmorland and Northumberland. I hope that the snapshot of local conditions that I have recorded in this book will be found relevant by future generations of Fell pony admirers, and that the breeders, if they read it, won't find too many faults. In a world which now expects instant results from instant experts, they are still conservative, and take the long

A young man and his colt at the Stallion Show 2004.

view. When they are reluctant to accept a newcomer, they make dry remarks that point up his ambitions as materialistic and short-term, because although they live for today and act for today, they breed for forever. They see themselves as just recent links in a very long chain of responsibility to their family and their ponies.

Helping to gather the ponies off the fell, opening and shutting gates, fetching and carrying, [children] would be 'serving their time' – learning the traditional ways from their parents and grandparents just as the generations before them had done. (Frank Wales and Family)

It was family tradition and we were going to hand these ponies on to t'next generation. That was the important thing. (Dargue Family)

It is sobering to realise that these farmers, most of whose families have bred Fell ponies for generations, consider 'only thirty years' to be a short time.

REFERENCES

Cumberland Chronicle or *Whitehaven Intelligencer*, http://www.pastpresented.info/index.htm Accessed 11 November 2004

FELL PONY SOCIETY 'History CD' 2002: digital archive of press cuttings, stud cards, notebooks and sales notices, mainly from Mr R B Charlton.

FELL PONY SOCIETY, 1980: Stud Book 1898-1980 and annual updates. FPS, Penrith, Cumbria.

FISHER, E, 2001: *We Ploughed by Moonlight*, Workington: Hills.

FITZGERALD, I, 2000: *The Dales Pony*. Suffolk: Whittet Books.

FITZGERALD, I, 2004: *The Dales and the Friesian,* article in 'Native Pony' April-May 2004.

GODWIN, B: http://www.communigate.co.uk/ryedale/in thepicture2/page5.phtml, Bernard Godwin, on accompanying a pit pony to Midland shows. Accessed 6 December 2004

HAYES, H M, FRCVS, 1877: *Veterinary Notes for Horse Owners*, 17th revised ed (Rossdale P, 1987). London: Stanley Paul.

HICKMAN, G, *Improving returns from common grazings in the New Forest.* Faunus, LSIRD Network, Macaulay Institute, Issue 6

JONES, Sir Clement, 1948: *A Tour in Westmorland,*

http://www.fivenine.co.uk/local_history_notebook/A%20Tour%20in%20Westmorland/chapter_2.htm Accessed October 2004

LAMBERT, J et al, 1996: *Transect Through Time.* Lancaster, UK: Lancaster Imprints

MILLARD, S, 2002: *The Fell Pony and Countryside Museums at Dalemain,* http://www.fellpony.f9.co.uk

MURRAY, D A, 2005: The Fell Pony: grazing characteristics and breed profile - a preliminary assessment. A feasibility study on the potential role of Fell ponies in conservation grazing post Common Agricultural Policy reform. MATILDA, Leicester, UK.

PRINGLE, A, 1794: *A General View of the Agriculture of the County of Westmorland* (Board of Agriculture, later the Royal Agricultural Society)

RICHARDSON, C, 1990: *The Fell Pony.* London: J A Allen.

RICHARDSON, C, 1995: *The Hackney.* London: J A Allen.

SHAW, A: http://www.healeyhero.info/rescue/com/pony_alf.htm Alfred Shaw talks of ponies at Mapperley Colliery. Accessed 6 December 2004

SHEARD, J: *The Dales in winter: dangers and delights for country folk,* http://www.daelnet.co.uk/news/weekend/weekend_15102004.cfm Accessed 5 December 2004

Somerset County archives: Cyril Wyburn interview: *Winter 1947.* http://www.somerset.gov.uk/archives/exmoor/wyburnsummary1.htm Accessed 5 December 2004

SUTCLIFFE, A, 1981: *Breeding and Training a Horse or Pony.* Newton Abbott & London: David & Charles.

HARDIMAN, J R: *The Thoroughbred Racehorse, Confused Pedigrees And Mistaken Identities.* http://www.highflyer.supanet.com/investigation2.htm Accessed June 2003

SCHOLES, S F, HOLLIMAN, A, MAY P D, HOLMES M A, *1998: A syndrome of anemia, immunodeficiency and peripheral ganglionopathy in Fell pony foals.* The Veterinary Record, 7 Feb 1998; 142(6): 128-34.

THOMAS G W; CARTER S D; BELL S C; PHYTHIAN C; TAYLOR; KNOTTENBELT D C, *Aid to the antemortem diagnosis of Fell pony foal syndrome by the analysis of B lymphocytes.* The Veterinary Record, 17 May 2003; 152 (20) 618-621 (4).

YOUATT, W, 1831: *The Horse* (4th ed, 1908) Longmans, Green & Co, London.